FROM RIGHTEOUSNESS TO FAR RIGHT

MCGILL-QUEEN'S STUDIES IN ETHNIC HISTORY
SERIES ONE: DONALD HARMAN AKENSON, EDITOR

1 Irish Migrants in the Canadas
 A New Approach
 Bruce S. Elliott
 (Second edition, 2004)

2 Critical Years in Immigration
 Canada and Australia Compared
 Freda Hawkins
 (Second edition, 1991)

3 Italians in Toronto
 Development of a National Identity, 1875–1935
 John E. Zucchi

4 Linguistics and Poetics of Latvian Folk Songs
 Essays in Honour of the Sesquicentennial of the Birth of Kr. Barons
 Vaira Vikis-Freibergs

5 Johan Schroder's Travels in Canada, 1863
 Orm Overland

6 Class, Ethnicity, and Social Inequality
 Christopher McAll

7 The Victorian Interpretation of Racial Conflict
 The Maori, the British, and the New Zealand Wars
 James Belich

8 White Canada Forever
 Popular Attitudes and Public Policy toward Orientals in British Columbia
 W. Peter Ward
 (Third edition, 2002)

9 The People of Glengarry
 Highlanders in Transition, 1745–1820
 Marianne McLean

10 Vancouver's Chinatown
 Racial Discourse in Canada, 1875–1980
 Kay J. Anderson

11 Best Left as Indians
 Native–White Relations in the Yukon Territory, 1840–1973
 Ken Coates

12 Such Hardworking People
 Italian Immigrants in Postwar Toronto
 Franca Iacovetta

13 The Little Slaves of the Harp
 Italian Child Street Musicians in Nineteenth-Century Paris, London, and New York
 John E. Zucchi

14 The Light of Nature and the Law of God
 Antislavery in Ontario, 1833–1877
 Allen P. Stouffer

15 Drum Songs
 Glimpses of Dene History
 Kerry Abel

16 Canada's Jews
 (Reprint of 1939 original)
 Louis Rosenberg
 Edited by Morton Weinfeld

17 A New Lease on Life
 Landlords, Tenants, and Immigrants in Ireland and Canada
 Catharine Anne Wilson

18 In Search of Paradise
 The Odyssey of an Italian Family
 Susan Gabori

19 Ethnicity in the Mainstream
 Three Studies of English Canadian Culture in Ontario
 Pauline Greenhill

20 Patriots and Proletarians
 The Politicization of Hungarian Immigrants in Canada, 1923–1939
 Carmela Patrias

21 The Four Quarters of the Night
 The Life-Journey of an Emigrant Sikh
 Tara Singh Bains and Hugh Johnston

22 Cultural Power, Resistance, and Pluralism
 Colonial Guyana, 1838–1900
 Brian L. Moore

23 Search Out the Land
   The Jews and the Growth of Equality in British Colonial America, 1740–1867
   Sheldon J. Godfrey and Judith C. Godfrey

24 The Development of Elites in Acadian New Brunswick, 1861–1881
   Sheila M. Andrew

25 Journey to Vaja
   Reconstructing the World of a Hungarian-Jewish Family
   Elaine Kalman Naves

MCGILL-QUEEN'S STUDIES IN ETHNIC HISTORY
SERIES TWO: JOHN ZUCCHI, EDITOR

1 Inside Ethnic Families
  Three Generations of Portuguese-Canadians
  Edite Noivo

2 A House of Words
  Jewish Writing, Identity, and Memory
  Norman Ravvin

3 Oatmeal and the Catechism
  Scottish Gaelic Settlers in Quebec
  Margaret Bennett

4 With Scarcely a Ripple
  Anglo-Canadian Migration into the United States and Western Canada, 1880–1920
  Randy William Widdis

5 Creating Societies
  Immigrant Lives in Canada
  Dirk Hoerder

6 Social Discredit
  Anti-Semitism, Social Credit, and the Jewish Response
  Janine Stingel

7 Coalescence of Styles
  The Ethnic Heritage of St John River Valley Regional Furniture, 1763–1851
  Jane L. Cook

8 Brigh an Orain / A Story in Every Song
  The Songs and Tales of Lauchie MacLellan
  Translated and edited by John Shaw

9 Demography, State and Society
  Irish Migration to Britain, 1921–1971
  Enda Delaney

10 The West Indians of Costa Rica
   Race, Class, and the Integration of an Ethnic Minority
   Ronald N. Harpelle

11 Canada and the Ukrainian Question, 1939–1945
   Bohdan S. Kordan

12 Tortillas and Tomatoes
   Transmigrant Mexican Harvesters in Canada
   Tanya Basok

13 Old and New World Highland Bagpiping
   John G. Gibson

14 Nationalism from the Margins
   The Negotiation of Nationalism and Ethnic Identities among Italian Immigrants in Alberta and British Columbia
   Patricia Wood

15 Colonization and Community
   The Vancouver Island Coalfield and the Making of the British Columbia Working Class
   John Douglas Belshaw

16 Enemy Aliens, Prisoners of War
   Internment in Canada during the Great War
   Bohdan S. Kordan

17 Like Our Mountains
   A History of Armenians in Canada
   Isabel Kaprielian-Churchill

18 Exiles and Islanders
   The Irish Settlers of Prince Edward Island
   Brendan O'Grady

19 Ethnic Relations in Canada
   Institutional Dynamics
   Raymond Breton
   Edited by Jeffrey G. Reitz
20 A Kingdom of the Mind
   *The Scots' Impact on the
   Development of Canada*
   Edited by Peter Rider and Heather
   McNabb
21 Vikings to U-Boats
   *The German Experience in
   Newfoundland and Labrador*
   Gerhard P. Bassler
22 Being Arab
   *Ethnic and Religious Identity
   Building among Second Generation
   Youth in Montreal*
   Paul Eid
23 From Peasants to Labourers
   *Ukrainian and Belarusan
   Immigration from the Russian
   Empire to Canada*
   Vadim Kukushkin
24 Emigrant Worlds and Transatlantic
   Communities
   *Migration to Upper Canada in the
   First Half of the Nineteenth Century*
   Elizabeth Jane Errington
25 Jerusalem on the Amur
   *Birobidzhan and the Canadian
   Jewish Communist Movement,
   1924–1951*
   Henry Felix Srebrnik
26 Irish Nationalism in Canada
   Edited by David A. Wilson
27 Managing the Canadian Mosaic
   in Wartime
   *Shaping Citizenship Policy,
   1939–1945*
   Ivana Caccia
28 Jewish Roots, Canadian Soil
   *Yiddish Culture in Montreal,
   1905–1945*
   Rebecca Margolis
29 Imposing Their Will
   *An Organizational History of Jewish
   Toronto, 1933–1948*
   Jack Lipinsky
30 Ireland, Sweden, and the Great
   European Migration, 1815–1914
   Donald H. Akenson
31 The Punjabis in British Columbia
   *Location, Labour, First Nations,
   and Multiculturalism*
   Kamala Elizabeth Nayar
32 Growing Up Canadian
   Muslims, Hindus, Buddhists
   Edited by Peter Beyer and Rubina
   Ramji
33 Between Raid and Rebellion
   *The Irish in Buffalo and Toronto,
   1867–1916*
   William Jenkins
34 Unpacking the Kists
   The Scots in New Zealand
   Brad Patterson, Tom Brooking,
   and Jim McAloon
35 Building Nations from Diversity
   *Canadian and American Experience
   Compared*
   Garth Stevenson
36 Hurrah Revolutionaries
   *The Polish Canadian Communist
   Movement, 1918–1948*
   Patryk Polec
37 Alice in Shandehland
   *Scandal and Scorn in the
   Edelson/Horwitz Murder Case*
   Monda Halpern
38 Creating Kashubia
   *History, Memory, and Identity in
   Canada's First Polish Community*
   Joshua C. Blank
39 No Free Man
   *Canada, the Great War, and the
   Enemy Alien Experience*
   Bohdan S. Kordan
40 Between Dispersion and Belonging
   *Global Approaches to Diaspora in
   Practice*
   Edited by Amitava Chowdhury and
   Donald Harman Akenson
41 Running on Empty
   *Canada and the Indochinese
   Refugees, 1975–1980*
   Michael J. Molloy, Peter Duschinsky,
   Kurt F. Jensen, and Robert J. Shalka

42 Twenty-First-Century Immigration to North America
Newcomers in Turbulent Times
Edited by Victoria M. Esses and Donald E. Abelson

43 Gaelic Cape Breton Step-Dancing
An Historical and Ethnographic Perspective
John G. Gibson

44 Witness to Loss
Race, Culpability, and Memory in the Dispossession of Japanese Canadians
Edited by Jordan Stanger-Ross and Pamela Sugiman

45 Mad Flight?
The Quebec Emigration to the Coffee Plantations of Brazil
John Zucchi

46 A Land of Dreams
Ethnicity, Nationalism, and the Irish in Newfoundland, Nova Scotia, and Maine, 1880–1923
Patrick Mannion

47 Strategic Friends
Canada-Ukraine Relations from Independence to the Euromaidan
Bohdan S. Kordan

48 From Righteousness to Far Right
An Anthropological Rethinking of Critical Security Studies
Emma Mc Cluskey

From Righteousness to Far Right

*An Anthropological Rethinking
of Critical Security Studies*

EMMA McCLUSKEY

McGill-Queen's University Press
Montreal & Kingston • London • Chicago

© McGill-Queen's University Press 2019

ISBN 978-0-7735-5688-1 (cloth)
ISBN 978-0-7735-5689-8 (paper)
ISBN 978-0-7735-5813-7 (ePDF)
ISBN 978-0-7735-5814-4 (ePUB)

Legal deposit first quarter 2019
Bibliothèque nationale du Québec

Printed in Canada on acid-free paper that is 100% ancient forest free (100% post-consumer recycled), processed chlorine free

We acknowledge the support of the Canada Council for the Arts, which last year invested $153 million to bring the arts to Canadians throughout the country.

Nous remercions le Conseil des arts du Canada de son soutien. L'an dernier, le Conseil a investi 153 millions de dollars pour mettre de l'art dans la vie des Canadiennes et des Canadiens de tout le pays.

Note: A version of Chapter 4 was originally published as "Solidarity and Gender Equality as a Discourse of Violence in Sweden" in *Gender, Violence, Refugees*, ed. Ulrike Krause and Susanne Buckley-Zistel (New York: Berghahn, 2017).

Library and Archives Canada Cataloguing in Publication

Title: From righteousness to far right : an anthropological rethinking of critical security studies / Emma Mc Cluskey.

Names: Mc Cluskey, Emma, 1981– author.

Series: McGill-Queen's studies in ethnic history. Series two ; 48.

Description: Series statement: McGill-Queen's studies in ethnic history. Series two ; 48 | Includes bibliographical references and index.

Identifiers: Canadiana (print) 20189065486 | Canadiana (ebook) 20189065494 | ISBN 978-0-7735-5688-1 (cloth) | ISBN 978-0-7735-5689-8 (paper) | ISBN 978-0-7735-5813-7 (ePDF) | ISBN 978-0-7735-5814-4 (ePUB)

Subjects: LCSH: Refugees—Sweden. | LCSH: Internal security—Political aspects—Sweden. | LCSH: Sweden—

Moral conditions. | LCSH: Sweden—Ethnic relations. | LCSH: Sweden—Emigration and immigration—Social aspects. | LCSH: Sweden—Emigration and immigration—Government policy.

Classification: LCC HV640.4.S8 M33 2019 | DDC 305.9/0691409485—DC23

This book was typeset in 10.5/13 Sabon.

Contents

Preface xi

Acknowledgments xv

Prologue xvii

1 Introduction: Thinking Righteousness and Far Right Relationally 3

2 Construction of the Self: Sweden as Morally Exceptional 27

3 Seeing Like a Good Citizen: An Anthropology of the Governmentality of Righteousness 68

4 Limits of the Governmentality of Righteousness: Counter-conduct and Moral Panic 105

5 Anthropological Rethinking of Critical Security Studies: Reflexivity, Metis, and Solidarity 139

6 Conclusion: The Devil in the Anthropological Detail 171

Notes 187

References 197

Index 219

Preface

The so-called refugee crisis of 2015 and 2016 in Europe called into question some of our modes of analysis and their implicit assumptions. Even the relative openness of Sweden and Germany and their "humanitarian superpower" status eventually turned to hostility toward refugees: political elites articulated justifications for closing borders clearly along security lines, as well as along more ambiguous lines of "burden sharing" and already having done enough. In both countries, far right parties made significant inroads into public life, and xenophobia and hostility toward refugees – once taboo – has become much more normalized and commonplace, not only in these countries but also arguably all over the Western world.

This book argues that existing approaches to so-called critical security studies, the body of international relations literature that has gone the furthest to examine the precise mechanisms through which migrants come to be constructed as a threat, goes little way in theorizing the textured, contradictory, and often resistant practices of everyday life present within societies. Instead, the field is inclined to focus on what is immediately visible: speech acts by politicians and sensational media or spectacular politics, such as the seizing of refugees' valuable possessions in Denmark or the building of walls in Bulgaria, Hungary, and Austria, among others. Though important, this type of analysis renders invisible less elitist sites and modes of political contestation.

What happens when you don't have an obvious politics of hate or racism but seemingly "good" and "decent" people come to be attracted to the far right, or come to view hardline practices toward migrants and refugees as morally right? The more interesting questions about how migrants are framed as "threatening" and the rise of xenophobia is not about party politics and speech acts, but about normalization, subjectification, and what is going on when people go about their day-to-day life, removed from the realms of high politics. What was deemed taboo not so long ago, slowly and gradually now becoming ordinary parlance amongst large swathes of people.

In this book, I argue that it is necessary to move beyond what is directly evident in terms of official narratives, however, and to shift the focus of investigation in terms of security, migration, and asylum into the day-to-day realm, where much of the controversy over migration and security is played out. Doing this also shows how practices of "security" are intertwined with notions of hospitality, generosity, and even solidarity, and that seemingly exceptional moments of identifying migrants as threats can be rooted in much broader politics of humanitarianism and righteousness.

The book proposes a more political-anthropological approach to analyzing securitization and sets out to explore alternative realms of understanding and the gravitas of political practices that are seemingly fleeting and insignificant, but that can nonetheless adopt enough uniformity to completely reconfigure social relations.

Using the case study of Sweden, labelled a humanitarian superpower for its response to the refugee crisis, the book follows the story of nineteen months of ethnographic fieldwork with a grassroots NGO in a small Swedish village where over one hundred refugees were housed. This embedded, anthropological study examines how a new way of thinking emerged whereby it became legitimate to openly speak of the refugees as undeserving and undesirable, and to take action to ensure that the perceived "generosity" of Sweden was not being abused. It demonstrates that microphysics and micropractices, not ideology, gave rise to this threat construction. Therefore, instead of identifying security as an enclosed, pre-ordained space or set of apparatus, the book puts forward a political-anthropological reconstruction of critical security studies. It argues that such an approach is best placed to examine how local communities can act to "take their security into their own hands" and formulate their own security practices in a horizontal fashion, through so-called hidden transcripts, and acts of appropriation.

With the far right and increasingly hardline practices toward refugees gaining popularity throughout the Western world and with the implementation of borders and even fences coming to represent not only a "normal" but also, in many cases, a "decent" response to the so-called crisis, study of these securitizing practices as they evolve requires a political-anthropological approach rather than a traditional political science approach, which can only offer a post-facto analysis focused on political parties and spokespersons.

This book will be of interest to social scientists across a variety of disciplines interested in the wider scholarly debate on the so-called refugee crisis and response to it throughout Europe and the Western world. It will particularly appeal to scholars of critical security studies, migration studies, international political sociology, and international relations theory more broadly, or those interested in ethnographic methodologies.

Acknowledgments

My thanks to the many people who contributed to the work presented in this book. First and foremost, I cannot adequately express my gratitude to Didier Bigo for his support and steadfastness, and for teaching me how to follow my curiosity. In Didier I could not have found a more perfect mentor. This project was made possible through the generous financial support of the Economic and Social Research Council of the United Kingdom (grant number ES/1017992/1). A contribution to book production costs was made by SOURCE, Societal Security Network, under the European Union's Seventh Framework Programme for research, technological development, and demonstration (grant agreement no. 313288). The Department of War Studies, King's College London also provided much-appreciated intellectual and fieldwork support.

As my research was based on in-depth ethnographic fieldwork, none of what I have written would have been possible without the generosity of those who so kindly gave of their time, befriended me, and invited me into their homes, particularly the Friends of Syria organization and the people of Öreby. To respect our agreement of anonymity and confidentiality, I have used pseudonyms throughout this work; however, I am grateful for everything that they did for me.

Of the many colleagues and companions who have supported me throughout this project, I especially thank Monique Jo Beerli, Hanna Ketola, Bruno Magalhães, Isabel Rocha de Siqueira, and Renata Summa for setting the bar so high on what it means to be a friend.

My sincere thanks to everyone who kindly offered comments on and critiques of various parts or drafts of the book – most notably

Claudia Aradau, Tugba Basaran, Peter Busch, Victor Coutinho Lage, Nicholas de Genova, Elspeth Guild, Peo Hansen, Jef Huysmans, Vivienne Jabri, Akta Kaushal, Ulrike Krause, Sankaran Krishna, Mariella Pandolfi, Ben Rampton, Jennifer Riggan, and Nisha Shah, as well as the three anonymous peer reviewers. Their suggestions helped focus and improve the project immensely.

To the team at McGill-Queens University Press, particularly Richard Baggaley and Eleanor Gasparik, thank you for your patience, encouragement, and attention to detail during the production process. Working with MQUP has been a pleasure from start to finish.

I am extremely grateful to Susan and Lasse Carlsson, the centre of my life in Sweden, not only for opening up their home to me during my time there but also for being research assistants extraordinaire. It is no understatement to say that this project would not have gotten off the ground without their dedication. I am profoundly indebted to my wonderful parents who, with boundless love and tolerance, have always encouraged me. My gratitude also to my sister Fi, for the music, the laughs, and the pep talks.

Special thanks, however, are reserved for Peter Carlsson and Svea Mc Cluskey. I remain most inspired and sustained by their love and their energy. This book is dedicated to them.

Prologue

SCENE 1.1: THE FAR-RIGHT BLOG

The following is an excerpt from a Swedish website known for its nationalist leanings:

> We read with alarm in today's newspaper that the Swedish Migration Agency, Migrationsverket (MV), is trying to force the municipality of Holmberg to receive a large number of asylum seekers, located in the village of Öreby. We have come to understand that there will be around 70 people placed here in the first wave, with the possibility that this will increase.
> We have been called by troubled villagers living in Öreby, who are understandably confused about what's going on. Unfortunately, we currently do not know more than what it says in the newspaper. However, we will not stand by idly and accept this. We encourage everybody to stage an intervention in the next council meeting, where we will be vocal and consistent in our message that we do not find this acceptable. This is a clear violation of the principle of municipal self-determination.
> The subject is apparently too sensitive for any of the local newspapers to open comments on, but everybody is free to discuss it here on our website instead. We uphold our right to freedom of speech and freedom of expression. Every comment and opinion, regardless of stance, will be published. Our only request is that tone of comments is polite and objective and everybody is respectful in their engagement with other people's comments.[1]

It was January 2013 and the small village of Öreby was about to receive a few dozen mostly Syrian asylum seekers. There were only a handful of comments posted below this particular blog, most of them from people claiming to be Öreby-dwellers who were concerned about their children's school becoming overcrowded or wondering if it would be more effective to use funds to help refugees directly in the Middle East, where they shared a similar culture to those already living there. Reading from a British perspective used to the tabloid press, with its consistent demonization of refugees and asylum seekers and the hundreds of comments decrying that the island is full and that all asylum seekers are bogus and responsible for all society's ills, I found the few comments on this self-proclaimed Swedish nationalist site to be rather civil in comparison.

In reaction, the Very Nice Lady from the Swedish Church who was dealing with helping the Syrians resettle was aghast. "That these frightening far-right people are talking about our village on their website is terrifying! Everybody knows everybody here and there's no way that any of the villagers would write on a blog like this. This is just trash." As it transpired, a meeting was scheduled, but not until a few weeks later, and it was organized by Migrationsverket, not the local council and certainly not the local right-wing representatives.

SCENE 1.2: THE MEETING

12 February 2013: Öreby Village School, Skåne

The meeting took place in the school hall. It was a Tuesday evening and it had already been dark for a couple of hours. The hall was completely full. Not only was every chair occupied but people were also standing along the back wall and in the doorway. The main stage of the hall was set up with three seats facing the audience: one for the representative from Migrationsverket; one for the head of the municipal council; and the last for the president of the Öreby Residents' Association, who was chairing the event.

It was only 7 p.m. but no one had brought along their children. It wasn't really a family affair. There was a sense of urgency about all of this. Of the three officials, only the man from the residents association was present, waiting patiently for the other two to arrive onstage. Audience members chatted to each other in hushed tones.

When the man from MV walked in with the councillor, the room quietened immediately. After very short introductions by the chair and allusions to this being the place where "everybody will be able to openly talk about what some of you have been concerned about privately," the MV representative took the floor.

His message was short and to the point. Öreby would be receiving around seventy, mostly Syrian, asylum seekers. This was just an initial phase with the possibility that more could be settled here in the near future. Everything was set up to go ahead, and the new arrivals would be housed as soon as possible, probably within the next three weeks. It was a prepared statement, read aloud from a piece of paper. The official had said nothing that had not already been stated in the local newspaper a few weeks earlier. After the official took his seat, the meeting was opened up for questions.

"Of course we do not object to helping people in need, but why were we not consulted on the issue?" The official assured the crowd that this was a temporary measure, that they could report any problems directly to him, and that they would certainly be consulted before any more families arrived. In fact, another meeting was already scheduled for the spring.

"Has anybody thought about the effect that this will have on our house prices?" Again, the official reiterated that this was temporary and house prices should not be affected.

"These refugees have come straight from a war zone and may be psychologically damaged. We have to consider the impact that will have on resources, especially at the school." Everything had been taken into consideration and planned accordingly. The MV representative was clear that there was nothing to worry about in that regard.

When the time came for a smartly dressed woman in her forties to ask her question, she stood up and looked around the hall. "Everybody has been very polite, but I, for one, would like to say that this is a disgrace, Mr Goran Bengtsson," addressing the MV official by his full name.

"Because of you and your organization, I will no longer feel safe walking around the streets of my own village and my two teenage daughters will no longer be able to go out on their own. The women of Öreby will be forced to stay locked away in our houses or else face sexual harassment, abuse, or worse."

After the woman's declaration, the room fell silent.

SCENE 1.3: SWEDEN'S U-TURN

24 November 2015: Essex, United Kingdom

Just over one year after I had finished my fieldwork, I was back home in the UK, with a newborn baby in tow. And the political landscape seemed to be hurtling in all directions at enormous speed. It was nearly wintertime again, after a summer that saw the start of the biggest humanitarian crisis in the last fifty years. Things were confusing on all counts. The big news in Europe related to the Swedish government and its response to this so-called refugee crisis.[2] Measures had just been announced to deter any more refugees from coming to Sweden. The move was largely seen as a U-turn to what was widely viewed as Sweden's previous generous policy: the granting of permanent residency to all Syrians arriving at the border, the right to family reunification, and the provision of a comparatively higher standard of welfare than that given by other European Union (EU) member states. As of the start of 2016, most refugees would only receive temporary residency permits, identity checks would be reinstated on all forms of transport along the southern border with Denmark, and the right to bring families would be severely restricted (Regeringen 2015b). My phone wouldn't stop beeping.

After announcing these new measures at a press conference, the deputy prime minister, Åsa Romson, broke down in tears. I watched this scene with a feeling of dissonance and unease while my baby slept in her crib. It seemed as though Romson was crying not only for the refugees but also for herself, her party, her government, and her country. She was crying about the loss of status that Sweden would suffer now that it could no longer act as a moral superpower. Sweden had been tainted by the far right. It was a moral disaster.

FROM RIGHTEOUSNESS TO FAR RIGHT

I

Introduction
Thinking Righteousness and Far Right Relationally

At a time when refugees are not treated so well … how nice to find people with such a heart! Sweden opens its borders, organizes language classes, gives economic assistance, and offers paths to join society. They do not have anyone in a concentration camp and other such terrifying places. That's an example we can present to the world. Because in reality it is the only country that is doing that, and is not filled with misery. It is not thereby suffering. This is the message Sweden presents: Open your heart to your brother, your sister, who has nowhere to live, to work, to sleep peacefully.

Pope Francis, February 2014

ETHNOGRAPHY AND THE FAR RIGHT: THE SHATTERING OF TABOOS

The title of this book is *From Righteousness to Far Right*. I was surprised that this project ended up speaking about nationalism, the far right, or thick friend-enemy distinctions. As with most ethnographic research, this was not my intention from the beginning. I had come to study refugee resettlement in one of the most humanitarian nations in the Western world. The "far right" had nothing to do with my research. They were skinheads or uneducated folk stuck out in backwater places. Or maybe this alt-right crowd that people had started to talk about back then – acne-ridden young men who lived in their parents' houses and spent all day on strange online forums. Whatever they were, they were nothing to do with me.

As the short vignette in the foreword showed, this was also the preconception of many of the villagers, the kind and generous people who volunteered time and donated clothes to help the newly arrived refugees. They saw themselves as upstanding people. The blog that raised objections to the resettlement of the Syrians in Sweden was not only "far right" but "frightening." Nothing to do with the village or the people who lived there. But as this book shows, what was labelled at the start of my research as "far right" by many in the village came to be normalized. Positions that were once considered taboo came, instead, to be owned and performed by the very same people who had contributed to making them a taboo in the first place. A shift had taken place.

Therefore, the term "far right" in the book title does not denote some objective political position but, rather, something relative, meaning different things to different people, at different times, and in different countries. In the context of the book, "far right" emphasizes this relational element. "Far right" was used specifically by many of the people in the village to describe specific behaviours, attitudes, and positions that they themselves deemed frightening and, initially, taboo but that they later came to rationalize and embody. Although this does include voting for a political party that is commonly presented as, and that the villagers themselves labelled, far right (though this party, the Sweden Democrats, has rejected this label and calls itself centrist), this does not completely capture the way in which I use the term. My usage also extends to broader practices that many of my actors articulated as being in bad taste at the start of my fieldwork; for example, labelling the refugees as violent, as undeserving and lazy, or as playing the system; or demanding action to stop the entry of refugees into the country.

To my surprise, as things progressed, I discovered that people who came to identify themselves with these once off-limits narratives were in fact very nice. A lot like the Brexiter and outright racist grannies and grandads at home who told me how they were "ethnically cleansed" from East London and that Brexit could help make Britain white again. "We're not racist. We just didn't feel like we belonged there anymore, love," they would explain in a kindly voice when I was campaigning for a "stay" vote. I sometimes felt a bit sorry for them. Of course, this project took place a couple of years before Brexit, Trump, etc., and the re-emergence of nationalisms in the West. This wasn't the first time I had my preconceptions challenged. But it was the most destabilizing. I felt sympathy for these people who came to align themselves with what they had once called "far right" in the village of Öreby. They were nice.

Indeed these latest events – the reaction to the so-called refugee crisis, Brexit, Trump, and the rest – came to frame how I pieced together my analysis. This story could have been told differently. But I hope my reasons for doing it this way will become clear. In framing the argument in terms of the shift from righteousness to far right, I have attempted to illuminate the conditions of possibility of a particular type of exclusionary and securitarian politics, one that is on the rise. Without a complete openness to the field, and the willingness to understand and empathize with the positions of *both* the refugees and the villagers, I would not have been able to bring these dynamics to light. Instead, I would have remained trapped with the explanatory mechanisms of my discipline: official documents and discourses, political entrepreneurs, speech acts, or bureaucrats vying for more money to control immigration and stop terrorism. Thus, this book suggests an anthropological rethinking of critical security studies that places ontological primacy on these micropractices of the everyday, by these seemingly unimportant actors, re-framing their significance in our understanding of issues of global politics and international relations. This rethinking, instead of working with ready-made explanations and categories, attends and opens up to the plasticity and fluidity of boundaries around far right politics and the manner in which, mechanisms through which, and points at which these boundaries crystallize.

What can be done with this new anthropological way of seeing political transformation on the ground? What is its significance and how can this approach help inform how we study the rise of so-called far-right politics, populist nationalism, and the resurgence of seemingly exceptional and extreme securitarian "answers" to the "problem" of migration and mobility?

I hope that the most important intervention of this book comes from the insistence on a focus on these everyday diffuse micropractices, in all their complexity, as a more open and subtle means of analyzing the rise of this far right as I've described it. Such an approach offers precious empirical insights and scale of analysis on what is usually addressed through the broader scope of media and public opinion or public policies and party politics. Though useful, this type of analysis can also have a deeply de-politicizing effect in rendering far right politics as something neatly demarcated and "over there," nothing really to do with us as academics (see Huysmans 2008 for an extended discussion on the idea of exceptionality as de-politicizing). In contrast, this anthropological approach aims to understand how these positions become normalized, how seemingly unexpected people can "own" this type of politics, and how we are all implicated in these sets of relations. Therefore, an anthropological rethinking of critical security studies, in documenting the interplay between righteousness and the far right, is one way of shedding light into this dark corner and helping us to examine exactly how, through a rich textured and nuanced analysis, this phenomenon can happen anywhere and to anyone.

THE MORAL EXEMPLAR AS BANAL: HUMANITARIAN REASON AS TRANSVERSAL

This book is not primarily a discussion on Sweden or Swedish domestic politics. It does not make recommendations to the Swedish government regarding its asylum policy, argue for the opening up of political discourse to allow for greater dissent from the so-called politically correct narrative, or suggest measures to better "integrate" the newly arrived refugees. Instead, it is a discussion on the sociology of power as a relation, at the level of micropractices: the relationship between welcoming and rejecting, between integration and violence, and between solidarity and security. These are broad questions that are relevant to all European and North American countries that have become countries of asylum and immigration, particularly those promoting immigration for humanitarian reasons, and not in terms of some kind of market logic. In Foucauldian terms, as discussed in the following section, it is a type of governmentality that is somewhat transversal, to greater or lesser extents, depending on how hardline or otherwise a state's stance is toward asylum.

In terms of national myths, moral exceptionalism is one that is rather banal. Certainly, it could be argued that most nations have a story that sets them apart as morally superior in one way or another – an inherent feature of the nationalist project. What is interesting about Sweden, and why I chose Sweden as my particular case study, is that this country has taken the idea of "humanitarian reason" (Fassin 2010) to the furthest extent, articulating its asylum policy not simply in terms of hospitality or humanitarianism, but in terms of solidarity, as further discussed in chapter 2. When I embarked upon my project, "Sweden" as a category of practice could be seen to exemplify the tension between framing in the international and the unease over asylum in everyday life. The controversy over immigration and asylum could be seen to be invisibilized to a greater extent in Sweden than in other Western European nations and an image of tolerance arguably still maintained there.

Throughout my research, however, the political landscape – both within Sweden and Europe more broadly – changed considerably as a result of the escalation of the Syrian Civil War and the subsequent refugee crisis that ensued. According to the United Nations High Commissioner for Refugees (UNHCR), the number of forcibly displaced people worldwide at the end of 2014 was the highest it had been since the Second World War, a 40 per cent increase since 2011 (cited in *New York Times* 2015). A rising number of these refugees fled to the EU, increasingly through means such as crossing the Mediterranean Sea in boats and other vessels, or overland via southeastern Europe. The majority of these arrivals, according to the UNHCR, were from Syria, though large proportions were also from other refugee-producing countries that had seen ongoing conflict (Amnesty International 2015).

In September 2013, roughly halfway through my fieldwork, Sweden saw its moral superpower image resurrected from the supposed dustbin of history (though it was never buried that deep, as we will discuss in chapter 2): it took the unilateral decision to grant all Syrians arriving at the border permanent residency and the right to family reunification. The move, which received cross-party support (aside from the anti-immigration Sweden Democrats party, which at that time occupied only ten seats in parliament), resulted in Sweden, alongside Germany, receiving roughly two-thirds of all Syrians arriving in Europe during 2014 and 2015 (see Sverige-Radio 2015).

At the same time, securitarian ideologies were also on the rise throughout the West. The Brexit debate in the UK saw the normalization of hostility toward migration within mainstream political discourse, and the vote to leave the EU was deemed to be responsible for a rise in xenophobic hate crimes (BBC 2017). Marine Le Pen's Front National came second in France's 2016 election, and Germany's Alternative for Germany (AfD), Hungary's Jobbik, Italy's Lega Nord, and Austria's Freedom Party all went from strength to strength (see *Telegraph* 2016). With Sweden's September 2014 election, the Sweden Democrats also became the third largest party in Sweden's parliament, attracting 13 per cent of the popular vote (*Dagens Nyheter* 2014). The relationship between welcoming and rejecting, between integration and violence, and between solidarity and security thus became ever more important to explore. The notion is that so-called good people are appearing to resist ideas of humanitarianism, hospitality, and solidarity and are generating a new way of thinking, whereby the exclusion and rejection of those most in need is normal and acceptable. "Nice" people say these things. We can no longer speak of the far right simply in terms of ideology, but in terms of local and situated actions, through practical operations that perhaps never make their nature explicit but, nonetheless, can add up to change.

INTERNATIONAL POLITICAL SOCIOLOGY: OPENING UP ALTERNATIVE SPACES AND MODES OF KNOWING THE INTERNATIONAL

The arguments put forward in this book contribute toward the intellectual project known as international political sociology (IPS), particularly research taking place within an IPS problematization of security, in discussion with the wider field of critical security studies (CSS). As a discipline, CSS emerged after the Cold War, when ideas of threats as "external" and "objective" began to be unsettled (Dunn Cavelty 2007). With the rise in importance of non-state actors and the broadening of the security agenda within security institutions beyond state-centric military understandings, CSS sought to interrogate these new understandings of "threat," examining exactly how these new definitions and classifications came into being and gained traction (see CASE Collective 2006). Therefore, engaging with the idea of the international not as an objective category of analysis but instead as a specific problem, an IPS take on CSS has been extremely successful in bringing together scholars from across different disciplinary traditions – political sociology, anthropology, political theory, geography, criminology, and the humanities – to challenge disciplinary boundaries, borders, and entrenched categorizations (Huysmans and Nogueira 2016, 299). IPS works more as a methodologically pragmatic approach toward particular research questions or "problematiques" (see Guillaume and Bilgin 2016), analyzing specific practices, their strategies of justifications, and their implications, particularly in terms of how they empower certain groups or individuals and reproduce dominant forms of knowledge (Basaran et al. 2016, 3).

In this sense, it is the horizontality of practices that is important. We do not have the international or local levels of analysis; we have "transversal lines" (Basaran et al. 2016, 1) opposing the false dualisms found in international relations and broader political science between structure and agency, between constructivist approaches reliant on norms and theories and empirical approaches so often reliant on positivist epistemologies, and, lastly, between the collective and the individual (Bigo and Walker 2007). Instead, IPS thinks in terms of processes and relations: how agents are constituted by these processes and relations, and how their identities are shaped and transformed (Basaran et al. 2016, 4). Huysmans and Nogueira (2016, 299) have used the terminology of "fracturing international relations" to speak of the particular intervention IPS makes as a method of enquiry, directing attention to how societies, states, and the international are continuously made and remade (see also Guillaume and Bilgin 2016), instead of adopting what Coleman and Rosenow (2017) have called "ready-made accounts of power." Thinking in these terms thus opens up for enquiry the realm of the seemingly insignificant, realms of intervention that have variously referred to the "routine," "everyday," "local," "vernacular," or "ethnographic," sometimes in relation to "turns," though this denotes some kind of homogeneity to the work that has taken place there.

An IPS approach to studying security can thus be positioned against how the once-dominant frameworks in CSS conceptualized the way in which threats are brought into being – not least, scholarship associated with so-called securitization theory (ST) and the Copenhagen School.[1] Though vital in de-essentializing the notion of threats and instead conceiving security as an intersubjective process, ST famously conceives of threats as brought into being through a speech act by a political elite who declares an issue an existential threat (Buzan, Wæver, and de Wilde 1998). This issue is then accepted (or not) by the intended audience, and the issue becomes "securitized," lifted from the realm of ordinary politics to a type of emergency or panic politics where exceptional measures are justified.

Critiquing this framework, Basaran (2008, 340) so eloquently points out that "the problem with security ... is not its exceptionality, but its banality." Security is not an elite, exceptional, decisionist phenomenon politics but a banal, routine practice of various professionals of security. Focusing on the notion of security practices, an international political sociology of security has been at the forefront in bringing to light the role in which routines of, for example, police organizations, customs and immigration officers, or private companies are able to dominate what constitutes the truth about risk and unease through the power-knowledge nexus and produce an image of the enemy that resonates throughout society (Bigo 2002, 63).

A great deal of discussion within IPS has unsurprisingly focused, therefore, on freedom of movement, mobility, migration, and borders, particularly a practice-based approach to the topic of borders (Côté-Boucher, Infantino, and Salter 2014; Davidshofer, Jeandesboz, and Ragazzi 2016; Magalhães 2016). Shifting the analysis from borders to bordering has shed light on the way the practice can become a mundane activity, both de-centred and externalized, taking place within different "social universes" – not only the military sphere, or even the realm of border guards and police, but also through the work of database analysts operating far from any popular notion of a "border" (see Bigo 2014b). The effect of this has been the production of new systems of decentralized border controls (Garelli and Tazzioli 2017; Andersson 2014; Frowd 2014).

Taking account of the "diffusing insecurities" (Huysmans 2014, 74) that have permeated people's day-to-day lives in the post–Cold War period, the shift from ideas of security to notions of risk that took place in global governance, dispersed across a multiplicity of institutions far from high politics and statecraft, has also contributed to the study of more seemingly insignificant practices. The logic of risk, and the social and political implications of this rationalization, has been examined mostly in relation to technologies of surveillance (see Aradau, Lobo-Guerrera, and Van Munster 2008; Amoore and De Goede 2008; Aradau and Blanke 2017), most notably within techniques of migration governance, where subjects deemed at risk are conflated with risky subjects in the production of legitimate knowledge on the management of migrants, producing indifference as well as hostility (see Aradau 2004; Tazzioli 2017; Basaran 2015).

In studying everyday routines of bureaucrats, IPS scholars have also demonstrated the way in which security logics have permeated neighbouring fields. For example, Beerli (2018) has shown how the humanitarian space has witnessed the bureaucratization and professionalization of security in contemporary times, thus destabilizing any distinction between practices of humanitarianism and practices of security (see also Pallister-Wilkins 2015; Gabrielsen Jumbert 2013). Similarly, logics of emergency, preparedness, and prevention within the field of global health (Lakoff 2015) and climate change (Dalby 2013) have focused on the implications of anticipatory logics within these realms.

A profound move made by those working with an IPS approach to studying routine practices of security has been the conceptualization of *insecurity* too as a political practice, and not an essential state, or something necessarily in opposition to security. If we can no longer see security as an objective value, it becomes necessary to study the way in which different bodies of knowledge are *labelling* security, examining the tensions and controversies between different actors in these labelling practices, as well as their wider effects. Through different intellectual moves, it is possible to study the relationship between the construction of the security label and the boundaries of the security practices that may in fact be labelled by others as freedom, mobility, violence, privacy, or indeed human rights or hospitality. As opposed to viewing the two in opposition, Bigo (2007) conceptualizes the relation between security and insecurity as a Möbius strip, a metaphor that demonstrates how one can never be certain of what constitutes the content of security and not insecurity. As such, it is necessary to turn attention to the study of everyday *(in)securitization* processes and practices.

Though this turn to routines and diffuse insecurities has been absolutely crucial in destabilizing the idea of security as an exceptional act or as something far removed from ordinary people, it has been inclined to undertheorize the vast array of contradictory narratives and practices within people's day-to-day lived experiences. The emergence of the notion of a collective threat, risk, or danger outside bureaucratic or technocratic settings is also underexplored, as well as any examination of threat perception from the point of view of the targets of these security practices: the general public (see Vaughan-Williams and Stevens 2016 and Jarvis and Lister 2013 for an extended discussion of the latter).

THE EVERYDAY AND STUDY OF MICROPRACTICES IN INTERNATIONAL POLITICAL SOCIOLOGY

In addressing security and surveillance not as an exceptional act but as a "little security nothing" (Huysmans 2011), a major recent move in IPS has been a focus on the everyday as a domain in which to unsettle and intervene in dominant understanding of where power is enacted and situations of significance are made (see Huysmans 2016; Guillaume and Huysmans 2013; Noxolo and Huysmans 2009; Summa 2016). Drawing primarily on de Certeau's notion of quotidian practices, the everyday is conceived as a mode of invention, constructed from moment to moment when it is created from a multiplicity of practices.

In this vein and gaining inspiration additionally from Enloe's ([1990] 2014) hypothesis that women's daily and seemingly unimportant experiences are the stuff of global politics, Huysmans (2016) has developed the idea of "democratic curiosity" as a means to contest the diffusion of security practices ever deeper in everyday life. Here, "everyday" is conceived differently than the security routines that Bigo et al. speak of in that it is a space to resist or, more accurately, *appropriate,* the micropractices of surveillance that permeate day-to-day life: the CCTV cameras recording our image on public transportation, the capturing of data when we make a purchase using a contactless credit card, or the box-ticking of a consent form to accept the terms and conditions of a new mobile phone app. The everyday for Huysmans et al. is specific in that it is a realm of intervention and disruption as well as just reproduction.

Further scholarship that has attempted to conceptualize the everyday lived experiences of subjects of security has been rather limited. The few notable exceptions are those who use the terminology of "vernacular (in)security" to examine citizens' perceptions of threats at an everyday level (Vaughan-Williams and Stevens 2016) and those writing from within a "critical anthropology of security" perspective (Goldstein et al. 2010; Maguire, Frois, and Zurawski 2014; Green and Zurawski 2015).

With regard to the second category, Juliana Ochs' (2011) ethnography of everyday life in Israel during the second intifada is exemplary. From a CSS and IPS perspective, Huysmans (2014) reads Ochs' study as a destabilization of the exceptional/everyday life dichotomy by highlighting how the very exceptional and elite security practices of exception deployed in the Israeli state permeated the most intimate of relations. This is fascinating, and the myriad ways (often contradictory) in which people internalized a state of emergency certainly erase any notion of a distinct elite or everyday sphere. However, relatedly, and more profoundly, Ochs' rich ethnographic detail documenting mundane activities – from café culture after a suicide bombing to the blossoming of interest in soft furnishings and home decor as citizens were obliged to stay indoors – shows that everyday practices are not reducible to this idea of reproducing or challenging dominant security narratives. The very idea of dominant narratives is completely unsettled.

In contrast to working with ideas of disruption, reproduction, contestation, or appropriation of elite narratives of security, writing from an anthropological perspective embraces the idea of "mess" and the capacity of subjects of security to *both* reproduce and appropriate prevailing security practices and knowledge, without making explicit conclusions regarding the capacity of everyday practice to either resist or reproduce. The theorization is instead within the very "thick descriptions" (Geertz 1973) of the seemingly trivial acts of day-to-day life. Ochs' example from a chat with a security guard at a café is telling: "'I myself can't do anything. If a terrorist comes what can I do? … There is no one who can protect you. Not you for yourself. Only –' and he again pointed up to the sky, leaving open whether security remains, in his opinion, a matter of chance, fate, divine will, or diplomacy." (Israeli security guard cited in Ochs 2011, 61).

Here, Ochs manages to empirically capture Bigo's notion of the Möbius strip perfectly: there is no essential state of security or insecurity; these values are always relational, and what somebody labels insecurity another will label as fate; it depends entirely on one's position. Some recent scholarship within the critical anthropology of security that has done similar work, but perhaps pushes this notion of the Möbius strip even further, examines how local communities construct threats far from any explicit securitarian ideology, particularly what could be seen as an elite one. Diana Fox (cited in Goldstein et al. 2010) is close to my approach in her study of the way in which Jamaican parents, with the prospect of corporal punishment being banned in Jamaican schools under pressure from international non-governmental organizations, constructed this possibility in terms of a threat to national security. Without the right for teachers to hit children in schools, Jamaica would become a country filled with "gangsters" and "prostitutes" as children would grow up without discipline or boundaries.

Here, a question of human rights, when examined ethnographically and through everyday lived experiences, can be perceived by some as a threat to security. Security is seen as emergent and contingent. As with the Möbius strip, the question of whether an issue signifies rights or threats depends entirely on the perspective from where one is standing. For a researcher developing the type of anthropological sensibilities we have spoken of, as well as an ontological and epistemological openness to the field and all its mess and controversies, these conclusions can be extremely destabilizing.

Coleman (2015) makes a similar point in arguing against "activist anthropology" within ethnographic engagements with security, as this leads to "conceptual enclosure." Instead, she puts forth an approach that gives weight to ontologies emerging from everyday struggles and all their complexities. Austin (forthcoming), too, looks to the "local," "lay," and "ordinary" in a re-jigged "style" of critique that advocates an empathy and openness to all life experiences in the field, no matter how problematic this may be ethico-politically, as a way to understand the emergent causality of our particular problematiques within international relations (IR). This aligns with the professional ethic of sympathy with all research subjects that ethnography demands, which can lead to dissonance and moral ambiguity when the intimacies required by such research unsettle our ideas of "responsible scholarship" (see Eckl 2008).

RETHINKING CRITICAL SECURITY STUDIES ALONG ANTHROPOLOGICAL LINES

When I speak of rethinking CSS, I am speaking of placing the ontological primacy on this anthropological mode of knowing. An openness to how Bigo's Möbius strip is played out through the very micropractices of day-to-day life. In the spirit of an IPS mode of enquiry and commitment to disrupting taken-for-granted reifications, the mobilizing not only of ethnography as a method but also of a specific political anthropological way of knowing allows me to treat security not as an a priori category, but as an emergent and contingent phenomenon.

In this spirit of, and in pushing forth, the ontological value given by the political- anthropological, Bigo and Mc Cluskey (2018) speak about a "PARIS" approach to studying practices of (in)security, signifying not to a city with a specific school of CSS but an acronym for Political Anthropological Research for International Sociology. For us, it is essential to understand the moments in which individuals in their practices feel that they are (in)secure because of the relations and processes in which they are immersed. To reiterate, this could be a set of relations that others label freedom, violence, or human rights – or, as this book shows, generosity and even solidarity. It depends on precisely where one is standing. In this vein we share a great deal with Appadurai's (1996) idea of the international conceived as different sets of "–scapes" and the crucial role played by *imagination*, particularly the imagination framed as a social practice in the creation of these –scapes. Our aim is to objectivize these power relations, to bring them to light in all their complexity instead of subsuming them under a single category or grand narrative.

I am well aware that issues such as urban vs rural, north vs south, political landscapes, and varying socio-economic situations are not covered within this book, and some would charge me with bias and partiality. Needless to say, however, conducting ethnography on some sort of pre-calculated representative number of sites would be absolutely futile. There will always be something left out, somewhere not accounted for, and someone who could say that my findings are not generalizable to the situation anywhere else. In response, I would say is that I never claimed my project gives access to the "really real" (Behar 2003, 16) or provides some sort of innocent knowledge. My project was not intended to be a comparative survey of attitudes toward asylum in different parts of Sweden. On the contrary, all this book has attempted to do is to tell a story, with Öreby seen not so much as a bounded locale, the village – a somewhat hackneyed image now in the anthropological context (cf. Candea 2007, 180) – but as a "conjuncture of social relations," a "conjuncture of the national and the transnational" (De Genova 2005, loc311). Instead of endowing actors with a preconceived subjectivity – Swedish, villager, female, "good" person – an anthropological approach enabled me to write in the constantly shifting formations of these subjectivities as they were happening, engaging with the temporality of this subject formation. As the following chapters show, for the members of the NGO, this ricocheted between being women, mothers, teachers, confidents, eyewitnesses, and law enforcers – all the time, however, being "Swedish" and representing the "decent citizen." For the Syrians, it bounced between victim, friend, professional, or member of a cosmopolitan elite. And crucially, as I try to show, my presence was a major factor in many of these subject formations. Therefore, this anthropological account of life in Öreby is not an attempt to build some sort of meta-narrative. Instead, my interpretation of the goings-on in the village simply build traces, with the manner in which I made connections between these traces also written into the story.

The specific conceptual apparatus that I use to tell this story are set out below. Firstly, Scott's (1990) notions of a "hidden" and "public" transcript, and the significance he places on local practices of appropriation and re-appropriation, or metis, are absolutely essential in making this anthropological rethinking possible. Secondly, Foucault's idea of "governmentality," treated here as a concrete ethnographic object, is used to illuminate the making of these particular governable subjects. Crucial to note, however, I do not use this literature or these frameworks as some type of canon to study the everyday, conceptualize micropractices in precisely the same way as does Scott, or mobilize a Foucauldian approach as a type of dogma. To be clear, for me, an anthropological rethinking of CSS means placing absolute primacy on the ethnographic knowledge derived from people's situated lived experiences and my interactions with them. Drawing on Scott's and Foucault's specific theoretical mechanisms is useful only in conceptualizing the story as I wish to tell it: the various spins that people put on their day-to-day experiences, the way these micropractices added up to something more tangible, and the way in which taboos came to be shattered.

BRINGING THE EVERYDAY TO THE FOREFRONT: JAMES SCOTT AND THE HIDDEN TRANSCRIPT

Resonating to some extent with the scholarship of the most prominent cultural theorist of everyday life, Michel de Certeau (de Certeau 1998), the political scientist and anthropologist James C. Scott conceptualizes everyday acts in terms of resistance to domination. In his 1985 ethnographic study of mundane, microscopic acts of resistance by Malay peasants in a small farming village, entitled "Weapons of the Weak" and refined in his later thesis "Domination and the Arts of Resistance: Hidden Transcripts" in which he supplemented these observations with other examples from history, the author develops his concept of resistance through microscopic acts (Scott 1985; Scott 1990). Such resistance, however, can appear from the outside as acceptance of such domination and works, almost paradoxically, by maintaining the illusion of a placid surface, while slyly making use of fleeting, seized opportunities that push the limits of what is permitted (Scott 1990, 196)). Indeed, according to Scott's observations, both the "ruling" and "subordinate" groups – as labelled by the author – stage a convincing performance of a "public transcript," but at the same time produce a type of "hidden transcript" when simply in the company of each other. He sees the public transcript as representing the maintenance work that is needed to uphold relations of domination through symbolic demonstrations and enactments of power (Scott 1990, 49) and the hidden transcript as going slightly beyond groans of complaint or grumbles of discontent under one's breath in that, in a given structural situation, these grumbles are created and shared collectively.

Scott (2010) fashioned his thesis as a challenge to mainstream political science at the time and what it considered "political," since concerns over water irrigation or farming are conceptualized as the centre of political struggles. For Scott, struggle is not at the level of parliament but at the level of the everyday. The author first set about investigating the notion of a hidden transcript among Malay peasants with the precise idea of examining how Gramsci's notion of hegemony would work on the ground at the micro-level, in a tiny community. However, such a notion of a hidden infrapolitics of subordinate groups as resistance disputed both the concept of hegemony and the idea (which Scott debated with Tilly) that a political movement must have a strong public presence, i.e., banners, organizations, and slogans as well as defined public goals (Scott 2010).

Scott's theorization of the everyday later extends to practices of "mētis," which I discuss in chapter 5. Scott borrows the ancient Greek term – meaning a type of practical knowledge that involves adapting quickly and well to unpredictable events – to talk about the idiosyncratic practices of day-to-day life that are almost second nature. Here, we are not talking about a calculated strategy but an action that is only implicit and experiential in nature, acquired through practice and exercised in environments so complex that rational processes of decision-making do not apply. Scott (2010, 311) calls this the "art of the locality." In my story of the Swedish village, I develop this notion of metis to conceptualize the various ways a national myth was appropriated and re-appropriated in day-to-day goings-on, though never really articulated. These non-discursive practices, the various twists and turns, are just "the way things are done around here" and, as such, can never be codified.

Unlike James Scott's work, resistance in my story is, therefore, not emancipatory. We do not have the case of the poor peasants, subverting and evading their dominators in order to liberate themselves from these power structures. Instead, we have what appears to be a white, middle-class elite – by and large people who identify themselves as good and decent – adopting hidden transcripts and appropriating ideas of solidarity ever so slightly against the grain, to construct the newly arrived refugees as a threat, willing to sacrifice them in the name of not only protection (cf. Balzacq et al. 2010) but also decency. However, as with Scott's thesis, these dynamics are largely invisible to a casual observer, who would see only a placid surface and things appearing to rub along nicely.

When applied to the field of CSS and international political sociology, a significant number of studies of processes and practices of (in)securitization can certainly be found guilty of looking only at the public transcript, what is immediately visible or social life that is more or less stabilized and where consensus has been reached. CSS offers little to examine concrete empirical practices of appropriation and metis: controversies and dissensions that are not directly evident to the observer and that require a more political-anthropological approach to be able to shed light on the social world *in its making*. Thus, directing analysis to these tiny struggles and all their intricacies is fruitful in keeping the door of an IPS problematization of (in)security firmly open.

GOVERNMENTALITY AS AN ETHNOGRAPHIC OBJECT: EMPLOYING A DE-ESSENTIALIZED NOTION OF POWER AND GOVERNMENT

As well as orienting my argument along anthropological lines, inspired by the ethnographic work of James C. Scott, the other intellectual point of departure for my project is the thinking of the late Michel Foucault, particularly his notion of governmentality and a "caring biopolitics" (cf. Foucault 2007; Rose 1999).

Unlike the types of crude domination present in Scott's fieldwork, such as that of the peasants and nobility, serfs and landowners, conceptualizing power in modern democracies sees power as diffuse, circulatory, and productive, permeating all social interaction. Particularly pertinent then to my project is Foucault's notion of modern government, which refers not simply to a state apparatus but also to a "conduct of conduct." This refers to all the more or less methodical and strategic ways of thinking or acting that aim to regulate and manage the action of others for specific ends (Rose 1999, xxi). Within this framework, the state and its institutions are but one element in manifold circuits of power. "Government" refers to any rational attempt to shape or direct the conduct of human beings by acting upon their hopes, wants, contexts, and environments (Inda 2008, 1).

In this respect, such an exercise of power in the form of government can be differentiated from simple coercion or domination. Nikolas Rose best articulated this distinction: "To dominate is to ignore or to attempt to crush the capacity for action of the dominated. But to govern is to recognize that capacity for action and to adjust oneself to it" (1999, 4). To think in these terms enables us to have a better understanding of how the type of power relations engendered within humanitarian governance are in part salutary; certainly, the productive element of this banal, everyday myth-making sees the generation of self-governing, happy, and contented subjects. "Biopolitical" was Foucault's label for the type of power concerned with managing not only life, death, health, and illness but also everything to do with what we call lifestyle, including the social, cultural, and environmental conditions under which we live (Dean cited in Selby 2007, 333). To think in this way, however, also enables us to envisage how notions of obedience, discipline, obligation, and taboo likewise are in play. To criticize the morally exceptional narrative with regard to refugee policy would be to criticize something that everybody has agreed is unequivocally "good"; therefore, particular debates are off limits, at least publicly and within polite company.

Thus, what we have at stake is not an official state narrative being imposed on an unwilling population, or individuals resisting an ideology or dogma. Instead, we have only practices of conduct (of conduct) and counter-conduct,[2] broadly correlating with Scott's idea of the public and hidden transcripts, which are further discussed in chapters 3 and 4. Through adopting this Foucauldian point of departure, we are able to understand the hatching of new discourses in the Swedish story, and their capacity to adopt enough uniformity to account for change, not by evolution or a gradual development, but by the capacity that each element within an episteme is now read differently, through a different episteme, allowing something new to emerge. At play is not an alternative meta-narrative, one that rejects moral superpowerfulness, but simply microphysics, these tiny practices of conduct and counter-conduct that carve out new terrain of acceptable behaviour.

As the subtitle to this section suggests, my project does not treat governmentality as an abstract notion or Weberian ideal type, but as a tangible, ethnographic object. This means that I am not attempting to build a grand meta-narrative of asylum and refugee issues in so-called humanitarian countries, but instead am examining the concrete manifestations of the type of governmentality at play in these contexts. In this respect, my fieldwork attempts to be a "biopsy"[3] or snapshot of a type of governmentality that is in some ways transversal, though particularly pronounced in the Swedish story, with its national myth of moral exceptionalism and humanitarian superpowerfulness.

In summary, by adopting this approach and telling the story as I have done, this book provides new insights into everyday (in)security by making the following innovative contributions to understanding: First and foremost, the book develops an approach to (in)securitization that redirects the focus from public statements and actions to the relation between public and hidden transcripts and between everyday practices of metis and problems of the international. This takes us beyond the main approaches that look at public speech acts, official documents and discourses, and security professionals and technologies and develops a truly anthropological approach of how security is enacted in mundane practices and spaces.

Secondly, the book demonstrates the great value of working at the intersection between anthropology and CSS for understanding the (in)securitization of migration by placing an absolute ontological primacy on the ethnographic, situated descriptions of people's everyday lived experiences as a mode of knowing and of knowledge.

Lastly, the book contributes to understanding ambivalences in humanitarian actions and in particular how humanitarian intentions and practices can relatively easily slip into their opposite. Unlike most analyses that focus on humanitarian organizations or logics, this analysis focuses on how humanitarian sentiments and practices are enacted in micro-situations in a village, and at the interstices between a national discourse and everyday experiences and expressions in an ordinary village.

RESEARCH STRATEGY AND OVERVIEW OF THE ARGUMENT

Of the four years I spent on this project, about nineteen months were spent in Öreby, a small village in Skåne, Sweden, in which about 70 Syrian refugees were initially resettled. Over the course of my fieldwork, the number gradually increased, reaching about 120 people by the end of my primary research period.[4] In February 2013, I joined the newly established grassroots organization Friends of Syria, which had been founded in the village a few weeks previously as a way to collect and distribute donations, and help the refugees settle into life in Sweden. Offering my services as a translator and interpreter, I followed encounters between the volunteers and refugees when new refugees arrived or when new volunteers joined the group. I was also present for many of the village special events – National Day, Children's Day, the anniversary of a walking trail to the next village, and the autumn market – engaging in the broader interactions between the refugees and the villagers. During my time in Öreby, my position bounced between being a foreign "expert" on refugees, a friend and supporter of the volunteers – especially Bodil, chair of the Friends of Syria – to being a sympathetic ear that some of the refugees could confide in about the problems they faced in Sweden, or at least somebody who could temporarily relieve their boredom for a couple of hours. I also conducted about two dozen more-structured interviews in people's homes – with volunteers, refugees, and figureheads in the village – about their feelings toward the resettlement and in an attempt to piece together events that had taken place before my arrival. In order to not identify any of the people who took part in the study, I chose to change all the names in my book, from the village and location of Öreby to the name of the NGO, the Friends of Syria. I have also used pseudonyms for everyone I have written into the story; however, I have endeavoured to convey conversations that took place as accurately as possible.[5] This is not to say that I have attempted to provide a fly-on-the-wall account of the happenings in Öreby while I was there. Recognizing that it is always the ethnographer and not indigenous voices producing the authority of the text (cf. Clifford 1983), the book is clear that the very dialogical nature of any ethnographic situation renders any representation characteristically "problematic, contested and thus political" (De Genova 2005, 24). Therefore, I hope that I have been sufficiently open in the chapters that follow about the political choices I made while undertaking this project and about the reasons I have told the story of Öreby in the way that I have.

To briefly reiterate, upon embarking on this project, I did not set out to document the rise of the far right in Sweden or to engage with anybody who identified with the far right. I did not approach my fieldwork expecting to work with ordinary, decent people – volunteers, various community figureheads, and altogether unremarkable villagers – who, upon receiving over one hundred refugees in their village, came to view these refugees in terms of being both victim and threat. Indeed, within my imagination, the far right were nothing at all to do with my research. Within the following nineteen months, however, what villagers once labelled as far right and off limits began to loom ever larger within my research, not in terms of ideology but through tiny acts or snatches of conversation, whereby these good and decent folk felt that they had no choice but to vote for an anti-immigration party and engage in a number of other practices that would have been seen as thoroughly indecent only a few months previously.

This book tells the story of this journey, the manner in which a small, rural community in Sweden acted to take their security into their own hands, not simply by voting for the far-right party (which over one in four people in the village did in the 2014 general election) but also by writing blogs for far-right websites conveying "first-hand," and "eyewitness" accounts of life in a refugee centre, by inviting TV crews to film the "real" goings-on in their village, by accusing the refugees of milking the system, and by warning them that they would be killed by the Swedish police if they did not "behave."

By drawing upon this particular case in detail, the book narrates ways in which the concepts of decency and righteousness were reconfigured over time and through various processes and mechanisms, and the manner in which a new arena of acceptable behaviour was carved out. It follows how an entire world view became contested, not by evolution or a gradual development, but because each constituent within this discursive framework was able to be read differently. What emerged was something new. Not an alternative meta-narrative, one that rejected moral superpowerfulness, but simply microphysics: tiny practices of conduct and counter-conduct, a hidden transcript of stigmatization of the refugees (never articulated in polite company) that eventually broke through and became public, carving out a new terrain of acceptable behaviour.

By the end of my fieldwork, relations between the refugees and the volunteers had been disbanded. The tiny grassroots NGO, Friends of Syria, which sprung up in reaction to the hostility some of the villagers had displayed toward the resettling of the refugees at an initial meeting, had disintegrated. The small activity centre, an apartment that the volunteers had co-opted as a space for the refugees to hang out and a location where the volunteers could run their various activities and classes, had been closed down. Migrationsverket (Swedish Migration Agency), which had established the centre, could no longer afford to fund it, and with fewer and fewer people turning up (both refugees and volunteers), nobody could be bothered to fight the government migration agency's decision. Bodil, the woman who founded the grassroots group, whom many of the refugees at one point described as a "gift from God," had distanced herself from the group, complaining of being sick and tired of the Syrians and wanting her life back.[6]

The broader political picture within the country very much mirrored the goings-on in Öreby. At the height of the so-called refugee crisis, the political landscape within Sweden also dramatically changed. As of November 2015, Sweden reversed the decision to grant asylum to all Syrians arriving at the border, issuing them with only temporary permits as well as reintroducing border checks on the Oresund Bridge and ferry (See *Dagens Nyheter* 2015a; *Guardian* 2015a). Sweden said it could no longer shoulder such a burden practically single-handedly (along with Germany). The numbers of people arriving were simply too many, according to most people – it no longer being taboo to say so. Therefore, by adopting a political-anthropological approach to security, we are best placed to understand the manifold array of practices and processes that lead to the generation of this new episteme as they evolve and how, far from any political ideology, such moves can still be conceived of as good and righteous. As Didier Bigo (2014a) forcefully argued: "The perspective from a very small, remote village may illuminate more about international life that a synthesis of the dominant perspective and its stereotypization of all others as 'the Other,' or the enemy, or the suspect."

In telling the story of the way in which the Syrian refugees in Öreby come to be seen as a threat to the village, legitimately articulated as unwelcome, undesirable, and even disposable, this book puts forward five hypotheses or signposts. Firstly, it argues that the idea of the Swedish national myth of moral exceptionalism, especially regarding its refugee and asylum policy, generates a particular type of subjectivity and plays a major part in the construction of governable subjects.[7] I label this type of governmentality the governmentality of righteousness, which I expand upon in the following three chapters. Secondly, it states that in generating this particular subjectivity of the good citizen, the governmentality of righteousness also renders certain behaviours and specific practices taboo. Open criticism of Swedish asylum policy is deemed in bad taste. This phenomenon is expanded upon in the chapter 4.[8]

Thirdly, and most importantly, the book argues that, within the axes of practices subsumed within this mode of governmentality, within the wiggle room and metis of this specific conduct of conduct, solidarity is appropriated and re-implanted as humanitarianism, hospitality, and generosity, with all the baggage this embodies. Refugees are provided with a high standard of living; however, as chapter 3 demonstrates, they are expected to play by all the rules of being a worthy guest.[9] Everyday interactions between the villagers and refugees are permeated with these obligations of reciprocity on the part of the Syrians. Building on this idea and developed in chapter 4, my fourth hypothesis goes on to state that the tiny practices of counter-conduct by the so-called good citizen, also embedded within the governmentality of righteousness, serves to form a type of hidden transcript. This transcript utilizes, re-utilizes, reinserts and re-implants, and recreates what it means to be a good citizen in terms of Swedish asylum policy, permitting the Syrian refugees to be viewed as undeserving and undesirable. Lastly, I put forward the idea that through the mechanism of a "moral panic" (Cohen 1980), these previously non-discursive practices and hidden transcripts can be openly voiced and social relations between the refugees and the good citizens are completely disbanded.

The core of my argument conceives of solidarity and metis as the base of an (in)securitization iceberg, the tip of which sees the sacrifice of the Syrian refugees as legitimate in the name of protection (cf. Balzacq et al. 2010). In the final chapter, I argue that it is the appropriation of solidarity toward the refugees not in rational and egoist terms but as a *free gift* that laid the basis for both the articulation of the refugees as undesirable and the disbanding of social relations to be justified. Though the Swedish national myth conceives of solidarity to such an individualistic extent that some theorists have likened it to the truest form of love (see Trägårdh and Berggren 2015), very local experiences and local understandings go somewhat against this. In his essay on the gift, Mauss ([1923] 1990) discusses the notion of "raising stakes" in the giving of a gift. Likewise, moral superiority and exceptionalism at an international level is conceived within the imagination of the good citizen in ever more demanding terms. Thus, Sweden's decision to be the "odd" country wanting to take more refugees (as referred to in a speech by then–integration minister Erik Ullenhag), at a very local level obliges greater and greater degrees of reciprocity from those "lucky" enough to be allowed in. These tiny practices of metis, these appropriations and re-appropriations of solidarity, moving ever further away from an abstract, rationalist conceptualization toward the embodiment of Mauss's free gift, gradually carves out an ever-wider area of acceptable conduct toward the refugees. Counter-conduct becomes conduct, the hidden transcript becomes public, and the boundary between the refugees and their hosts becomes crystallized, not through spectacular politics, ideology, or a competing meta-narrative, but through the tiny interactions of metis and solidarity, through the microphysics and hatching of new discourses. Social forces that begin as small and seemingly insignificant nonetheless go on to underpin these seemingly exceptional moments of exclusion.

OUTLINE OF THE CHAPTERS

In the telling of the story, chapter 2 introduces my case study of Sweden and foregrounds my ethnographic analysis in the broader domain of Swedish nationalism. Drawing primarily on the work of Charles Tilly (1999, 2002), it examines this nationalism as a type of standard story that, although actively promulgated by various political elites from the 1950s to the 1980s, is now (re)produced through more banal nation-centred practices and in relation to other EU member states. Though argued for some time as being an old-fashioned and outdated idea, the strategic resurrection of the national myth of moral exceptionalism is looked at in this chapter with regard to the refugees from the Syrian Civil War.

Chapter 3 introduces the village of Öreby, the refugees who were settled there, and the Friends of Syria local organization. Taking as a point of departure Tilly's standard story, but viewed through a Foucauldian lens, the chapter focuses on the productive element of the governmentality of righteousness and the myriad everyday practices available for the so-called decent citizen within the wiggle room of this modality of government. With open criticism of refugees deemed taboo in polite company, it looks at the "onstage posturing" of villagers in welcoming the refugees – publicly performing their generosity and tolerance – as well as the actions by the villagers that went ever so slightly against the grain of this idea of decency. The hierarchization and stigmatization of the refugees, with obligations placed on them to play by all the rules of being "deserving," is also examined.

Chapter 4 continues the story of Öreby and the way in which these tiny acts of marginalization set the foundation for much more overt exclusionary practices. It speaks of the hidden transcript of unease that manifested as the result of the refugee taboo, particularly along the lines of gender equality and good parenting whereby the Arab men were deemed to be hypersexualized and the children war-damaged, deficient, and deviant. It analyzes how through various moral panics – momentary eruptions of frenzy – the refugees were legitimately able to be openly spoken about as undesirable and the whole arena of what was deemed acceptable behaviour toward the refugees shifted significantly.

Chapter 5 looks at the more conceptual questions raised by my research and the main interventions my project has made into the CSS and anthropology of security literature. It stresses, firstly, the role of reflexivity in generating any meaningful dialogue between the two disciplines before then focusing on metis and arguing for attention to be paid to local knowledge and practical operations in any study of (in)securitization. Lastly, it examines the important role played by the idea of solidarity, arguing that it was the abnormailization of this concept and its reconstruction as a free gift that was central in enabling the refugees to be cast as dispensable.

The concluding chapter moves away from Sweden and reflects more broadly upon the developments that have taken place since I conducted my fieldwork, most notably the rise of so-called populism, nativism, and far-right parties across Europe and the West, and the seeming shattering of taboos whereby it becomes normal and, indeed, acceptable to speak in xenophobic and hostile ways about migrants. Here, I argue that a political-anthropological approach to the study of (in)security practices is the best framework for analyzing the challenging and changing of established norms. Engaging with localized, practical, and perhaps seemingly unimportant everyday practices can inform a more far-reaching phenomenon. In light of the 2015 and 2016 refugee crises, the way in which fears are manifested, exploited, and managed is best studied through such an approach, enabling engagement with these processes as they develop and evolve.

2

Construction of the Self

Sweden as Morally Exceptional

Before moving to my fieldwork in the village of Öreby, I'll first examine the cherished notion of Sweden as morally exceptional and shed some light on exactly how this myth was brought about and continues to be reproduced. As the introductory chapter discussed, in bringing their subjectivities into being, the volunteers and villagers I worked with bounced between identifying themselves as women, mentors, confidants, eyewitnesses, and law enforcers. However, as we will see in the following two chapters, a somewhat constant subjectivity was the self-identification of the villagers in very nationalistic terms as "good Swedes." In performing the role of welcoming the refugees into their village, the Öreby folk were keeping with their idea of what they considered a decent citizen did and how a decent citizen behaved. Unlike the countrymen and women in their fellow EU member states such as Denmark, the UK, or Italy, the "good Swede" was somewhat unique in displaying solidarity with the refugees, in offering them a safe haven and a new life for their families.

This chapter aims to foreground my ethnographic work in these broader nationalist narratives, looking at exactly which national identifications and stories the villagers of Öreby were drawing upon in their stance toward the refugees. The chapter examines this idea of Swedish moral exceptionalism as a popular national myth and cherished narrative, one that is constantly reconstructed and redefined to embody slightly different characteristics and markers, sometimes contradictory, but that nonetheless come to form a dominant narrative, or even nationalist dogma. In drawing primarily on the work of Charles Tilly (1999, 2002), Swedish nationalism is examined as a set of stories, emulations, and cultural modelling, all the time recognizing that nationalism has a performative element and embodies very real aspects of people's lived experiences. Moving away from the traditional international relations idea of looking at a nation's brand through a strategic soft-power lens, the idea of Sweden as progressive, open, free-thinking, caring, and unpretentious is seen as crucial in the production of a certain subjectivity, unique among Nordic countries in its combination of embracing modernity while retaining (secularized) Lutheran values.

The first part of the chapter examines the trajectory of the historic moral superpower regime of Sweden in international relations, examining the practices that went on performing and reproducing this myth from a more elite-manipulation view, stressing the importance of politicians such as Hansson and Palme in propagating the idea of Sweden as a truly modern state during the 1950s, '60s, '70s, and '80s. Particular attention is paid to the concept of solidarity and the way in which this notion was and is envisaged within the Swedish standard story, traditionally through the state's non-aligned security doctrine, its generous welfare program (*folkhemmet*), large developmental aid budget, and openness to refugees.

Though this national myth of moral exceptionalism is now argued as being a somewhat old-fashioned idea, confined to the dustbin of history, the second half of this chapter demonstrates the way in which it was never buried that deeply and, instead, was generated through more indirect means. Drawing additionally on Billig's idea of "banal nationalism" and Brubaker's notion of "nation-oriented practices," the chapter examines the production of exceptionalism through much more routine and diffuse activities. Introducing briefly the idea of the governmentality of righteousness (a concept that is much expanded upon in the following chapter), it examines the way the nationalist narrative is produced nowadays mostly in relational terms through practices of rankings, indices, opinion polls, nation branding, and popular representations of "the other," who are never quite as good, moral, or generous. Following Miller and Rose (2008), I conceive of these benchmarking practices as technologies of this type of governmentality.

Lastly, the chapter examines the very conscious and considered resurrection and triumph of the myth of the "Swedish model" in relation to its asylum and refugee policy vis-à-vis the Syrian Civil War, which has cemented Sweden's position as once again morally exceptional, unique in its position as most open to those fleeing war and persecution.¹

NATIONALISM AS ANTI-NATIONALISM: THE ROLE OF THE NATION IN THE SWEDISH EXPERIENCE

> Man is an animal suspended in webs of significance he himself has spun.
> Clifford Geertz (1973), *The Interpretation of Cultures*

The project of Swedish nationalism has been the subject of a great deal of literature within the country, most notably the scholarship of Orvar Löfgren (1990, 1993), Ake Daun's (1996) famous study of "Swedish Mentality," and Jonas Frykman's important contributions of "The [pure and rational] Hygienic Vision" (1981) and "The Swedishization of Sweden" (1993).

The stereotype of Sweden as the perfect society – good, moral, and champion of human rights – is a cherished narrative, a popular national myth. Historically, the image of Sweden as a moral superpower (Ruth 1984; Nilsson 1991; Dahl 2006) was centred on its activist foreign policy after the Second World War from Vietnam to South Africa, an interventionist approach that gained Sweden this label ahead of, among others, Canada, Norway, and the Netherlands (Dahl 2006). Indeed, Sweden's model could not be seen as merely passive, but as a guide or role model that was actively promoted. As a small state with no colonial history and a non-aligned security doctrine that had been in place since the Napoleonic Wars, Sweden came to see itself as "the conscience of the world," traditionally taking an active role since the Second World War in highlighting the plight of powerless actors, standing in solidarity with the dispossessed, and making it its duty to speak out against US interventions.

Ann-Sofie Dahl (2006) likens Sweden's moral superpower discourse with the Dutch notion of *gidsland*, a Lutheran almost missionary-like zeal (though without the same support of free trade as a means of universal progress). The moral superpower narrative presumed Sweden as a state to be more enlightened than other nations, thus rendering it obliged to spread the message and to better humankind (Nilsson 1991; Dahl 2006). Trägårdh (2007) also runs with this idea of Sweden as crusading and proselytizing, conceptualizing the Swedish model as on a "holy mission to spread the good message of Swedish social democracy to the world."

The many ethnologists studying nationalism and nationalism in Sweden firmly situate the country within, indeed sometimes even the embodiment (along with France) of, what Kohn famously typified as "Western" nationalism, as opposed to the more backward and reactionary nationalism of the non-West, which was seen as more emotional and authoritarian. This Western nationalism supposedly emerged out of the spirit of the Enlightenment and was connected in its genesis with ideas of individual liberty and rational cosmopolitanism (Kohn 1961).

This tendency to equate nationalism with its extreme manifestations was, in fact, a reason why a great deal of the literature on national myths dealt with the processes taking place in parts of the periphery; "problems" of nationalism, as pointed out by Ozkirimli (2010, 5) belonged to "them" and were not "ours." As this so-called Western nationalism was seen as good and harmless, it was not subject to the same degree of critique. As Michael Billig (1995, 55) asserts, "our" nationalism is not framed as nationalism per se, with all its connotations of irrationality, excess, and unfamiliarity, but instead is seen as patriotism, which is inoffensive, sometimes even beneficial. In his famous study of "materializing the nation," it was Swedish nationalism that Löfgren (1993) contrasted with the US to exemplify this type of unconscious (re)production of nationalism through everyday practices, as opposed to rhetoric: "The old nations have images of operetta states and banana republics, and in these caricatures we see clearly the institutionalized patterns for what a proper nation is supposed to look like. Successfully accomplished national projects, such as that of the Swedish and French, are quickly taken for granted; unsuccessful examples, on the other hand, serve as examples of unrealistic ambitions or airy-fairy dreams, or merely comic attempts to initiate the old national giants" (Löfgren 1993, 166).

This banal nationalism, as articulated by Billig (1995) is especially salient in the Swedish case whereby nationalism is especially seen to be something increasingly associated with the far right, a subject of embarrassment and disdain. For Billig (1995), nationalisms of the West should not be viewed as emerging only in extraordinary situations such as times of crisis, but instead be conceptualized as habits that are reproduced daily. He states that "this reminding [of nationhood] is so familiar, so continual, that it is not consciously registered as reminding ... The metonymic image of banal nationalism is not a flag which is being consciously waved with fervent passion; it is the flag hanging unnoticed on the public building" (Billig 1995, 6–8). Indeed, a well-worn cliché, particularly in recent popular culture, is the mocking of the seemingly overly nationalistic Norway, which is the subject of ridicule and teasing in Sweden especially regarding the celebration of their National Day on 17 May, complete with national costumes, flag waving, and street parades. The commemoration of their democratic ideals dating back to the 1815 constitution – regarded with such reverence in Norway that all amendments are written in its original language, Danish – is framed as a source of bemusement by Swedes (see Ruth 1984). Any sense of collectivity in Sweden is also thought to pale in comparison to that of the Danes, who are seen to rally around their national hero, nineteenth-century cleric, historian, and educator, N.F.S. Grundtvig (Ruth 1984), as well as that of the Finns, who are seen to have a shared sense of unity brought about by experiences in the Second World War (Ruth 1984). Somewhat paradoxically then, to be nationalistic is to be un-Swedish, antithetical to what it means to be modern and outward looking. Booth (2014), in a recent travelogue of Scandinavia, even jokes how the Swedish national anthem doesn't even once mention the word Sweden.

As Brubaker (1996, 10) has successfully argued, however, viewing nationalism as some kind of force that resurges and recedes would be a certain error. A more accurate understanding would be to conceptualize the nationalism as a heterogeneous set of nation-oriented practices, idioms, and possibilities that are endemic in contemporary social and political life. Nationalism cannot be understood without taking into account its "everyday manifestations" (Ozkirimli 2010, 231). Important to look at is the way in which ideologies, myths, and dominant narratives are reproduced through routine and often bureaucratic practices of everyday life: the mundane opinions, attitudes, and blasé acts of discrimination (cf. Billig 1995; van Dijk 1998). For Billig (1995), social scientists themselves contribute to this process by defining nationalism in too restricted a way, confining it to nationalist movements based on irrationality. The literature on Danish nationalism, discussed later in this chapter, is crucial in this process. The spectacle of the "cartoon affair" and the anti-immigration rhetoric of the right-wing government is held up as a sort of re-emergence of nationalism. It can be pointed to as an example of crisis or calamity, worthy as an object of study while other Scandinavian nationalisms are seen as uninteresting, unproblematic, and certainly unworthy of the same level of scrutiny.

Charles Tilly was one of the most important, though arguably underestimated, authors in this regard, with his focus in the latter years of his career on nationalism as performance, stories, and cultural modelling (Brubaker 2010). His notion of "emulation," or the idea of the "visible, prestigious and transferable models" of successful nationalism projects, is seen as one of the most important contributions to the field (Brubaker 2010). The outcome of this process was a world in which "administrative structures, constitutions, and declared commitments of regimes to development, stability, and democracy came to resemble each other far more than did the diversity of their populations, material conditions, and actual accomplishments" (Tilly, cited in Brubaker 2010).

For Tilly (1994), the mundane terrain of the quotidian serves to conceal the array of networks and resources that depend on the existence of the nation for their very being. Furthermore, the performative element of nationhood is enacted through what Tilly (2002) calls "standard stories" that emphasize the cultural homogeneity and cohesiveness of the nation. He insisted on the way in which, "for reasons that lie deep in childhood learning, cultural immersion, or perhaps even in the structure of human brains, people usually recount, analyze, judge, remember, and reorganize social experiences as *standard stories* in which a small number of self-motivated entities interact within a constricted, contiguous time and space" (Tilly 2002, 47, emphasis in original). The importance of these performances for Tilly was their external audience, "disciplined, stereotyped public demonstrations of nationness" (1999, 179) were crucial for recognition and the granting of statehood.

Resonating strongly with Tilly's conception of the standard story is the notion of the national myth, taken as something inherently primordial to nations in much of the nationalist literature (cf. Smith 1986; Armstrong 1982) but recently studied in more sociological terms. For example, in Miller's (1995) famous defence of nationality, he writes how all national identities contain a substantial element of myth, some being complete invention but most being based on a specific interpretation of events whose occurrence is accepted by all. He cites Orwell in defending this claim: "Myths which are believed tend to become true, because they set up a type of 'persona,' which the average person will do his best to resemble" (Orwell, cited in Miller 1995, 37).

In this way, national myths take on a life of their own. For Calhoun (1994, 3–4), these self-understandings, although "dubious," are also very real as aspects of lived experiences. People identify with certain stories as being "theirs" and, hence, collude to a degree with the production of these fictions, even to the extent that they are recognized as a sort of background condition of everyday life.

THE TRAJECTORY OF MORAL EXCEPTIONALISM IN THE SWEDISH MYTH-MAKING MACHINE

Writing in the mid-1980s, Swedish ethnologist Ruth notes that it is the idea of being exceptional that still united social consciousness in Sweden. For Ruth (1984), this myth is interesting in that, unlike its counterpart in the United States, it has never *officially* been articulated as an ideology as such, though always implied. Therefore, in tracing back this national myth of Swedish exceptionalism and moral superpowerfulness, one finds most of the scholarship united around the idea of the element of *conscious* nation-building practices by elites in twentieth-century Sweden in transforming their nation's small state position from being a handicap to a benefit (Ruth 1984). This suggestion of some kind of instrumental element to the generation of a nationalist dogma and national myth-making that is devoid of any type of binding moral tradition is more in line with the elite-manipulation view of nationalism than a type of banal practice as in Billig's conception, though of course without the element of violent conflict, and is led by so-called modernists such as Paul Brass: "The study of ethnicity and nationality is in large part the study of politically induced cultural change. More precisely, it is the study of the process by which elites and counter-elites within ethnic groups select aspects of the group's culture, attach new value and meaning to them, and use them as symbols to mobilize the group, to defend its interests, and to compete with other groups" (Brass, Taylor, and Yapp 2000, 40–1).

In this respect, nationalism as a political movement is seen in the Swedish context as a type of *ideology*, a particular social democratic movement and dogma embodying and combining the seemingly contradictory elements of a sense of common purpose, hostility to pre-industrial values, a rationalistic futurism taking the place of religion, and anti-traditionalism as, somewhat paradoxically, the dominant tradition (Ruth 1984). For Ruth, this emerged as a reaction to Sweden being a country of self-doubt and intense vulnerability. He points to August Strindberg, writing as early as the 1880s, openly criticizing the political elite and professing cosmopolitanism as the only tenable attitude for a Swede.

Although the first few decades of the twentieth century saw the Social Democrats in Sweden fashion Sweden as a vanguard of modernism, which the entire nation embodied, it was foreign writers and scholars who identified Sweden as a model. In the 1930s, writing for a US audience, Marquis Childs generated the image of Sweden as the "Middle Way," an exemplar of how freedom could be preserved with a relatively large amount of state intervention (Childs 1966 [1933]). The Anglo-Saxon world, as well as left-wing politicians and journalists from Germany and Austria, also propagated the myth of Sweden as a progress machine in the post-war period, with foreign journalists often said to be visiting Swedish institutions to study the secrets of their success (Ruth 1984).

It was, of course, during this time that Social Democrat Prime Minister Per Albin Hansson's famous concept of *folkhemmet* (the people's home) was brought into the popular imagination, whereby the previously vague, organicist concept of a cohesive society was transformed to incorporate a radical program of social reform (Lawler 1997, 568). The *folkhem* concept became so successfully engrained in the Swedish episteme that it came to be viewed as bipartisan, even perhaps apolitical, and thus serving to solidify the hegemony of social democracy in the region for many decades to come (Lawler 1997). The notion that Sweden should be like a good home – devoid of inequality and marked by mutual understanding – set the course for introduction of free education at all levels, including tertiary, and free universal health care, which was enacted between 1947–55 (Hentilä 1978). It was also with the birth of *folkhemmet* that the oft-cited notion of solidarity first came to the fore. Indeed, the welfare state saw the linking of solidarity with notions such as egalitarianism and social justice (Lawler 2007): solidarity conceived as a type of insurance incorporating every citizen into the fold.

However, this discourse of moral exceptionalism did not take hold in Swedish public consciousness until the 1950s, when the concept became more overtly instrumentalized by political elites. This socialist, ideological model cherished among the Social Democrats (who, aside from a few years in the early 1990s when Carl Bildt's Conservative-led coalition were in power, monopolized government until 2006) reached its climax in the mid-1980s under Olof Palme, who positioned Sweden publicly as detached from both superpowers throughout the Cold War, with especially vociferous criticism of US foreign policy at the time.

It was also during this time that concern for the suffering of those in the then Third World became a feature of elite Swedish rhetoric. Sällstrom (1999) writes of this phenomenon as one of the most path-breaking dimensions of Swedish internationalism. Interestingly, Gustavsson (1998) ascribes these feelings not only as a desire by Sweden to break away from its isolated position on the periphery of Europe but also as a way to assuage its feelings of guilt due to military, economic, and political security. This new notion of Swedish internationalism saw journalists and writers from inside Sweden run with this idea of Sweden as the embodiment of utopia:

> We are experiencing today in Scandinavia one of the most important experiments of world history. That may sound pretentious, yet it isn't. Scandinavia of today is the world's avant-garde society. What is taking place among us will happen in other countries tomorrow, as soon as they have reached a comparable level of freedom and welfare. We have an almost unlimited freedom of speech and freedom of the press. We have a standard of living that is the envy of the whole world. We simply have every imaginable opportunity to lead our lives in free development of our human and creative possibilities ... If we only know how to use our freedom and to realize it in our lives, our experience ... will be of profit [to] the entire world around us. (Gustavsson 1998)

Thus, the notion of solidarity emerged once again, but this time embodying a sense of compassion for distant others.[2] This was amplified throughout the following two decades when, absorbed into the moral superpower narrative, Sweden's reputation grew as a welcoming and open country for those fleeing war and persecution.[3] Throughout the 1970s, the passing of legislation that saw non-citizens resident in Sweden for three years having the right to vote in, as well as stand for office in, local elections cemented this progressive identity, as Bjork noted in his discourse analysis of newspaper articles during this time: "Editorials [during the 1970s] were often characterized by a pronounced self-righteousness, an unshakeable belief that Sweden really was the best in the world at formulating immigrant and refugee policies. A fundamentally ethnocentric worldview was manifested" (Bjork, cited in Pred 2000, 44).

The mid-1970s also saw the adoption of multiculturalism as a political doctrine, whereby immigrants were given the opportunity to decide the extent to which they adopted a Swedish cultural identity. The term *"invandrare"* was initiated as something forward-thinking and egalitarian in the late 1960s. Introduced by the Ministry for Employment and adopted shortly afterward by several other governmental agencies, the aim was to move away from the supposed dehumanizing term "imported foreign labour" (Molina 1997, 23). However, with the word "immigrant" or *"invandrare"* becoming divorced from actual processes of migration, and with the absence of ethnically determined categories of identity within Swedish society (compared, for example, with Britain's ethnicity categories of British Asians, Black Caribbean, or Black African), the terms "immigrant" and "Swede" came to represent two mutually exclusive categories. An immigrant could not be a Swede and vice versa. However, an immigrant's culture, in keeping with the doctrine of multiculturalism, was to be respected and tolerated according to the Social Democratic governmental ideology (Molina 1997).

For many scholars within international relations, this very instrumentalized view of elites fashioning the state as possessing desirable, attractive elements is purely a strategic measure designed to build the political and diplomatic clout of states within institutions. The idea of states having the capacity to influence other states without the use of force is an old and well-established one in mainstream liberal IR theory, evident all the way back to discussions about the importance of winning "hearts and minds" in British Malaya. Framing oneself in a positive way through a certain cultural identity or through political institutions is thought to serve as a way of attracting others to your ideas. Most famously, this idea of "soft power" was embraced and instrumentalized by Joseph Nye, who sped down the road of strategically wielding "culture" and "values" as a way to seduce and persuade "the other" – without so much as a backward glance during the Clinton administration. "You can get others to admire your ideals and do what you want, you do not have to spend as much on sticks and carrots to move them in your direction. Seduction is always more effective than coercion and many values like human rights, democracy and individual opportunity are deeply seductive" (Nye 2004, x).

The notion of Europe possessing some sort of "moral authority" as an "island of peace" grew out of this particular narrative, where the presentation of the self as somehow innately imbued with democratic governance, human rights, and gender equality is central. In Nye's example, Norway is trumpeted for its "attractiveness" – most notably for its efforts in "peacemaking " – though all of the Nordic countries are lauded by this particular author for their moral authority, in this respect framed against all the brutishness of the death-penalty-condoning, war-instigating, and gun-toting United States.

This line of thought in IR lies on the same continuum as broader reflections on power as subtle and diffuse; for example, the phenomenon of an actor being rendered as powerful without actually having to act (Lukes 2004, 86). Furthermore, the attraction or magnetism that derives from status, in which Lukes includes notions of deference, alleviates those actors who are already comfortable in their positions from acting and instead allows focus on preservation (Lukes 2004, 86). For James C. Scott, "the impact of power is most readily observed in acts of deference, subordination and ingratiation" (Scott 1990, 9).

For both Ingebritsen (2002) and Bergman (2007), the shift toward internationalism in the Scandinavian states can by no means be explained only by their geopolitical location and a desire to break away from a peripheral role in world politics, though this is part of the reason. These writers point to a consistency between domestic policies and exporting these policies abroad. The "shared social democratic institutions" of the Scandinavian nations, as well as their "ideologies of social partnership" (Ingebritsen 2002, 13) and a consensus-based policy-making machine, enable the states to effectively and unhypocritically export the model of environmental policy-making, peace-keeping, and development aid. This type of internationalism is conceived of as "a *logical extension* of the idea of social solidarity at home to solidarity abroad" (Ingebritsen 2002, 18, emphasis added). Bergman (2007) uses to approach of the English School of IR, particularly the notion of "solidarism" or a "thin cosmopolitanism" to argue that Sweden's notion of good international citizenship is grounded in a rule-bound international society that is sensitive to issues of redistributive justice, regardless of borders. Citing various Social Democratic political elites from the last century, she thus conceives of Swedish solidarity as "the ability to extend one's loyalties to members of one's own political community as well as distant others" (Bergman 2007, 81).[4]

It is within Sweden's generous developmental aid program and practices after 1949, however, where the concept of solidarity can be witnessed most prominently. David Lumsdaine (1993) points out that this approach toward overseas aid was shaped by humanitarian concerns within the country and were closely linked with what he labels a "moral vision" in international politics. For Hook (1995), the construction of a generous overseas aid program as a feature of Swedish foreign policy was seen as a conscious strategy by the Swedish parliament in the early 1960s to extend the idea of solidarity within the state to solidarity outside. He points to a 1962 speech in which the Riksdag declared the Swedish aid program to be "an expression of a much deeper recognition that peace, freedom and welfare are not exclusively national concerns but are increasingly something increasingly universal and indivisible" (Hook 1995, 8).

And so we have seen with the emergence of Sweden's national myth of moral exceptionalism an evolution of the concept of solidarity: the egalitarianism of the welfare state broadening to the idea of extending a hand of friendship to those suffering in the global south through both a generous refugee policy and a developmental aid budget. In the final chapter of the book, we return to the concept of solidarity, examining how tensions between how it is conceived and how it is appropriated at a day-to-day level permit quite a bit of wiggle room. We will see how solidarity in its relation to violence and security is absolutely critical in enabling the refugees to be legitimately conceptualized as non-deserving. The remainder of this chapter, however, examines the myriad ways in which the perseverance of this myth is enabled, in spite of EU harmonization and globalization.

THE SWEDEN-IN-CRISIS NARRATIVE: MORAL EXCEPTIONALISM AS CONSIGNED TO THE DUSTBIN OF HISTORY?

Looking at any of the literature on the Swedish model in the fields of political science, sociology, anthropology, or migration studies, the consensus seems to be that the idea of Scandinavia – and Sweden especially – standing out as somehow exceptional is now an old-fashioned idea that has been firmly consigned to the dustbin of history (Hansen 2009). Sweden is seen to have lost its shine and is now simply yet another neo-liberalized Western country, no different than any other and certainly no longer placing itself up on a pedestal. Sweden is framed, in one way or another, as having failed its utopian promise.

In this vast array of literature on the demise of the Swedish model, a uniting feature is the idea of crisis of some sort. These crises are framed in a variety of ways: the crisis of social democracy after the death of Olof Palme (indeed sometimes even before); the crisis of Swedish identity in joining the EU; the crisis of Swedish neutrality at the end of the Cold War, and of migration and integration with the rise of certain ghettos and no-go areas, racist crimes, riots within "immigrant" neighbourhoods. Cited also are the rise of the nationalist Sweden Democrats (Sverigedemokraterna) party and the various economic crises: firstly, in the 1990s when globalization and consumerism was framed as the ultimate challenge to the *folkhem* model and, secondly, the current economic crisis, complete with very high youth unemployment. Interestingly, the idea of the death of the Swedish model, whether defined by focusing on the welfare state, foreign policy, migration, or asylum policy, has been an ongoing phenomenon for about thirty years, with various scholars proclaiming at various times that Sweden was now in decay.

The idea of Sweden in decline has entered the popular episteme to such an extent that it has become a kind of clichéd narrative. Even much of the English-language travel-writing genre talks about Sweden having lost its social democratic essence, as the country now witnessing the destabilization of the foundations on which it was built. For example, in his influential travelogue, Brown (2011) writes at length about his return to Sweden in 2006, after a thirty-year absence, noticing how everybody seemed "fatter, dirtier and shorter" and noting with disdain the proliferation of McDonald's, which had popped up all around the country. Such narratives are so commonplace that journalist Henrik Berggren, in a review for another British travelogue that pokes fun at the Swedish model, shrugged off the critique by pointing out how people "have been writing off Sweden since the seventies, and even after the early nineties when the Swedish model did appear to be fatally undermined by its economic imbalance, it recovered quickly and strongly" (Booth 2014).

This theme of writing about the death of the Swedish model probably first emerged in the article entitled "Swedish Autumn" by German author Hans Magnus Enzensberger writing in the Swedish newspaper *Dagens Nyheter* in 1982. Enzensberger conceptualized this period of the early '80s as Sweden's decline: the glory years of the nation were now firmly behind it and Sweden was now a spent force. Writing as early as 1984, Ruth's shattering article on Sweden's fall from international grace picks up on Enzensberger's theme and lists an array of so-called scandals generated by the much-cherished social democratic ideology, from forced sterilization to the relatively widespread removal of children from their parents, which saw the image of Sweden transformed into one whereby the *fears* as opposed to the hopes of modernity were projected (Ruth 1984).

The literature on the demise of the Swedish welfare state is also extensive and spans several decades (Hansen 2009; Lawler 2005, 2007; Hedberg 2009; Pred 2000; Dahlstedt 2005; Dahlstedt 2008; Schierup and Ålund 1991, 2010). Much of this came about at the end of the 1980s when neo-liberalism came to the fore, and when, for the first time, Sweden's "natural" party of leadership, the Social Democrats (who had been in government virtually uninterrupted from 1932 to 1976), had lost power to a centre-right coalition. Much of the literature on this phenomenon is in keeping with the narrative of the general shift to the right that took place throughout Europe during this time, with the exception of Hedberg (2009), who attributes this shift toward the right in Swedish politics to lower election turnout among the working class since the 1970s.

Lawler (2005, 2007), in writing about Sweden's "moral" foreign policy, frames the decline of the Swedish model as far more recent and as seen to be at least partly brought about by the discrediting of the idea of a normative foreign policy at all, after the failures of the strategies adopted by the US and the UK as a result of the War on Terror. In any case, the Scandinavian approach can no longer be seen as exceptional, due to the general trend toward more overtly normatively infused foreign policies following the Cold War (Lawler 2005).

However, the Swedish entry into the EU in 1995 is certainly held as most responsible for the demise of exceptionalism on account of the greater harmonization of foreign policy, placing Sweden firmly within the Western camp for the first time. Hansen (2009) conceptualizes Sweden's entry as the success of the Swedish right in restraining the nation's so-called bad habits of international solidarity and cosmopolitanism. He points to writings by then-incoming conservative prime minister Carl Bildt in 1991, which labelled as scandalous the idea that "more Swedish cabinet members and official delegations [are] going to Gaborone than to Brussels." Bildt continued that "it became more natural for Swedish prime ministers to give speeches at meetings in Mozambique or before the revolutionary masses in Managua than to hit on the idea – nobody did it! – of going to the European parliament in Strasbourg ... Europe was a white spot on the map of Swedish foreign policy and public debate." It seemed, Bildt went on, "as if South-East Asia was situated just east of Stockholm" and "Southern Africa just south of Malmö" (Bildt cited in Hansen 2009).

In examining this shift to the right, the admission of Sweden into the EU in 1995 was said to have resulted not only in an attempt to consign the moral image to the dustbin of history in terms of foreign policy but also a marked discursive shift in political language on refugee and asylum policy. The notion of refugees being a "problem" can be seen to have emerged during this time, with greater European co-operation and harmonization also been argued as warranting a "race to the bottom" of restrictive migration and asylum policy with "more Europe" being argued as equalling "less migration" (Hansen 2009). Migration scholars writing from within Sweden talked about the "thorny road to Europe" and the "worrying shift" toward what they labelled "illiberal practices" that are more in line with those of Denmark, France, and the United Kingdom (Schierup and Ålund, 2010).

Pred's (2000) book, based on research from the same period, talks instead about the tensions of racism and prejudice rising to the surface of social life as the result of the economic crisis that affected the country in the 1990s. Pred conceptualizes the end of the last century as the era that saw the "reawakening of racism" throughout the whole of Europe, characterized by an intensification in ethnic and cultural stereotyping. In his many interviews with non-European and Muslim migrants, the recurrent theme that Sweden was more open, tolerant, and welcoming to foreigners in the previous decades is clear. Pred cites the newspaper *Dagens Nyheter* in stating in 1988 that "it is high time that Sweden reconsider its image as the stronghold of tolerance" (cited in Pred 2000).

It is fair to say that the criticism of Sweden's more restrictive migration refugee policy and rhetoric was not unwarranted. Throughout the last decade, Sweden has witnessed the introduction by parliament of a financial support or maintenance requirement as a condition of family reunification, a policy in line with other European member states (European Migration Network 2013).[5] As a member of the EU, Sweden participates with other member states at a meta level in activities that administratively serve to expel and exclude the migrant and thus generate a general sense of unease around the notion of migration: for example, the implementation of the VIS (Visa Information System), the active participation in FRONTEX projects involving border surveillance and forced repatriation flights following failed asylum applications, and working with airlines to prevent undocumented migrants from boarding flights to Sweden at the point of departure (see European Migration Network 2013).

And certainly, many migration scholars writing from within Sweden talked about an end to Swedish exceptionalism and the increase in racial hostilities following the discursive moves toward more negatively charged rhetoric around migration and asylum. In terms of outwardly xenophobic and far-right political parties, 2010 saw the election to parliament for the first time of the Sweden Democrats, with its blatant anti-immigration rhetoric such as calls for "a multicultural world, not a multicultural society" (see Sverigedemokraterna.se 2010). This inevitably increased the number of debates around migration and integration in the Riksdag and a gradual discursive shift of the mainstream political parties toward the right regarding the subject.

It would certainly seem, therefore, that the myth-making machine of the once much-cherished Social Democratic elite is a thing of the past, eroded by decades of globaliaztion, Europeanization, and neo-liberalisation. As stated by Ruth back in the 1980s, Swedish identity is now shattered into bits and pieces, leading the author to claim that *"there [now] needs to be a new source for national myths"* (Ruth 1984, 92, emphasis added).

In contrast to many of these scholars, however, I argue that though the idea of Sweden as morally exceptional may have been discarded to some extent, it was never entirely buried. Rather, it lingered around and was reproduced through much more subtle and indirect means. As discussed in greater detail in chapter 3, I argue that the Swedish national myth of moral exceptionalism generates a particular type of subjectivity and plays a major part in the formation of governable subjects. In drawing on the scholarship of Michel Foucault, I label this specific configuration of power relations a type of governmentality, one that I call a governmentality of righteousness. Departing from the notion of the instrumentalized elite myth-making machine, which frames the construction of the Swedish model throughout the twentieth century, the second part of this chapter goes on to examine national myth-making as a more diffused, routine, and bureaucratic activity, much more in line with what Foucault talked about in terms of governmentality. Following the scholarship of Tilly, Billig, and Brubaker, it locates this new source for myths within the more banal, taken-for-granted practices that reproduce this very peculiar Swedish nationalism and the social relations that enable Swedes not only to buy into this myth as "theirs" but also to actively reproduce it. Many of these technocratic comparative practices, particularly benchmarking and the use of indices, I conceive of as technologies of this type of governmentality (cf. Miller and Rose 2008), embodying the extension of the rationality and ethos of the market into other spheres of life. These practices of ranking are a fundamental technique of advanced liberalism, important for the (re)construction of spaces and subjects and for rendering the "incommensurable commensurable" (Larner and Le Heron 2004, 227).

MORAL EXCEPTIONALISM AS RELATIONAL AND TRANSINDIVIDUAL: SWEDEN AS THE BEST OF A BAD BUNCH

Once generated and expressed, [myths] can acquire a considerable life of their own.

Halliday 1995, 7

Halliday's assertion that myths aren't so easily killed off and buried is especially pertinent in the Swedish case. Though the myth of moral exceptionalism has been trampled on in academic fields from migration studies to economics, the notion of Sweden as somehow better than everywhere else still remains a popular theme, both within Sweden and internationally.

Some of the literature on state identification can help shed light on the way in which a national myth can linger and be continually reproduced, despite changes in context and environment. From the late 1980s and early 1990s, critical constructivists and postmodern scholars within the field of IR have successfully argued that the very constitution of the state depends on the continuous construction and differentiation between the state "self" and others. Therefore, as opposed to viewing a state's identity as an already existing set of characteristics, identity is instead viewed as a dynamic process, a practice of boundary drawing that renders the state coherent as a social and political actor. Much of the scholarship of this era examined how states come to see themselves as democratic, liberal, and human rights exemplars by a process of continuously defining others who were non-democratic, illiberal, and human rights violators (e.g., Ashley 1988; Campbell 1992). Traditionally, the focus of this work was on how a dangerous or threatening other was brought into being, thus justifying violent practices such as intervention in the name of both state security and human rights. It was this body of work that played an important role in conceptualizing the relational element of identity. In terms of Sweden, its role in IR was defined not against a dangerous other but against other states that were less democratic, less moral, or less gender equal (cf. Towns 2002).

Outside of IR, scholars within both political and linguistic anthropology produced some very interesting work on the more mundane elements of (re)producing a particular nationalism, specifically against migrants or refugees already within a nation, or within conflict situations. For example, De Genova (2005) looks at the production of a US nationalism (a "nation of immigrants") against Mexican migrants through English-language classes via the deployment of discourses of "immigrant Americanism" and the construction of the "hardworking immigrant." Charalambous (2009) also looks at language classes to demonstrate how Cypriot nationalism is (re)constituted as particularly Greek by the teaching of Turkish as a foreign language, positioned alongside Italian and French and associated not with Cyprus, but with a multilingual Europe. Similarly, Gullestad (2002) demonstrates the increasing ethnification of Norwegian nationalism against Muslims through the press and wider media.

In the remainder of the chapter, I draw upon the insights of these scholars in looking at the contingent and relational elements of national identity. However, in the same vein as those mentioned in political and linguistic anthropology, I move away from notions of identity politics to look at the many ways the reproduction the national myth of Swedish exceptionalism comes about through the much more banal and heterogeneous processes and nation-oriented practices that position Sweden as "the best" in relation to the rest of Europe, and the wider world.

THE DRAMATIC DEMISE OF DENMARK AS A PROGRESSIVE NATION

For Mouritzen (1995), the generic Nordic progressivism includes as an important facet the ideas of hospitality to migrants and refugees, and solidarity with the Third World as well as the more traditional ideas of peacefulness, egalitarianism, and environmentalism. Lawler (2007) and Ingebritsen (2002) are among the many in political science to point out how the former two characteristics jar, both in theory and in practice: "As the populations of Northern European states have become more diversified, Scandinavian governments have confronted an internal conflict over cultural preservation versus multiculturalism. Even though Government goals promote equality, many citizens are sceptical about the effects of immigration on Scandinavian societies. How will Scandinavian welfare systems survive with a new class of participants who do not share a common religion, language or understanding of widely held social norms?" (Ingebritsen, 2002, 21)

Interestingly, the identification of Denmark as embodying the inevitable consequence of this tension has acted to reproduce and solidify Sweden's identification of itself as tolerant, rational, and generous against its southern neighbour. Indeed, it is Denmark that is seen as the Scandinavian country in crisis, epitomizing the breakdown or perversion of internationalism to come to mean a more restrictive asylum and migration policy in the name of protecting the welfare state and national norms and values. The Danish experience is one of "differentiation" (Lawler 2007, 103) in relation to the rest of the region, whereby the Nordic model is seen as fracturing along individual state lines and following a plurality of very different pathways.

Most academic study about securitization of society in terms of the Nordic countries – moves by politicians to cast a nation's identity as somehow under threat – has been with reference to Denmark. Linde Laursen (2007) talks about "something rotten" in the state, while Lawler (2007) points out how Denmark has shown that a collective identity as internationalist and cosmopolitan becomes something that a nationalistic dogma can utilize, whereby popular affection for the flag is grounded in a high level of consensus over what are perceived as core values, cosmopolitanism being one. The academic literature on securitization of migration in Denmark is huge, serving to produce, as a by-product, ideas of Sweden as much more competent and able in addressing these tensions. For Lawler (2007), in his focus on the "Janus faced Solidarity," it is Danish internationalism that is to be "reconsidered." The Swedish government is commended for being "proactive" in addressing the dilemmas that Danish internationalism has faced. "During the (cartoon) crisis the brand of Denmark most likely moved from being a positive stereotype among Muslims – an image of the friendly, Scandinavian welfare state – to being more firmly associated with a more negative stereotype of 'The West.'" (Stig-Moller cited in Lawler 2007).

Within Swedish popular culture, the "racist Danes" theme became a common feature of both popular and political discourse after the election to parliament of the anti-immigration Danish People's Party in 2001, and their subsequent electoral success in 2006. Before the Sweden Democrats rose to prominence in the 2010 general election thus forcing the mainstream political parties to engage with them on issues of immigration and integration, political debates between mainstream political parties in the 2006 Swedish general election seemingly revolved around which party was most opposed to the anti-immigration policies of the Danish People's Party (see, for example, Local 2006).

What were portrayed at the time in Sweden as "Europe's strictest immigration laws" – introduced by the governing Liberal-Conservative coalition government in Denmark – were widely criticized in both governmental and popular discourse. This legislation, which saw the Danish government reliant on support from the Danish People's Party for a parliamentary majority, introduced new provisions, stipulating that a Danish citizen could not bring a spouse from a non-EU country into Denmark without lodging a bond of 93000 Krone, passing a solvency test, and demonstrating that both parties have stronger bonds with Denmark than any other country (see Dansk Folkeparti 2010). At the time, these policies led to a large proportion of Danes with spouses due to join them from non-EU states migrating to Malmo in South Sweden and commuting to Copenhagen daily (BBC 2005). Popular discourse saw Swedes take pride in their generosity and humane treatment of migrants vis-à-vis the Danish, to the extent that the Oresund Bridge connecting the two cities was commonly referred to as the "Love Bridge" (Bloomberg 2006). Furthermore, critique of Danish immigration laws was so vocal in Sweden that Pia Kjaersgaard, leader of the Danish People's Party, commented that "if they [Swedish people] want to turn Stockholm, Gothenburg or

Malmo into a Scandinavian Beirut, with clan wars, honour killings and gang rapes, let them do it. We can always put a barrier on the Oresund Bridge" (Kjaersgaard, cited in BBC 2005).

Swedish cultural conceit against Denmark regarding openness was at a peak during this time. The Danes were portrayed as xenophobic and Islamophobic compared to the Swedish culture, which was characterized as much more rational and mature around the issue of migration. Indeed, Denmark was made an example of, a warning to all good Swedes to be on their guard against the hatching and growth of those sorts of discourses in Sweden to ensure that their country avoided blindly following a similar path to its southern neighbours.

The most striking example of this kind of discourse was a book published by journalist Lena Sundström in 2009 entitled *Världens Lyckligaste Folk* (The world's happiest people), which criticized Denmark's migration policies. This book went on to be awarded the Gleerups Literary Prize, was nominated for the August Prize, and was commissioned to be made into a TV documentary on TV4. Sundström is now political commentator on the same channel, the most viewed non-publicly funded channel in Sweden.[6]

THE ROLE OF OPINION POLLS

The politician who yesterday said "God is on our side" today says "public opinion is on our side."

Bourdieu 1993, 150

In framing nations and cultures in a particular way, the role of opinion polls, particularly comparative opinion polls that quantify and compare people's opinions and values across different countries, is also crucial. Popular media often abounds with claims of nations being happiest, most or least racist, most trustworthy of governmental or intergovernmental institutions or of the media, and so forth. Politicians who claim to have the population on their side gain a huge amount of political clout. Most-democratic societies or populations with the highest levels of subjective well-being are lauded, viewed, sometimes in caricature, as beacons of enlightenment with an educated, broad-minded population. Such comparative polls enable nations to effectively be ranked in terms of niceness.

The well-known Eurobarometer public opinion survey is thus a main actor in the reproduction of the still-cherished Swedish national myth of modernity, with its connotations of rationality, tolerance, and internationalism. In terms of reproducing the myth of Sweden as the least-racist European country, a "Future of Europe" report on Sweden from 2010, for example, showed the country as having the highest proportion of people (80 per cent) who agreed with the statement, "People from other ethnic groups enrich the cultural life of my country," (European Commission 2010, 53) and the highest proportion of people (77 per cent) who agreed with the statement, "Immigrants play an important role in developing greater understanding and tolerance with the rest of the world" (European Commission 2010, 58). In a similar survey undertaken in 2006, Sweden also had by far the highest proportion of people who agreed with the statement. "Immigrants contribute a lot to our country" (European Commission 2006, 48).

Furthermore, Sweden was the only nation to have the highest proportion of answers to the question, "Which characteristics are most important for being a national of any one country?" saying "exercising rights" was most important, and the country to place the absolute least importance on having parents of the nationality in question or being raised in the country (European Commission 2010, 44). These results, though widely problematic, as acknowledged by Eurobarometer itself as well as a broad range of sociologists, are nonetheless widely reproduced in European media, enabling the cherished national myth to once again run away with itself.[7]

The myth of Scandinavia as a land of happy, fulfilled citizens is also reproduced through such opinion polls (though famously, Denmark is ranked in first position on well-being indices). According to Eurobarometer, after Denmark and in comparison with the other member states, Sweden had the second-highest satisfaction rate among citizens with the lives they lead (European Commission 2011, 2). It was also classified as being the most optimistic of the member states, with the highest proportion of people saying that they felt the next twelve months would be better than the last (European Commission 2011, 15). Trust in political institutions was also high: Sweden's citizens were the most likely in the twenty-seven member states to trust their national parliament (European Commission 2011, 46), the second most likely in any EU member state to trust their government (European Commission 2011, 45), and the second most likely to trust local authorities and the United Nations (European Commission 2011, 48–9). They were also the least likely to complain about paying tax or how this tax money was spent (European Commission 2013, 20). Sweden had the highest proportion of people rating their national economy as good (European Commission 2013, 7). Interestingly, Sweden was the second most likely nation to have citizens state that they trusted TV reporting (European Commission 2011, 42) and had the third-highest satisfaction rate with how democracy worked in the country (European Commission 2011, 71).

The most widely reported results of the Eurobarometer poll, however, were perhaps those from a 2010 survey conducted on social attitudes. Sweden was ranked as having the second-highest number of people (after Czech Republic) responding that they had no belief in God (European Commission 2010). These findings mirrored a similarly widely reported Gallup poll conducted in 2012 that placed Sweden as having the fifth-lowest proportion of people identifying themselves as religious compared to the rest of the world (Gallup International 2012).

Within this discursive framework sits the World Values Survey, which claims to be "the most comprehensive investigation of social and political change." Carried out by a network of social scientists in about one hundred countries, it monitors and analyzes support for democracy, tolerance for foreigners and ethnic minorities, the role of women, the place of religion within societies and the changing levels of religiosity, the impact of globalization, attitudes toward the environment, work, family, politics, national identity, culture, diversity, insecurity, and subjective well-being. Unlike the Eurobarometer, whose own analysts suggest that the findings be interpreted with an element of caution, the World Values Survey appeals for rigorous academic research papers based on their data. The World Values Survey also presents itself as surpassing many of the most common methodological critiques, including that of Eurocentrism, by employing researchers from all one hundred countries surveyed to help develop the questions and ensure accurate translation, both linguistically and culturally, though this occurred only during the later waves of the survey.

Analysis of this data then plotted these values along two different dimensions or axes that the survey argues much of the variation in values between societies boils down to: traditional values versus secular-rational values, wherein traditional values are said to emphasize the importance of religion, parent-child ties, deference to authority, and traditional family values (World Values Survey 2013). The analysts claim that "people who embrace these values also reject divorce, abortion, euthanasia and suicide" and that "these societies have high levels of national pride and a nationalistic outlook." In contrast, according to the survey, secular-rational values are said to have preferences opposite to the traditional values. These societies, according to the survey, place "less emphasis on religion, traditional family values and authority, and divorce, abortion, euthanasia and suicide are seen as relatively acceptable" (World Values Survey 2013). Nations are then grouped together according to cultural proximity in a sort of Huntington-esque cultural map of the world identified as eight distinct domains: Protestant Europe, English speaking, Catholic Europe, Confucian, Islamic, Orthodox, South Asia, and Africa.

With the Bourdieusian critique of public opinion polls in mind, specifically the idea of the "imposition of the problematique" (Bourdieu 1993), it comes as no surprise that Sweden features at the very top right-hand side of the map, as the nation with the highest level of "self-expression" values as well as the highest level of "secular-rational values." Sweden is also the country identified by the survey as being "the least racist," based on questions centred on possible objections to having a neighbour of a different race, of which only 1.4 per cent of the population expressed disapproval (World Values Survey 2013).

Based on research from the World Values Survey, Swedish public intellectuals have run with this idea of Sweden as once again distinctly and exceptionally modern and moral, which has again captured popular imagination both internationally and within Sweden. The most striking example is the provocatively titled book *Är svensken människa? Gemenskap och oberoende i det moderna Sverige* (Is the Swede human? Autonomy and community in modern Sweden) (2015). Here, citing the results of the World Value Survey, historians Lars Trägårdh and Henrik Berggren put forward the hypothesis that the supposedly socialist and consensus-orientated Swedes are in fact hyper-individualists, pursuing personal autonomy to a much greater extent than even citizens of the US. The authors go further, placing at the heart of their model a deeply rooted conception they label a Swedish "theory of love," whereby they argue that authentic love is only possible between people who are truly independent and equal. As Swedes fulfil these criteria, the authors hold relationships between Swedes as being more meaningful and more loving than in other nations. For Trägårdh especially, this is "spectacular," as other cultures see mutual dependence, not radical independence, as the very stuff of love.

Based on Rousseau's social contract theory and the idea of the *volonté générale*, the authors claim that this particular moral logic is distinct from the types of social contract at play in, for example, the US or Germany. Once again we see the notion of solidarity as key to the national myth, this time likened to the ideals of independence and economic equality, institutionalized by the authors in what they call a "radical alliance" between the Swedish state and the individual, what they label "statist individualism." This has served to balance the "deep existential desire" for personal freedom and, simultaneously, social cohesion, thus on the one hand, liberating the individual from what they call unequal and patriarchal forms of community, such as the bonds to family, churches, and charities, while on the other hand, leaving the individual relatively powerless against the state. Within Sweden, this book received widespread acclaim, and in 2011 Trägårdh was appointed a member of then–prime minister Reinfeldt's Commission on the Future of Sweden.

Sweden's self-confessed rationalist secularism, viewed as respectful and tolerant by many academics and commentators, again serves to position the country as hyper-modern, most evolved, and most enlightened. This move away from rooting values in Lutheran Christianity and toward more vague notions of decency and humanity again enables a Swedish way to be envisaged as universal, the epitome of the good life, according to Swedish sociologists, while more overt religious values are viewed as particular, marginal, and somewhat quirky. For Richard Tomasson (2002), resonating strongly with Trägårdh's conception of the "Swedish social contract," Sweden is the nation that comes closest to Alan D. Gilbert's famous conceptualization of a "thoroughgoing secular society" as "one in which norms, values and modes of interpreting reality, together with the symbols and rituals which express and reinforce them, have been *emancipated* entirely from assumptions of human dependence on supernatural agencies or influences. In it, the natural world would be regarded as autonomous, and knowledge, values and social structures would be ordered upon purely mundane principles" (Gilbert, cited in Tomasson 2002, 72, emphasis added).

Interestingly, however, the Church of Sweden itself can be seen as playing a crucial role in (re)producing these secular, humanitarian identities. In his essay "Why Are the Swedes so Secular," Tomasson (2002) traces the historical trajectory of the Swedish church, pointing to the strong influence of Enlightenment traditions from France in the eighteenth century as further secularizing what was already a very low-temperature religion. By the beginning of the nineteenth century, being appointed a bishop was based on scholarly and cultural attainment with notions of piety firmly subordinated. He argues that, within the Swedish strand of Lutheranism, there has thus never been much resistance to secular thought, science, and evolution, with issues such as abortion and euthanasia barely registering in debate. The decision to ordain women in the 1950s was again seen as a logical and progressive step with very little opposition from religious conservatives.

As a result of these developments, the Church of Sweden thus fashions itself as embodying Swedish humanitarianism more generally, particularly in terms of solidarity with developing countries and concepts of charity and volunteering. A highly educated clergy and rational theology as well as the hegemony of the Social Democrats have further solidified the secularization of the Church in that it now frequently acts more as a vague, fluffy non-governmental organization and organ of civil society embodying Swedish niceness and progressiveness as opposed to anything more overtly religious. Uppsala University professors of sociology Beckman, Ekstrand, and Pettersson (2006) have even come to characterize the Church of Sweden as an "agent of welfare."

The most striking example of the Church of Sweden positioning itself in such a manner was the 1997 exhibition in Uppsala Cathedral of Ecce Homo (Behold the man) in conjunction with the gay and lesbian international conference. Among the exhibits was a re-appropriation of Da Vinci's *The Last Supper* in which Christ is dressed in high heels and the twelve apostles are portrayed as transvestites, and another portraying Christ as an AIDS sufferer. The high degree of support from the archbishop, members of the clergy, and Swedish politicians – along with Vatican disapproval of the exhibition – cemented the position of the Swedish church as the manifestation of the Swedish imagined collective identity: standing up for the weak and vulnerable and firmly ahead of the pack, even, or perhaps especially, when deemed as unpopular (Beckman, Ekstrand, and Pettersson 2006).

Within some of the more critical scholarship, in the United States especially, Sweden's secularism is held up as a cause for celebration.

The most striking illustration of such discourse is that of Phil Zuckerman, who presents Sweden's irreligiosity as example par excellence of how so-called Godless societies are not devoid of morals but are pleasant places in which to live (Zuckerman 2008) in response to the increasingly powerful claims of the Christian right of the US, which claim otherwise. The framing of Swedish secularism in such a manner by US scholars seems to be the latest manifestation of the ongoing competition in popular literature between Sweden and the United States for the most evolved notion of modernity, a discourse that can be traced back to scholars such as Thomasson (cited in Zuckerman 2008), who used the Swedish model to demonstrate the inherent injustices embedded in the American Dream.

THE ROLE OF STATISTICS, RANKING, AND BRANDING AS GENERATORS OF COMMUNITY MOBILIZATION

Aside from comparative opinion polls and the huge amount of data, reports, and scholarship drawn from such polls, the subtle stories of Swedish superiority are reinforced through the now ubiquitous range of international rankings and indices. These statistics and indicators – a collection of named, rank-ordered, simplified, and processed data about a named social phenomena in a manner that enables the comparison and evaluation of different units (Davis, Kingsbury, and Merry 2010, 16), albeit in a different context – have been shown to have a community-mobilizing effect, designating insiders and outsiders and fixing a certain identity to a group.

Furthermore, as discussed previously, these indicators can be seen as the embodiment of "governing at a distance" (Miller and Rose 2008), enabling certain actors to exercise influence over the conduct (of conduct) of actors scattered all over the world (Davis, Kingsbury, and Merry 2010, 23). These technologies thus act as a form of "global governance," rendering the sphere of the global more knowable by positioning the experiences and performances of others into immediately comparable proximity (Larner and Le Heron 2004, 417). It is important to point out, however, that these comparative techniques, such as benchmarking, are not a neutral expression of underlying realms, such as society, but instead are an inherently political act, helping to constitute and exist relations of power (Davis, Kingsbury, and Merry 2010, 23). They are presented as efficient, consistent, transparent, scientific, and impartial by reducing complexity to a series of numbers and blurring the division between the governed and the governors (Davis, Kingsbury, and Merry 2010, 23).

With that in mind, it has become somewhat of a cliché to see Scandinavian nations, particularly Sweden, featuring at or near the top of these various indices and values that measure overall societal health or progressiveness. The dissemination of these indices and rankings throughout the press and wider media can then be thought of as a practice of "banal nationalism," in Billig's words, not as overt as newspaper references to a homeland, "us," or "we," but nonetheless a reminding that is so familiar, so continual "that it is not consciously recognised as reminding" (Billig 1995, 6)

The broadest of these indices is arguably the United Nations Human Development Index, published as part of the Human Development Report and ranking 175 countries based on three factors: a long and healthy life (measured by life expectancy), knowledge (measured by school enrolment numbers and levels of literacy), and standard of living (measured by GDP per capita). In 2013, Sweden ranked eighth in the world (UNDP 2013a). Concerning life expectancy, infant mortality rates, and child welfare, Sweden ranked eighth, fourth, and fifth respectively (UNDP 2013a). According to Save the Children, Sweden was also the second-best place, after Finland, to be a mother in 2013 (Save the Children 2013).

In terms of its welfare system, inequality of income distribution in Sweden was the second-lowest of all EU member states (Eurostat 2011a, 10); material deprivation rate, i.e., the proportion of persons who cannot afford to pay for selected items, was also the second-lowest of the member states, after Luxembourg (Eurostat 2011a, 12; Eurostat 2010, 331). Social protection expenditure as a proportion of GDP in the twenty-seven EU countries was the second-highest in Sweden, after France (Eurostat 2011b, 19), and expenditure on care for the elderly was far higher in Sweden year-on-year compared to other member states (Eurostat 2011b, 24). This has led the United Nations Global AgeWatch Index to label Sweden the best country in the world in which to grow old (see DN 2013).

With regard to the environment, Sweden was ranked seventh by NGO Germanwatch (2013) in its Climate Change Performance Index of the country doing the most to improve environmental conditions (though this is technically fourth place as the first three were left blank to demonstrate how no nation is doing enough). Transparency International's Corruption Perceptions Index ranked Sweden as having the fourth-lowest perceived levels of corruption in the public sector, and the World Justice Project ranks Sweden in third place regarding rule of law and government effectiveness (Transparency International 2013).

It is also a fairly clichéd narrative to see Sweden constantly featured in these indexes as one of the most gender-equal state. In her study of how immigrant identity in Sweden is constructed vis-à-vis gender-equal Swedes, Ann Towns (2002) points out that not until the mid-1990s and entry to the EU did Sweden see itself positioned at the forefront of women's rights, being ranked as the most gender-equal state in two new indices that materialized in the same year: the Gender Development Index (GDI) and the Gender Empowerment Measure (GEM). The GEM measures economic participation, political participation and decision-making, and power over economic resources, according to which Sweden ranked fourth in 2013 (UNDP 2013a).

In contemporary times, interesting results regarding gender equality in Sweden can also be seen in the data published by the Inter-Parliamentary Union, which examines the number of women in parliaments of various states. In 2011, for example, Sweden had the second-highest number of females in parliament, behind only Rwanda and Andorra (IPU 2011). Furthermore, Sweden was the only state, according to the European Union Agency for Fundamental Rights, to introduce legislation against discrimination covering several areas of society that actually went beyond the scope of the European parliament's Directives on Gender Equality and Anti-Discrimination (FRA 2008, 62). Resonating strongly with this are public opinion polls according to which Sweden vis-a-vis other EU member states is said to have the highest proportion of citizens in favour of gender equality in pay, with 99 per cent agreeing that females and males should receive equal pay for carrying out the same job (European Commission 2011).[8] Finally, Sweden is one of the only nations in which the female poverty rate is equal to or, in some cases, lower than the male poverty rate.

Sweden can still be seen to be one of the largest development aid donors,[9] praised by the Development Assistance Committee (DAC) for remaining focused on poverty reduction as well as three thematic properties: democracy and human rights, environment and climate change, and gender equality and the role of women in environment (OECD 2013). In addition, Sweden can be seen as spending the highest proportion of its GNI on official development assistance of the twenty-seven EU member states (Eurostat 2010, 150). This was also seen in earlier reports, with Sweden spending the most on development assistance from 2005 to 2007 (Eurostat 2009, 126). In the 2010 report, Sweden was praised as being one of only four EU states to reach targets set by the United Nations, with Sweden the only state to actually *exceed* these targets (Eurostat 2010, 150).

The majority of Sweden's bilateral developmental aid assistance is committed to low-income countries (those countries classified as long-term recipients of humanitarian assistance), and to "fragile states" (OECD 2013). The DAC also praised Sweden for being the first state to publish a "policy coherence document," a strategy for considering the actual impact of domestic policies on developing countries, thus positioning itself as a powerful advocate on this issue within the EU (OECD 2013).

Motivations for developmental assistance has been a long-running topic of discussion within the scholarship on development finance. A common dichotomy within the literature is that between the altruistic donors, which allocate funds based on the needs and merits of the recipient countries, and the egoistic donors, which donate based on prospects of political gain and self-interest (see Hoeffler and Outram 2011). Though a lot of the more recent scholarship (as highlighted, for example, in Alestine and Dollar, 2000), tends toward conceptualizing motivations for developmental assistance as some sort of convergence between altruism and egoism. An interesting study of all 130 members of the OECD (DAC) between 1980 and 2000 shows the Nordic countries as well as the Netherlands, Switzerland, and Ireland as least egoistic, i.e., refraining from using their developmental assistance to reinforce particular political linkages or targeting aid to the most significant trading partners (Berthélemy 2005).

In terms of a generous image around migration and asylum statistics, indicators generated by Eurostat, the European Union Agency for Fundamental Rights, the Migrant Integration Policy Index, the UNHCR database, and the European Urban Knowledge Network have received a great deal of press attention within Sweden since 2005, enabling headlines such as "Axen (Swedish MP) proud of Europe's most humanitarian laws" (*Dagens Nyheter* 2010) and "Sweden is top country at integrating immigrants" (*Dagens Nyheter* 2012).

Even before the onset of the Syrian Civil War and Sweden's unilateral decision to grant permanent residency to all Syrians arriving at the border, Sweden was ranked as having the highest number of citizenships granted per inhabitant, the highest ratio between the number of citizenships granted by each member state and the respective size of the resident population of non-nationals, the highest absolute number of asylum applications lodged, and the highest number of positive asylum applications (Eurostat 2011a). Reports from the European Union Agency for Fundamental Rights at the same time showed that Sweden had the highest awareness among minority groups of equality bodies and the most progressive data collection system for anti-hate crime (European Union Agency for Fundamental Rights 2010). The Migrant Integration Policy Index also ranked Sweden in first place in Europe for its ability to integrate immigrants (Migrant Integration Policy Index 2010).

The accumulation of these rankings and their constant reproduction and dissemination can be seen to capture public imaginations and ascend into popular discourse. Through these rankings and indices, Sweden is seen as something attractive and seductive, something that can be drawn upon as nourishment for the reproduction of the national myth at a more instrumentalized, political level. Within this context, a soft-power survey carried out by Monocle, a media company and lifestyle magazine that, in conjunction with the Swedish Institute, comes up with "the thirty countries which best attract favour from other nations through culture, sport, cuisine, design, diplomacy and beyond" (Monocle 2013), ranked Sweden sixth and applauded it for being the "leading Nordic nation" and scoring highly on "the boring stuff," which Monocle defines as education, good governance, and gender equality. On the topic of asylum, the magazine states that "Sweden's stance is something which they should be proud of." Though lighthearted and apparently tongue-in-cheek in its presentation and propagation, the survey nonetheless makes a large impression, with stories devoted to it in most of the mainstream Swedish dailies, and spokespersons from the Swedish government making sure to comment: "We interpret this as a sign that we are heading in the right direction when it comes to the foreign ministry telling the story about Sweden. We all invest a lot in social media, the ministry itself, the embassies and the foreign minister … It's unique for such a small country to be on this type of list. It shows that, despite us being a nation of only nine million people, we have been successful at 'nation branding' and Sweden thus has a relatively loud voice on the global arena" (Mats Samuelsson, Local, 2013).

The attention given to this magazine ranking does suggest that a nation's brand is more important than it first appears. Furthermore, the type of soft power exerted by countries is deemed important, with some power seen as softer and thus perhaps even more seductive than other. Unlike some of the super soft power exerted by such as countries as the United States, whose image is based on corporations such as McDonald's, Olle Wastberg points out how Sweden's desire to "execute soft power" is "all about values." He argues that when people envisage Sweden, interestingly enough they don't imagine a geographical place but instead come up with a "bundle of values," for example, "peace, gender equality and caring." Wastberg sees this as a "stepping stone," making it easier for Sweden to promote its "core values" in International politics (cited in Visit Sweden 2013).

The principle Swedish agencies dealing with propagating "Sweden" as an international brand – Visit Sweden, the Swedish Trade Council and Invest Sweden (merged in 2013 to form Business Sweden), and the Swedish Institute – have jointly developed a brand platform, concentrating on the concept of progressive, with four core values around it. The first value is "innovative," meaning the embracing of new ways of thinking and seeing things from a new perspective as well as "having faith in a better future." The second is "open," meaning having a positive approach toward "free thinking" and toward people from different cultures and lifestyles. This idea also has a geographical element as it embodies the idea of people having space, not only to be creative but also to be free from overcrowding and able to readily access the countryside. The third value is "caring," conceived of on an individual basis, referring to feeling empathy and consideration for those who are most vulnerable. Lastly, the agencies promote the value of "authenticity," which they define as being "reliable, honest, and informal." Also included within this value are ideas of being unpretentious, clear, and unafraid to stand up for one's values, even if it is very uncomfortable (Wastberg, cited in Visit Sweden 2013). This interesting concoction of core values points to a very specific image of Sweden, different from other European or Nordic soft powers in its combination of embracing modernity while retaining the Lutheran idea of individual respect and care and protection for weaker members of society.

SWEDEN AS SAVIOUR OF REFUGEES: THE RESURRECTION AND TRIUMPH OF THE MYTH

Sweden has a moral obligation to assist the vulnerable Syrian population. We have contributed over 580 million kronor to the humanitarian effort in Syria and its neighbouring countries. Swedish money has been converted to medical care, food, maternity support and support for the most vulnerable groups such as children and has improved the situation for many ... When I look around at the great needs of people around the world, I feel a sense of pride when I think about what we have done as a nation.

Hillevi Engström, Swedish minister for
development co-operation, September 2013

Sweden's migration and citizenship statistics were comparatively high throughout the last two decades, with Sweden receiving a relatively much greater number of asylum seekers and refugees than other member states, thus leading it to be ranked as most open in the various statistical analyses mentioned. However, the emergence of a much more conscious and considered reawakening of the national myth was brought about as a result of the ongoing Syrian Civil War and Sweden's unilateral decision to grant permanent residency and the right to family reunification to all Syrian asylum seekers arriving at the border.

This move, a decision undertaken in September 2013 by the Swedish government, received broad cross-party parliamentary support.[10] According to reports by Eurostat on asylum applications in 2013, Sweden received 16,695 asylum applications – the second-highest absolute number after Germany; however, the highest number (together with Malta) of asylum applications per million inhabitants (Eurostat 2013). As of July 2013, Sweden received 11,605 applications from Syrians for asylum, second to Germany's 12,088, with the two countries jointly receiving 57 per cent of all Syrian asylum applications in the EU (UNHCR 2014). However, as a result of Sweden's decision to grant permanent residency to all Syrians, Tobias Billström, Sweden's minister for migration at the time, predicted that the number of asylum applications in Sweden would rise to between 59,000 and 67,000 during 2014 (*Local* 2013).

In interviews with the Swedish press, the spokesperson for migration and asylum from the main opposition party at the time, the

Social Democrats, applauded the decision "given the situation in Syria" but criticized the government for not acting quickly enough. In the same vein, the migration spokesperson from the Green Party, also welcomed the decision, stating that the granting of permanent residency status to all Syrians as well as the right to family reunification would be good for integration as Syrians would be able to immediately begin to study, look for employment, and "start their lives for real." Within the mainstream Swedish press, the decision to grant permanent residency to all Syrians was also greeted largely positively, with most newspapers arguing for the EU to follow Sweden's example. For example, main editorials in *Sydsvenskan* (2013) stated that "more needs to be done," especially at the European level, in order to accommodate more Syrian refugees. In *Dagen* (2013), the decision was deemed "excellent" and something that should be viewed as a source of pride by all Swedish citizens. In the larger national dailies, editorials were along similar lines. For example, *Dagens Nyheter*'s (2013) editorial page the day following the decision stressed the position of the UNHCR regarding the war in Syria, likening it to the genocide in Rwanda. The piece pointed out Sweden's generous attitude, quoting a study by the SOM Institute at the University of Gothenburg that showed that 85 per cent of Swedes regarded war as an acceptable reason to be granted asylum in Sweden.[11]

The spotlight from international media then shone on Sweden, with a great deal of press from both Arabic-language and Western news outlets devoted to Sweden's decision. CBC News in Canada hailed Sweden a "bastion of tolerance" in relation to its doors "open[ing] wide for Syrian refugees" and supposedly "forcing Europe to respond" (CBC 2014). In a slightly more reserved measure, the BBC spoke of Sweden "welcoming Syrian refugees and their families" (BBC 2013a), while al-Arabiya, a Saudi-owned pan-Arab news channel, singled out Sweden for being "the country most worthy of praise, aside from Syria's neighbours" (al-Arabiya 2013).

The very powerful and confident re-articulation of the Swedish national myth of openness toward those fleeing persecution enabled the political establishment in Sweden to accrue a great deal of symbolic capital in negotiations around refugee resettlement within the wider EU and to act as the spokesperson for a fairer and more humane asylum policy within the Union. This constant re-articulation of Swedish niceness at such a level once again enables the myth to be perpetuated at an everyday, almost-banal level, embedding its immediacy and givenness even further into the fabric of Swedish society. The "Swedish approach" to issues of migration, according to the newspaper *Dagen* (2013), is no longer in doubt.

RESETTLEMENT VS RELOCATION: SWEDEN AS SPOKESPERSON FOR A MORE HUMANE EUROPEAN ASYLUM POLICY

It was during the so-called refugee resettlement versus relocation debate within the EU that Sweden's old-fashioned moral superpowerfulness manifested itself once again. As Pred (2000, 44) points out, since the 1950s Sweden has differentiated between quota or resettlement refugees and those refugees who arrive individually at the border with no guarantee of residency, with the former category comprised of people whom the Swedish government committed to resettle directly in a local municipality in an agreement with the UNHCR. For the UNHCR, this practice is seen as one of the most "durable" methods through which to offer protection to refugees who are unable to integrate into their host country and who are unable to return to their country of origin (UNHCR 2014). The process involves selection of refugees from a state, usually from one of the large refugee camps in which the UNHCR operates, and their transfer to a third state that has an agreement with the agency on how many refugees will be taken. These refugees are then settled, with full permanent residency status, enjoying many of the rights afforded to nationals and the chance to become naturalized citizens of the resettlement country (UNHCR 2014).

During 2013 and 2014, apart from Sweden, twelve of the twenty-eight other EU member states offered some sort of regular resettlement program: Belgium, the Czech Republic, Denmark, Finland, France, Germany, Ireland, the Netherlands, Portugal, Romania, Spain, and the UK (UNHCR, 2014). The majority of these resettlement states assess UNHCR cases either by interviewing the refugees during selection missions undertaken in the host country or by deciding on a refugee's status based on a dossier approach (UNHCR 2014).

Here, the Swedish ideal of solidarity comes to the fore once again, with the UNHCR pointing out that resettlement provides a central element of the external dimension of the EU's asylum policy, demonstrating solidarity with third countries.[12] A tension emerged, however, in relation to the notion of solidarity in the EU's internal element, which came to be interpreted by many member states as not refugee resettlement (from a third country) but refugee relocation, an intra-EU "burden-sharing exercise."[13] For the Directorate-General for Internal Policies, this notion of solidarity within the treaty was considered poorly defined, either deliberately or confusingly so (Vanhuele, van Selm, and Boswell 2013). The narrow legal definition presented a limited relationship between articles 77–79 and article 80 of the Treaty on the Functioning of the European Union (TFEU), with most member states viewing solidarity as a response to immediate crises and member states' calls for assistance. (Vanhuele, van Selm, and Boswell 2013, 16). Some European resettlement countries thus allocated places for intra-EU relocation from within their annual resettlement quota, providing long-term protection for refugees from traditionally heavily burdened members such as Malta, while simultaneously reducing the overall number of places available for refugees resettled from outside the EU (European Migration Network 2013).

In practice, therefore, there was a significant disparity in how member states approached their international obligation to refugee protection (Vanhuele, van Selm, and Boswell 2013, 19). It was within this context that Sweden stepped up as the member state that was most adamant that relocation should in no way compromise resettlement program or come at the price of resettlement. Then–minister for immigration and asylum policy Tobias Billström was clear that resettlement should serve two priorities: first, in acting as a burden-sharing exercise with the countries of first asylum only, and second, in providing protection for the most vulnerable refugees. For Sweden, the reasons put forward for relocation by member states such as Malta or Italy, which were claiming to shoulder most of the burden, were deemed unconvincing, as Swedish ministers pointed out that, statistically, Sweden was under the same strain (Interview with Swedish Ministry of Justice in Perrin and McNamara 2013).

As the member state that was technically under the same level of pressure as Mediterranean member states but that at the same time did *not* lobby for relocation as a burden-sharing instrument, Sweden put itself in the position to strongly argue for resettlement as a tool of solidarity, actively encouraging member states that did not as yet have any sort of refugee resettlement agreement with the UNHCR to adopt one. As the member state that had resettled a significantly larger number of refugees in conjunction with the UNHCR,[14] the

Swedish government was in the strongest position to put pressure on the fifteen member states that did not participate in the UNHCR resettlement program. This stance by the Swedish government first grew momentum during the Iraq War when Tobias Billström, minister for migration and asylum policy, made a point of inviting his ministerial colleagues from the Justice and Home Affairs Council on a trip to a UNHCR camp in Jordan, to demonstrate the work carried out there by Migrationsverket. This move was designed to raise awareness of the positive impact of the resettlement policy with the aim of encouraging member states without a quota to take part in the scheme (Regeringen 2009).

It was during the start of the Syrian Civil War, however, when Sweden positioned itself at the forefront of lobbying for greater participation by EU member states in the resettlement program. Using as a point of departure Sweden's decision to grant permanent residency to all Syrians arriving at the border as well as the drowning of over 350 migrants outside Lampedusa, Italy, Billström campaigned within the Justice and Home Affairs Council for greater EU co-operation regarding asylum policy, pointing out how Sweden and Germany alone had taken two-thirds of all Syrian refugees to have entered the EU and that all twenty-eight member states should respond to the UNHCR's "call for need" (BBC 2013a). In press interviews around the topic, for both domestic and European audiences, Billström stressed that the position of the other members "vexes him … If all member states were to admit as many refugees as Sweden had done, the EU would be able to resettle 100,000 refugees per year; not a drop in the ocean" (BBC 2013b).

Within this narrative of lobbying for resettlement rather than relocation, the Swedish myth of moral exceptionalism and solidarity with refugees was fuelled with even more ammunition, able to be reproduced rather than simply inherited. These myths and standard stories were applied and adapted, much more explicitly, to a new set of circumstances in order to keep them meaningful (cf. Calhoun 1997). The words of the Swedish minister for justice resonated once again with the days of moral superpowerfulness, emphasizing Sweden's so-called uniqueness: "In the Swedish context, it is very important that politicians are not afraid to stand up for refugees. They dare saying that it is an important issue and that Sweden needs to show solidarity. Moreover, the Minister of migration always mentions resettlement when he talks about asylum issues. Often, at the

EU-level, Sweden stands out as the odd country proposing to improve asylum policy, to receive more refugees etc. This positive approach is considered peculiar by the other Member States. The Member States often have to deal with negative public opinion and politicians/parties that are unreceptive towards the asylum issue" (interview with Swedish ministry for justice in Perrin and McNamara 2013).

Building on this narrative, the narrow interpretation of EU legislation by certain member states was then linked by Swedish politicians to the rise of xenophobia in parts of Europe, which leads to "protection gaps" in terms of obligations toward refugees: "At the root of some of the restrictive provisions and interpretations of laws, policies and practices giving rise to protection gaps, is a resurgent racism and xenophobia. Despite the efforts of *some* governments and much of civil society, promoting tolerant and diverse societies remains an enormous challenge … multi-ethnic, multi-cultural and multi-religious societies are not just good but inevitable. We need politicians everywhere to unapologetically recognize and extol this. The exploitation of fear and hatred should never be allowed to win media audiences or votes" (Billström, citing the High Commissioner whom he "couldn't agree with more," cited in Regeringen 2013, emphasis added).

Sweden was thus once again reproduced as Europe's least-racist and least-xenophobic nation, by far the best at "doing" solidarity. If everybody else were to act as Sweden acts, the world would be a much better place. Therefore, much of the discourse around refugee resettlement from the Swedish government reinforced how well the Swedish approach worked in providing a safe, legal way for refugees to be resettled and stressed the fact that Sweden wanted to see greater responsibility taken at the EU level and from other EU member states (BBC 2013b). "If all EU Member States contributes to a common programme, we could reach the volumes necessary to achieve a strategic impact" (Billström cited in Regeringen 2013).

Swedish exceptionalism also emerged in the inter resettlement debate regarding so-called integration potential criteria and Sweden's lack of it. These criteria were adopted by several of the member states taking part in the UNHCR resettlement program, with the aim of easing integration into the host country, sometimes on the basis of a pre-existing labour diaspora community in that country (Perrin and McNamara 2013).[15] This process has been criticized by the UNHCR for the overlaps in profile restrictions – categories of refugees who are deemed undesirable for resettlement by the member state – resulting in competition for favoured caseloads and exclusion of certain groups (European Resettlement Network 2013).

As one of the minority of member states who did *not* specify any integration criteria, Sweden was highly critical of the notion of member states expecting to receive some sort of return on their investment regarding refugee resettlement or of attempts by states at only resettling refugees who were unlikely to run up excessive expenses in health care or social welfare systems of the member states. Sweden stated that, although this was the position taken after the Second World War until the mid-1970s, Sweden now "believes that the integration element can be evaluated in cases of labour migration but not in the case of refugees, where the need for protection should be decisive" (interview with Andreas Ollinen, in Perrin and McNamara 2013).

In terms of their resettlement program then, Sweden was extremely highly regarded by both the UNHCR and various NGOs and networks that work on resettlement. The European Resettlement Network, for example, held up Sweden's policy as exemplar, with particular credit given not only to the large quota but also to the strong coordination between partners both pre-departure and post-arrival, which they claim facilitates the quick departure and resettlement of a large number of emergency cases (European Resettlement Network 2013). This process sees refugees being met by municipality representatives upon arrival and accompanied to their accommodation. As of the end of 2013, 150 of the 290 municipalities in Sweden received refugees (including resettled refugees). The number of refugees allocated to each municipality is decided by a county-level quota system, jointly established by the migration agency, the employment office, and the county administrative boards. Migrationsverket is in charge of negotiating accommodation and placement of both asylum seekers and resettled refugees; however, accommodation for all other refugees is negotiated by the employment office, into whose care asylum seekers are transferred after residency is granted.

In 2011, the organizations also welcomed the creation of a pool of 250 emergency cases (which exists alongside Sweden's 350 other emergency places incorporated in the quota). For six months of the year, this new pool of cases is reserved for the sole use of unforeseen emergencies. For example, it was used in 2011 to respond to the refugees displaced in North Africa. Furthermore, access to citizenship is available to resettled refugees in Sweden (as with all refugees) within a relatively short period – four years – and without any requirement to pass a citizenship test or to demonstrate a capacity to speak the language (European Resettlement Network 2013). The network also exemplify Swedish efficiency regarding the granting of permanent status to refugees before their departure and the provision of residency permits in field situations through the use of portable equipment (European Resettlement Network 2013).

In addition, Sweden's placement program for resettled refugees was praised for its diligence, exemplified by its cultural orientation program, which prepares refugees for their resettlement ahead of their departure. This program, organized by Migrationsverket, sees representatives from particular municipalities and individuals from the employment office fly out to the UNHCR camps to show the selected refugees about nine to ten hours of videos about life in Sweden and to hold discussions and forums (European Resettlement Network 2013). Ideas of gender equality and women's freedom is a central feature of these cultural orientation programs (Muftee 2014).[16]

Furthermore, Sweden considered all categories of refugee in its resettlement quota: girls and women at risk; children and adolescents at risk; family reunification; those with medical, legal, and physical needs; survivors of violence and torture; and those with no possibility of foreseeable alternative solutions. This was again, among all EU member states, one of the least-restrictive sets of criteria for refugees who are to be resettled.

CONCLUSION

Although some sort of consensus appeared to have been reached on the decline of Swedish moral exceptionalism, this chapter has demonstrated the many ways in which this much-cherished myth was reproduced and re-enacted. Moving away from the notion of Swedish national myth-making as a conscious ideology in the early twentieth century, it has shown the variety of strategies through which a collective identity of being the most modern, most tolerant, and most progressive was generated by comparative opinion polls, rankings, and popular literature on Denmark as "the other"; by never living up to the standards set by its northern neighbour; and through various statistics and indices. This chapter has also shown how these low-temperature national myths, always forming a sort of vague background to everyday life, were more overtly used to fuel and nurture more explicit nation-oriented practices and discourses on the Swedish model, utilized by politicians and nation branders alike. Tightly intertwined into this national myth is the notion of solidarity, a dynamic and ever-shifting concept, first conceptualized in egalitarian terms in connection with the genesis of the welfare state but expanded to include an idea of compassion for the global south, both through the country's developmental-aid budget and through its asylum policy.

Lastly, the chapter has shown the way in which Swedish exceptionalism was so easily resurrected in all its former glory with the Syrian Civil War and the Swedish unilateral decision to grant asylum to all Syrian refugees arriving at the border. The practice was made all the simpler for its ability to tap into the immediacy and givenness of this myth of generosity, internationalism, and tolerance and to resonate so strongly with very real aspects of people's lived experiences. Here, the concept of solidarity is present once again, not only with regard to the refugees themselves but also in relation to the EU's resettlement policy where Sweden was incredibly vocal about being the best at doing solidarity, while never complaining about their burden even though it was as high as that in the southern European member states.

As I stated earlier, the slippery notion of solidarity is one that emerges throughout my fieldwork and one that I return to in chapter 5, where I examine the theoretical implications of the tensions present within these different types of solidarity and how this affects its appropriation at an everyday level. The next chapter, however, turns to my fieldwork in the village of Öreby, Skåne. Taking the idea of Tilly's standard story as a point of departure, it examines the various performances of nationhood through a Foucauldian lens, conceptualizing day-to-day practices between so-called good citizens and refugees as a biopsy of a particular form of governmentality – what I label the governmentality of righteousness. In examining how the Swedish national myth comes to form a type of *governable subject*, it explores the vast area of practices subsumed within the wiggle room of this particular governmentality: the conduct of conduct of oneself and others and the very local forms of knowledge embedded in local experiences between the refugees and the good citizens.

3

Seeing Like a Good Citizen

An Anthropology of the Governmentality of Righteousness

The previous chapter examined the way in which the Swedish national myth of moral exceptionalism and a cherished narrative of solidarity is constructed and invoked, particularly nowadays through statistics and rankings and in relation to the practices of other EU member states. We examined how, with Sweden's unilateral decision in September 2013 to grant asylum to all Syrians arriving at the border, this national myth was immediately resurrected from a supposed dustbin of history and firmly implanted into public consciousness once again – thanks to the proximity and givenness of the concept. We discussed the way in which professionals of politics play the game of enacting this narrative of moral exceptionalism but also how, through examining answers given to opinion polls and through various rankings, the national myth is enacted at a more banal level through the so-called good citizen. In blurring this line between national myth as an elite narrative and national myth as a standard story (Tilly 2002) enacted by all, we have straddled ourselves firmly between the field of IR and the discipline of anthropology.

It is toward the anthropological that this book now turns, recognizing that the national and international are always a form of local and that an in-depth study of micropractices at a very local level can help illuminate more about international life than dominant IR perspectives (cf. Bigo 2014a; De Genova 2005). This chapter takes as its point of departure from the previous chapter Tilly's concept of the national myth as a standard story, one which is not an elite narrative imposed on a docile public but which is in fact performed and embraced by members of society, and examines these performances through a Foucauldian lens. Recognizing the salutary element of the power relations at play within these standard stories, and their role in the generation of a certain subjectivity, I thus examine day-to-day practices between so-called good citizens and refugees as a snapshot of a particular form of governmentality, which I have labelled the governmentality of righteousness. This assertion really means two things: firstly, governmentality and the scholarship of Michel Foucault is used to shed light on a particular conduct of human beings that goes to the very core of how we view ourselves and others as moral beings. Far from being conceptualized as dramatic and catastrophic (as is the case with much of the Foucauldian literature within IR), the governmentality of righteousness is seen as being largely benevolent, seemingly benign, and linked much more to pastoral modalities of power and its secular variant, a caring biopolitics.

Secondly, governmentality in this regard is conceptualized here not as an abstract concept or ideal type. Instead, it is investigated in terms of its concrete manifestations: governmentality is treated as an *ethnographic object*. In referring back to the hypotheses posed in the introduction, we look at the way in which this Swedish national myth comes to form a type of governable subject. The good citizen is one who is also a good human being. Though in the Swedish story, any conception of "God" can be seen to have been replaced by vague ideas of "the future" and "modernity," we will see how ideas of obedience and sacrifice still come into play.

In the move to the study of micropractices and everyday life, the chapter goes on to examine some of the practices incorporated within the wiggle room of this particular form of governmentality. As asserted in the first chapter, governmentality should not be seen as some kind of Weberian ideal type; instead, it embodies a whole host of everyday practices of metis (cf. Detienne and Vernant 1991; Scott 2010 de Certeau 1988; Neumann 2002). Thus, the first section of the chapter introduces us to the village of Öreby in Skåne, South Sweden, in which about 120 Syrians and about 20 refugees of other nationalities were resettled and where I spent about nineteen months conducting fieldwork in 2013 and 2014. We are introduced to the Friends of Syria, a group of volunteers within the village who formed an ad-hoc non-governmental organization based on helping the refugees settle into their new life, and to key actors and events that gave rise to some of the many practices of everyday life that not only welcomed and cared for the refugees but also acted to marginalize, stigmatize, and oblige certain modes of behaviour from all parties.

In telling this story, we bring in the work of James C. Scott in conceptualizing certain practices as a type of transcript. As the notion of moral superiority goes straight to the very core of what it means to be a good citizen, certain types of behaviour, such as open criticism of Sweden's asylum policy or of the resettlement of refugees in Öreby, is rendered somewhat taboo by the good Swede. (I go into discuss of the manifestations of this taboo in chapter 4.) However, the corollary of this taboo is that a certain public transcript of emphasizing one's tolerance and decency is expected and practised within certain social settings, whereby an identity of righteousness can be maintained. In popular imagination, racism is thus confined to fantasy hillbilly communities, populated entirely by skinhead, uneducated men.

The remainder of the chapter explores some of the other practices between the villagers and the refugees subsumed within the governmentality of righteousness, such as prohibiting any grumbles or complaints on the part of the refugees and requiring the refugees to be suffering (but only the type of spectacular suffering that the villagers demanded) while at the same time compelling them to be stoic and resilient. However, this appropriation of solidarity as hospitality, humanitarianism, and charity, with all the baggage this embodies, it will be concluded, is completely subsumed within acceptable conduct of what it means to be a decent citizen. It hierarchizes, marginalizes, and excludes, and by no stretch could be seen to embody solidarity in the Swedish rationalist and egoist sense of the word – however, it is undoubtedly good when viewed through the eyes of neighbours, friends, and colleagues.

THE STORY OF ÖREBY, SKÅNE

Öreby is a leafy, picturesque village of about 1,600 inhabitants in Skåne, Sweden's most southern county. The majority of the houses are built along the main through road, which connects the nearest big town in the region in the south to a smaller settlement, the seat of the local municipality, in the north. A rather affluent village, most of the houses in Öreby are large, detached villas, occupied mostly by families with young children or by older, retired couples, and as such are largely very well turned out. Most have large, well-maintained gardens filled with apple and pear trees, flower beds and vegetable patches, children's swings and trampolines, or barbecues and outdoor furniture. The library and local school are both housed in a large, modern glass building that lies at the farthest end of the road, about a fifteen-minute walk from the centre, across the street from the local mini-mart, which sells basic everyday essentials between the hours of 9 a.m. and 12 p.m., then again from 2 p.m. to 5 p.m. As you enter the village from the south, a right turn would lead you onto *Blomgatan* (Flower Street), a narrow road that ends at a cul-de-sac bordering the car park to the village church, a huge whitewashed stone building dating back to the 1400s. Across the road from the church lies the village green, with a little stream running through the centre and two or three picnic benches scattered around. Large green fields surround the village.

Before the arrival of the refugees, Öreby was a completely mono-ethnic village, with everybody living there being Swedish, white, and largely born and raised in Öreby. The exceptions were Magda, a teacher in the local primary school who was originally from Poland but moved to Öreby in the 1980s after falling in love with a Swedish man, and Mikael, a man in his fifties originally from Serbia who did occasional shifts in the mini-mart. In February 2013, however, the demographics of Öreby changed overnight as the village became host to a fairly large number of refugees, resettled in an attractive little apartment complex off *Blomgatan* (which quickly became known in the village as *flyktingförläggningen* – the refugee camp, or simply the camp): fourteen or fifteen small, two-storey red-brick buildings surrounding an open, green communal garden housing some children's swings, slides, and a see-saw.

My connection to the village came about while I was studying in Lund and began to follow the story in *Sydsvenskan* newspaper of the generous donations and support given to one group of, at that point, seventy Syrian refugees who had just been placed by Migrationsverket in the Skånska village. In an area of Sweden with slightly higher-than-average national income, with a local municipality whose composition roughly reflected that of the national legislature, and with only two seats on the local council belonging to the far-right Sweden Democrats party – coupled with the glowing stories in the media of the kindness of this village – I felt it was an interesting site in which to engage with the day-to-day effects of this progressive identity.

I called the telephone number supplied in the newspaper, that of Bodil Petersson, a local woman affiliated with the Church of Sweden who was in charge of collecting donations for the new arrivals in

Öreby. I introduced myself as a researcher from London who was interested in following the story of Öreby as part of my fieldwork into refugee resettlement and in helping out in any way that I could. Somewhat flattered, and happy at the prospect of a much-needed Arabic, Swedish, and English speaker to help translate and interpret things for the new arrivals, Bodil jumped at the chance and a friendship was quickly formed. Over the course of the nineteen months that I carried out my research, the initial group of Syrian families was gradually joined by about forty more Syrians, as well as about a dozen refugees or asylum seekers from other parts of the world – Georgia, Uganda, and Eritrea – until about 120 new arrivals had been resettled in the town.

As opposed to an abstract notion of solidarity based around the national myth, I found that the particular dynamics between the villagers of Öreby and the refugees in this site were extremely illustrative of all the taboos, obligations, and negotiations of norms in play among those who are identified as, and identify themselves as, good citizens in the context of refugees *actually* being resettled in their neighbourhood. Indeed, the villagers of Öreby only came to be informed about the arrival of the refugees three weeks before the first arrivals; most found out after reading the news in the local paper. Migrationsverket then promptly arranged a meeting at the school to listen to locals' concerns, with promises of a spring follow-up meeting, which never materialized.

The meeting at the school, rather than performing the role of solidarity with the refugees became a terrain in which all notions of decency were abandoned, or at least put aside momentarily, in order to counter the imminent threat – in the eyes of the people of Öreby: the reality of refugees being placed in their village. For this brief moment, it was more important for the villagers (or at least some of the villagers) to prevent the refugees' resettlement at any cost, rather than maintain the appearance of being a good citizen to the other residents of the village present at the meeting.[1]

Disappointed at her fellow villagers' reactions to the news of the guests, Bodil organized a Facebook page and founded, with six other local people, the small NGO Friends of Syria (of which I later became a member) to collect donations of clothes, blankets, and kitchen utensils for the refugees. The six women and one man who made up the Friends of Syria were all locals, middle class, and aged in their forties or fifties. Despite the negative comments at the meeting,

Bodil, with the help of the other volunteers, accumulated a huge amount of goods that she took upon herself to distribute among the refugees. As a member of the village community, Bodil was not part of any wider humanitarian organization and was only loosely affiliated with the church. As opposed to the usual working practices of NGO workers, it was the Friends of Syria who initiated contact with the Syrian refugees. They knocked on each of their doors a few hours after the officials from Migrationsverket had settled them into their new homes, introduced themselves as fellow villagers and neighbours, and volunteered themselves as the first point of contact should the new arrivals need any assistance. A few months after the first refugees arrived, the Friends of Syria campaigned for a nearby house to be rented by Migrationsverket to be used as an activity centre for the new arrivals, which became the scene of Swedish lessons, clothing-donation collection and distribution, and general hanging out. I arrived on the scene about three weeks after the first refugees had been resettled in the village, just as the activity centre was about to open. Life at the camp seemed happy and laid-back; the refugees appeared to have, materially, everything they needed thanks to the donations; and many of the Syrians were extremely grateful to the Friends of Syria in creating such a friendly environment. Many people referred to Bodil as "*hadiyyat min Allah*" (a gift from God) and held her in great esteem.

SWEDISH NATIONAL MYTH AS A GOVERNMENTALITY OF RIGHTEOUSNESS: SEEING LIKE A DECENT CITIZEN

As I stated in the chapter 1, in the permeation of the national myth throughout society, it is useful to follow the language of Michel Foucault and think of this narrative of moral superiority regarding solidarity with refugees, and its re-appropriations, as functioning as a particular type of governmentality, what I have called the governmentality of righteousness. This concept allows us to illuminate the art of control by complicating the question of state power, relating state governance to the subjugation and subjectification of individuals. In this respect, such an exercise of power in the form of government can be differentiated from simple coercion or domination.

When I set out my first hypothesis of this book – the idea that the Swedish national myth of moral exceptionalism, especially regarding

Sweden's refugee and asylum policy, generates a particular type of subjectivity and plays a major part in the construction of governable subjects – it was based on this notion that no pre-given self exists prior to subjectification. It is through the conduct of individuals, which modern forms of government take as their referent object, that we come to constitute ourselves as moral subjects. To think in these terms enables us to have a better understanding of how the type of power relations engendered within these standard stories are in part salutary. Foucault labelled as "biopolitical" the type of power concerned with managing not only life, death, health, and illness but also everything in between: working conditions, family, standards of living, and the general "biosphere in which humans dwell" (Dean cited in Selby 2007, 333). However, unlike many of the Foucauldian writers within IR, I conceive of the nature of the biopolitical within the governmentality of righteousness as seemingly benevolent, benign, and linked more explicitly to older modalities of pastoral power.

I thus use the term "righteous," with its theological connotations, to refer to the type of governmentality I am discussing, with the aim of linking the type of pastoral power at play within the Swedish standard story to the production of a certain notion of oneself as completely just in one's actions. The term *"rättfärdig"* (righteous) was used by two of the actors during my fieldwork to discuss Swedish asylum policy in terms of the Swedish approach being so obviously good and noble that it was somewhat beyond reproach.

A governmentality of righteousness overlaps to a great extent with what Fassin (2012) has labelled "humanitarian reason." The author sees this particular rationality not only embedded within our immediate present but also in our long modernity (Fassin, 2012, 247–9). Within humanitarian government, Fassin sees the survival of the notion of human life as the highest good, quoting Hannah Arendt in examining how this principle derives from a much older one: "The reason why life has asserted itself as the ultimate point of reference in the modern age and has remained the highest good of a modern society is that the modern reversal operated within the fabric of a Christian society whose fundamental belief in the sacredness of life has remained completely unshaken by secularization." In asking, "why does politics have to be compassionate?" he traces this rationale back to Augustine of Hippo's observation that we *enjoy* feeling pity for others and being moved by their suffering. In this sense, humanitarianism has redemptive properties, albeit secular ones. It gives a façade of a viable, global moral community in which any barriers and inequalities can be overthrown. Fassin (2012, 252) points to this humanitarian rationale as embodying the ultimate "theological-political" recess. It thus has a distinctly salutary element in that, in saving others, humanitarian reason allows us to save something of ourselves.

However, a governmentality of righteousness departs somewhat from Fassin's (2012) humanitarian reason by focusing more on the ironic element of solidarity (Chouliaraki 2011, 2013) than an Arendtian solidarity of pity as is the case in Fassin's conceptualization. I feel that righteous best captures the rationale at play whereby because "we" feel good and proud because of "our" acts of altruism, any action that "we" take cannot be criticized.[2] In coming back to Foucault's pastoral power, though the author himself was hesitant to engage with any psychoanalytical terms, Jung's (2012) reflection on the shadow in relation to the author's examination of righteousness as a concept – a notion referring to an element of the self that enables denial and projection when one is absolutely certain of one's rightness – is also extremely telling regarding the propagation of pastoral power in the Swedish case. I return to this element of projection later in the chapter.

As we have seen so far with the story of Öreby, many of the villagers saw it as their moral duty to take care of the refugees and help them settle in. Within the space of eight months, over 120 refugees, most of them Syrian, had been resettled in the village. The type of decency engendered by this type of governmentality ensured that conditions for the refugees were quite comfortable, going way beyond notions of a bare life and generation of a narrow biopolitical subject as advanced so regularly in ethnographies of refugee camps and the anthropology of hospitality and humanitarianism (cf. Agier 2011; Redfield 2013; Fassin 2010). The huge bank of donations from the locals ensured not only that everybody had warm clothes for the winter, bicycles for the children to travel to and from school, and basic household utensils but also that each family had a television, toys, board games, and books in both Swedish and English. As a British person living in a similarly sized rural village in East Anglia, it would be incredibly difficult to imagine such a generous response to such a relatively large number of refugees being resettled in my home community.

To think in this way also enables us to envisage how notions of obedience, discipline, obligation, and taboo are also in play. To criticize the morally exceptional narrative with regard to refugee policy would be to criticize something that everybody has agreed is unequivocally good; particular debates are therefore off limits, at least publicly and within polite company, as I set out in the second hypothesis in chapter 1. The policing of the taboo and its repercussions are something I come back to in the next chapter; however, its corollary – the acting out of solidarity, humanitarianism, and hospitality for the benefit of oneself, one's neighbour, a newly settled refugee, or indeed a visiting researcher, what Scott has labelled a public transcript – is a subject I address in the following section.

Secondly, and as I stated in the introduction to this chapter, governmentality in this regard is conceived of as an ethnographic object, an entire axes of practices available for the so-called decent citizen while still maintaining an identification of oneself as a good, moral human being. It is not a Weberian ideal type, but instead a repertoire of available actions. When we talk of governmentality in this very concrete, anthropological manner, it thus avoids the problems of reification or essentialization we have seen with some of the Anglo-Foucauldian literature (cf. Dean 2002, 2010). Instead, we are able to bring to light exactly which practices are incorporated within this wiggle room and whether these practices can adopt any kind of uniformity. These kind of practices need not be openly articulated or codified. Instead, they point to more or less taken-for-granted actions that embody "how we have always done things around here" (Neumann 2002, 237). As we have discussed in chapter 1, anthropologists James C. Scott and Michel de Certeau utilize the ancient Greek term *"mētis"* to describe these type of practices, a way of behaving in the world that is learned simply by local knowledge and cunning as opposed to hard and fast rules or principles (see de Certeau 1998; Scott 2010; Neumann 2002).

As the third hypothesis of this book asserted in chapter 1 that within the axes of practices subsumed within this mode of governmentality, within the wiggle room and metis of this specific conduct of conduct, solidarity is appropriated and re-implanted as humanitarianism, hospitality, and even generosity within everyday practices between good citizens and refugees, with all the baggage that this embodies, I discuss below the manner in which this conduct of conduct, though outwardly decent, is inherently hierarchical in its performance and appropriation. As opposed to a rational idea of solidarity, refugees are instead obliged to play by all the rules of being a "worthy guest": visibly demonstrate their suffering, be ready to mend their "deficient" ways, and be loudly and constantly grateful for the refuge they are given by the good Swedish people. As I discuss throughout the rest of the chapter, however, this hierarchization, disciplining, and, in some instances, stigmatization of the refugees cannot be seen to go against the grain of the governmentality of righteousness, or be viewed as a modality of resistance or counter-conduct. Such behaviour, though far from acting in the ideal of complete solidarity with the refugees as per the national myth, still fits very much within the wiggle room of this type of governmentality and enables all notions of decency to be kept intact.

And so now back to the story of Öreby, and the axes of practices available for all its good citizens. With the topic of refugee resettlement in the village now rendered taboo, the role of the decent Öreby-dweller was to move on with life, demonstrate (within polite company) that the new arrivals were of course very welcome, and display tolerance and generosity whenever the occasion called for it.

A PUBLIC TRANSCRIPT OF SOLIDARITY: ETHNIC MINORITY CHILDREN, CHICKEN SAUSAGES, AND THE IMAGINED HILLBILLIES OF SJOBO

Welcoming the Syrians to Öreby: Onstage Posturing

Around five weeks after the first refugees had moved to Öreby, the local Residents' Association, chaired by an extremely genial gentleman called Lasse, decided to hold a barbeque in the village green to officially welcome the Syrians to Sweden. I had only met Lasse earlier that same afternoon and immediately warmed to his boisterous, somewhat unruly, take-me-as-you-find-me character. In attendance that evening were about twenty or thirty local residents, some local councillors, and about a dozen children, running around the green and enjoying the unusually mild weather. The Friends of Syria – Bodil, Monnika, Åsa, Ava, and Annika – could not attend the barbecue, citing family commitments (Benny had yet to join the group), and at the start of the barbeque no Syrians were yet present. Lasse, president of the association, had provided fifty traditional Swedish *korv* sausages as well as fifty chicken sausages to serve to the Muslim guests and had taught everybody to say "*Ahlan wa sahlan*" (Welcome), in anticipation of meeting the new residents. He further explained that as they were Arab, they were not very good with timekeeping and that everybody should expect them to be an hour or two late. I arrived at the barbecue around twenty minutes after it was planned to start, just in time to be offered a freshly grilled *korv*, presented to me by a smiling teenage boy (who I later learned was Lasse's son).

As this was my first meeting with many of the villagers, several took a great interest in my research and role working with the refugees, and I quickly found myself the centre of attention. "It's very different here to your country," one older, female resident offered. "Our Syrians will get a warm welcome from all of us here." I confided that I had certainly found the village very welcoming and conceded that the huge amount of donations and help given to the new arrivals would probably be unusual in Britain, although it was difficult to say. The theme of how terrible and right-wing British asylum policy was in relation to Swedish policy quickly became the favoured topic of conversation and remained that way throughout the afternoon and evening, with Swedish policy also compared favourably to that of the Danes and Finns: "Could you imagine how the Danes would react if they tried to dump a hundred refugees in Kvistgard or Espergaerde? [Two small municipalities just over the Oresund in Denmark.] They'd have a riot on their hands," an elderly gentleman offered, to which everybody laughed. "I refuse to go to Denmark anymore after how racist they've become over there," the man's wife interjected, in a more serious tone. "Why should we give the Danes our money when they treat foreigners so badly? After all, we are foreigners over there as well," she reasoned.

The rest of the evening then lent itself to discussing the tragic conditions the Syrians had fled. "You just have to look at the videos on YouTube to see how terrible it is there, bodies in the street and people being shot in front of their children," one resident narrated for the rest of the group, before becoming visibly saddened. "*Usch*, Inga, take it easy," her friend interceded, sympathetically putting an arm around her shoulders, just as the woman dramatically lifted a hand to her forehead. After two hours had passed, still no Syrians had arrived at the barbecue, despite living only two minutes away. It then became clear that, despite all the preparation, nobody had remembered to invite any of the refugees. This caused great embarrassment to Lasse, who felt the need to rush to explain himself to me: "We thought that the kids would pass on the message to their kids at school."

The particular discursive practice of the Syrians receiving a warm welcome in Öreby compared, for example, to the UK or Denmark revealed the way in which a certain social setting requires a very particular type of behaviour. We recall that Scott (1990, 49) conceives of the public transcript as the maintenance work needed to uphold relations of domination through the symbolic demonstrations of power. In terms of applying Scott to a Foucauldian framework, moving away from Scott's rather narrow and polemical definitions of domination and resistance and instead drawing inspiration from his musings on ideas of politeness and good taste, Scott concedes that some displays and rituals are closely choreographed to limit wiggle room, and that these rules of etiquette are too pervaded by power. In the instance of the barbecue, we see how a certain public transcript is performed In accordance with the governmentality of righteousness. Identity is constructed among the villagers in national terms: they were first and foremost Swedes and thus had a responsibility to stand in solidarity with their new Syrian neighbours, to express empathy toward their suffering and offer them a peaceful and secure place to live. As an external actor to a certain extent – both a foreigner and an academic – my presence constructed a dominating effect of sorts: Scott's "powerful stranger" (1990, 47).[3] I acted as a type of external critical parameter through which a unifying identity could be formulated and the public transcript enacted most coherently. Naturally, however, the barbecue was not arranged for the benefit of a visiting researcher/translator, and the president of the Residents' Association admitted feeling a sense of duty to organize something to show that the Syrians were welcome. The large turnout and much of the performance – discussions on what they had already donated to Bodil's Facebook campaign, what else the Syrians needed, and what they could do to help – were, of course, well-intentioned but were also a way of enacting the decent citizen to neighbours and friends. The fact that nobody actually remembered to invite the Syrians is testament to the extent of onstage posturing that the public transcript embodies.

The Skinheads of Sjobo: Projection and Denial

In order to keep this public transcript intact, it was important to erase any memory of the initial resistance to the refugees. Certainly, the initial meeting – the only occasion at which there was vocal resistance to Migrationsverket's plan to settle refugees in the village – was completely downplayed by the residents of the village, both at the barbecue and in interviews I conducted with locals throughout the first few weeks of my fieldwork. A few people referred to it as "hysterical"; however, the main narrative was one of lighthearted dismissal and even denial. Of course, it was understandable that the villagers were a bit concerned about the unknown, but nobody was *really* against the Syrians coming to Öreby. Some rationalized the actions at the meeting as a little bit over the top, but reasoned that now that the Syrians were here, and everyone could see that they were just normal families like "us," albeit needing a bit of help and support, nobody from Öreby would begrudge them making a new life for themselves in the village. A few people were of the opinion that the majority of Öreby dwellers would, under no circumstances, tolerate racism from their neighbours and fellow villagers and that the meeting was simply one or two loud people trying to make their voices heard above all others. As I was not present at the initial meeting and was denied access to the official minutes, I cannot comment on the extent of the resistance to the resettlement of the refugees and could only gauge it by the second-hand accounts from people I chatted to in the village or from the volunteers within the Friends of Syria.

In distancing oneself from the resistance, however, the notion of, in this case, being a village – as opposed to a town or a more rural, scattered community – was crucial for maintaining this identity. This was interesting as it was only in connection with the meeting, in the face of a clear occasion of resistance to the refugees, that the public transcript of solidarity was not conceived in purely nationalistic terms. The racists could never be from a village within this narrative as villagers (*byboarna*) were a distinct type of people who knew what it was to look after one another and support each other in hard times. They saw themselves as embodying Swedish ideas of solidarity and generosity vis-à-vis people who lived in the bigger towns and cities and who had lost touch with their roots. "Real" Swedes, then, were the Öreby folk, the polar opposite of these imagined others.

Throughout the first few weeks of carrying out my fieldwork and chatting to residents of the village, specifically about the meeting at the school, mysterious references to "what happened in Sjobo" were often made. Seven or eight people in the village, including the head teacher of the school, spoke derogatorily of the place. "The meeting wasn't anything like what happened in Sjobo, if that's what you're imagining. We're not like that here," an elderly man told me while trimming his hedge. This was the first time I had heard Sjobo mentioned by anyone in Öreby, though the name of the little village rang a faint bell somewhere in my memory. I had visited Skåne regularly for fifteen years and recalled seeing signposts for the town while on my way to Malmo. I also remembered some friends in Lund referring to how racist Sjobo was and the backwardness of the people there. Bodil, Åsa, and Monnika were also very quick to distance Öreby people from the type that lived in Sjobo: "There are no racists and skinheads here in Öreby like there are in a place like Sjobo," Bodil explained to me in one of our first meetings. "It's just not that sort of village. You wouldn't want to set foot in a place like Sjobo if you were an immigrant."

This demonization of Sjobo, a town only 100 kilometres or so from Öreby, draws on a referendum that took place in 1988 whereby it was decided that, against pressure from Migrationsverket in Stockholm, Sjobo would not accept refugees into its municipality. This controversy was a source of great embarrassment for the Swedish political elite, with then–prime minister Thorbjörn Fälldin stating that, "When Sweden has internationally pledged itself to receive refugees, a single municipality cannot hold a referendum about refusing to take part" (cited in Pred 2000, 191). The fact that this town still occupies a prominent place in Swedish, or at least Scanian (*Skånska*), public imagination as pervaded by racist, ignorant thugs some twenty-five years later – when I conducted my fieldwork – is a testament to the success of the Swedish media in criticizing the referendum decision and demonizing the inhabitants of Sjobo.[4] As such, the idea of the skinheads and neo-Nazis of Sjobo, a world apart from the kind, decent villagers of Öreby, was hugely successful in enabling the public transcript to function. So long as there were these imagined racist others, the Öreby dwellers could quite legitimately maintain the performance of the good Swedish citizen.

When it was not spatial, this type of projection was framed in terms of the demonization of certain organizations. For example, this was most noticeable in Öreby with regard to the actions of the generous villagers in contrast to the cold, uncaring bureaucracy of the Migration Board. It was well known in the village that, when the first refugees were settled in Öreby in the middle of an exceptionally cold winter, Migrationsverket provided only two thin duvets per family. Nobody from the agency showed the Syrians how to regulate the central heating within the apartments or advised them where to go for inexpensive warm clothing. The inadequacies and cold-heartedness of Migrationsverket was used as a mobilizing force to encourage donations via Facebook. Everybody in Öreby knew of Migrationsverket's clinical approach to dealing with the Syrians and spoke in terms of stepping up to the plate to help the Syrians. In this way, the image of the good Swede was maintained in the face of internal dissonance witnessing the inadequacies of the state apparatus that was supposed to represent the once-again cherished Swedish model of refugee and asylum policy.[5]

Aside from this projection and denial, the public transcript also required notions of one-upmanship in order to function effectively. For Scott, the public transcript can only be expected to function properly if maintained by what he called "guardians of taste and decorum."[6] In our specific example, these guardians set the bar of what it was to be a decent citizen, a standard that everybody else was required to match in order to preserve a righteous identity. The introduction of Benny to the Friends of Syria demonstrates these ideas of one-upmanship, as the next vignette illustrates. In his instance, Benny played the role of exemplar of decency, thus obliging others to follow suit.

"I'm One of the Good Guys": The Decent Citizen Par Excellence

Benny's introduction to the rest of the Friends of Syria group took place around mid-September, by which time the activity centre was in full swing and in use every day as a place where the Syrians could simply drop in and hang out, share a cup of coffee and supervise their children playing, bring any letters or e-mails they needed translated, or get assistance with phone calls to Migrationsverket.

Pleased to have a new volunteer at the activity centre, Bodil welcomed Benny into the small apartment, offered him a cup of coffee, and outlined to him our plans for the day, which were simply to bake cinnamon buns with whoever turned up and to make a start on arranging the clothes that had been donated. Upon hearing about my role as both a volunteer and researcher, Benny's face illuminated. He explained that he was a well-travelled man, having lived in Nigeria and Canada for the best part of twenty years, and that some of his best friends were Muslim. Excitedly, he asked Bodil if she had received his e-mail, sent that morning with the picture of his son. When she answered that she hadn't had time yet, he removed his wallet from his pocket and took out a carefully stored photograph that he laid on the kitchen table. A black teenage boy in full ice hockey uniform stared back from the picture. "You see, my son is black. He's adopted from Nigeria. You see? I'm one of the good guys," he said, and laughed.

This was the third time that an individual from the village had exhibited a photo to either Bodil or me of an adopted child belonging to an ethnic minority. On all three occasions, a proud parent had produced the picture to demonstrate what a generous and tolerant individual they were, drawing links with the Syrian refugees. On all three occasions, the pleased parent proceeded to relay a story of the terrible childhood their son or daughter had experienced in China, Thailand, or Nigeria and how they were now flourishing in Sweden. This type of action served to provoke others to bolster the public transcript by articulating their particular good deeds, whether this be how much they had donated to a particular cause or how many friends or relatives from ethnic minorities they had. Here, the public transcript could be viewed as one of complete solidarity with the refugees: they are likened to sons, partners, or friends who are also brown. In performing this transcript, however, it is clear that the refugees (along with brown friends and relatives) are placed into a hierarchy of individuals: they are the beneficiaries of the goodwill of the decent Swedes, a source of a certain type of social capital in certain settings to be drawn upon and presented when required. This demonstrates the point that, in its very nature, the governmentality of righteousness is somewhat hierarchical and exclusionary.

As we discussed in the third hypothesis of the book in chapter 2, the appropriation of complete solidarity with the refugees as generosity, humanitarianism, and even hospitality is completely in keeping with the public transcript of decency we spoke about above, even though these framings place certain demands and obligations upon these refugees to be worthy guests. In the everyday practices of metis and wiggle room of the governmentality of righteousness, refugees are obliged to play by all the rules of hospitality: be loudly and constantly grateful for the refuge they are given, accept their lot without complaining, visibly demonstrate their suffering when required, and be stoic and resilient when visible suffering is no longer desired by the host community. As we discuss in the following section, however, all these re-appropriations and re-implantations, though exclusionary, are still very much in keeping with, and are subsumed by, the many axes of practices available to the actors operating within the governmentality of righteousness. As long as everybody plays by the rules, no challenge is posed to the notion of the villagers as good and decent citizens.

APPROPRIATING SOLIDARITY AS HUMANITARIANISM, HOSPITALITY, AND GENEROSITY: THE OBLIGATIONS OF THE GOOD REFUGEE

Accept Your Lot!: The Prohibition of Criticism

Öreby, though nowhere near as isolated as many Swedish villages in the rest of the country where asylum seekers had been resettled, was nonetheless about a forty-five-minute bus journey from the nearest sizable town with its shops, restaurants, cinemas, and cafés. The bus, though reliable, was rather infrequent with one bus per hour during morning and evening peak times, reduced to once every two hours at all other times of the day, with the last bus departing for town a little after 7 p.m. Malmo, the nearest big city in the region, with its comparative abundance of narghile houses and Arabic restaurants, was a further hour away, requiring a trip on the relatively expensive Öresundståg train. Apart from the single pizzeria *Smak*, owned by an elderly couple from the next village along, everything in Öreby was closed and locked up by about 5 p.m. It was extremely rare to see anybody, other than a few children playing or cycling, on the streets after this time. Though many of the Öreby folk worked in town and commuted in and out every day, trips to Malmo, or further afield to Copenhagen (a further half an hour or so across the Oresund Bridge), were very rare. They seemed to take place only a few times a year for special occasions like the Christmas market or a day out with the children to the Tivoli Gardens amusement park. In contrast, many of the newly arrived Syrians were from big cities – Damascus, Aleppo, Dera'a, Homs, and Hama – and unaccustomed to the very quiet and slow pace of countryside living. As a Londoner, and having spent a considerable amount of time in Damascus myself between 2006 and 2009, I was viewed by some Syrian people as an empathetic ear for their grumbles and observations about the culture shock they faced: "What are we supposed to do? In Haleb all the stores were open till midnight or later. We could go for a stroll, grab a shwarma and a beer, listen to some music. You know how it is. Here, everybody just seems so *tired*," remarked Nivine, a recently arrived woman from Aleppo who dragged out the last word to signify her mind-numbing boredom. "They have heavy blood, eh?" she would often assert – a common lighthearted Arabic expression used in Syria to describe guests who lack a sense of humour, are a burden to entertain, or suck the life out of a party.

What struck me about Nivine the first time I met her was not only her straight talking, which I found fun and refreshing, but also her stylish, glamorous clothes and impeccable makeup. No matter whether she was nipping out to the mini-mart or popping into the activity centre for a cup of coffee or to take part in one of the volunteer's cooking classes, Nivine always looked immaculate and smelled of expensive perfume. She told me that she and her husband, Omar, had been quite well off back home in Aleppo, with their own textile business, but had used all their savings to organize their flight to Europe: new passports and €15,000 flights into Sweden from Beirut. As I was usually dressed in jeans and a ski jacket, an ongoing joke with Nivine – with a ring of truth to it – was that she always made me feel drab and dowdy (I found myself re-applying lip gloss or combing my hair with my fingers whenever she was around).

Nivine's very glamorous and confident character appeared to make some of the other volunteers also feel somewhat frumpy and plain. Annika, for example, in her early forties, would often remark on the amount of makeup and gold jewellery that Nivine wore to the activity centre, commenting that Nivine "thinks she's better than all of us, with all her fancy jewels." On occasion, Bodil too would try to co-opt some of the other Syrian women into talking about Nivine after she had left the activity centre: "That woman wears a lot of perfume, eh?" she would half-joke. Some of the older, more conservative Syrian women would agree and assert, disapprovingly, that Nivine was "not a good type of woman," a declaration that would cause Bodil to quickly backtrack and revert to some form of to-each-their-own platitude. However, none of the younger Syrians in Öreby seemed to take any offence or pay any attention to Nivine's appearance and character.

Nivine's husband, Omar, too was branded "flashy" and "brash" by the Friends of Syria volunteers, though in a much more lighthearted manner. A very tall and broadly built man, Omar came to the activity centre relatively infrequently – only when he needed a letter from Migrationsverket translated from Swedish – and spoke with a bellowing, though jovial, voice. Omar also was always as well groomed as his wife, wore an expensive-looking watch, and owned the newest model of iPhone, upon which he showed photos of their home city, Aleppo, before they left and since. As Nivine and Omar were about my age and were relatively open and fun to be around, I spent a few evenings hanging out with them in their apartment while they talked about life in Sweden compared to life back home. It turned out that they travelled to Sweden because Omar had an uncle and some cousins living in Malmo and they hoped to eventually use these connections to find jobs in the area. Though they never openly complained of boredom to any other members of the Friends of Syria group (they were not at all impolite), Nivine and Omar were very open with me in talking about the culture shock and how they were both struggling with the very slow pace of life in Sweden.

At the beginning of September, about four months after Omar and Nivine first arrived in Öreby, Nivine excitedly approached me as I was walking from the bus stop to the activity centre. "Come and check out what Omar has bought," she said. As we approached their apartment, I noticed Omar out in the parking area next to an old, burgundy BMW convertible, which he explained he had bought from a friend of his cousin in Malmo. The car, though from the 1980s, was in perfect working order, they explained. The pair were excited that they would now be able to go on day trips, out shopping, or out for a meal whenever they pleased, without having to rely on local transport. Omar then opened the trunk of the car and pulled out a full-sized narghile pipe that they had found in a shop in the Rosengård shopping mall in Malmo, inviting me in to the apartment for a smoke and some snacks.

The purchase of a car was the source of some envious comments among a few of the other Syrians. A couple of the older, more well-established families who had been settled in Öreby for the longest and had a closer relationship with Bodil enquired how it was possible to buy a car in Sweden without yet having being granted permanent residency and the all-important *personummer*, insinuating that there was something very dodgy going on. However, what aggrieved Monnika, Bodil, and Åsa more that the illegality of the car purchase was the need for the pair to own a car whatsoever, though this manifested itself in more socially acceptable complaints about the perceived flashiness of the car. There was a consensus that, though Omar and Nivine may have led a very privileged life in Syria, buying a convertible BMW to drive to and from Malmo was in somewhat bad taste. As I had the closest relationship to Omar and Nivine, I felt obliged to defend their car purchase, pointing out how impractical going anywhere by bus was, especially in the evenings. As I was the only member of the group who did not own a car and who travelled back and forth to Öreby by bus, nobody challenged my opinion about the feasibility of bus travel. Indeed, it was largely only teenagers too young to obtain a driving licence or the elderly who used the bus network anyway. But it was acceptable to criticize the choice of car model. Though I argued that it was an old car and cheap to buy, Bodil and Åsa were aggrieved at the amount the car would cost to run: it was not fuel efficient and petrol is not at all cheap in Sweden like it is in Syria. This was especially annoying to the volunteers since Omar and Nivine were benefiting from Swedish taxpayers' money. Furthermore, they pointed out, buying such an ostentatious car was not a typically Swedish thing to do, a notion the volunteers did not expect me to fully grasp as I too was a foreigner.[7]

The behaviour of Nivine and Omar, their purchase of a car (and a not very practical car at that), and the disapproving reaction of the volunteers demonstrates the unease felt when a refugee stepped outside their place within the hierarchy and pushed the boundaries of what it meant to be a worthy guest. It was clear that even the purchase of a car to travel to and from Malmo was deemed somewhat insulting to the group. Why was there such a great need to go to Malmo so frequently when nobody else in the village did so? The Syrian couple were deemed rude in not accepting their lot, even though most Swedish people in the village owned a car. If all the other Syrian people in the village were happy to travel by bus or by train, then Omar and Nivine should not think themselves as better. Furthermore, the couple's perceived ostentatious display of not simply their wealth but also their personhood, self-esteem, and sense of fun went very much against the grain of what the volunteers perceived a good refugee to be. Nivine and Omar were not obviously needy or vulnerable. At the same time, this was received as a sort of lack of gratitude toward the generous Swedish people.

These thoughts were never expressly articulated by any of the volunteers. Nonetheless, it was the attitude picked up on whenever the couple either was around or had just left, hinted at through little off-the-cuff remarks or a rolling of the eyes. It was difficult to argue against any of the volunteers on this point. I could see how Nivine and Omar's car was rather vulgar by the standards of the village, and it was not an overreaction to deem the pair insensitive as they sped away from the car park with the roof of the car down. To disapprove of the pair thus again fit very much within the conduct (of conduct), wiggle room, or practices of metis within the governmentality of righteousness I wrote about previously. In its appropriation, showing solidarity with refugees demanded adherence to a relatively strict set of criteria. Far from recognizing the agency and choices of the couple, there was an expectation of reciprocation for the generosity shown by the villagers. In embedding itself within a national myth of moral exceptionalism and solidarity, Omar and Nivine's behaviour was thus conceived of as going against an imagined Swedish way, not simply against the hospitality of the villagers. As a foreigner, I was also often subject to these lectures: "That's not really how people behave here in Sweden," or "That's just not the way things are done." The conduct of conduct is thus expressly nationalistic in its action.

The worthy guest is not one who complains about their circumstances or conditions, a practice that is considered deviant, or at the very least unusual. Though Omar and Nivine could by no means be accused of grumbling about their resettlement in Öreby, their obvious refusal to simply accept their lot, and the way in which volunteers viewed this behaviour, is telling. The perception of deviance from the expected behaviour of the worthy guest became increasingly pronounced within the village as more and more Syrians began to be resettled there and became more heavily sanctioned. From the outset, it could never be said that complaining about one's situation as a Syrian in Öreby engendered a huge amount of sympathy (the indignation and resulting vilification of Migrationsverket's uncompassionate attitude toward the Syrians was witnessed by Bodil and Åsa, not brought to light by any of the new arrivals). However, reactions to these complaints shifted from attempts to rectify the situation for the refugees to increasing irritation and even indignation amongst the volunteers and within the village more widely.

The peak of this indignation, however, came about when one of the Syrians, Rifat, who was part of the first group to arrive in Öreby, gave an interview to a foreign newspaper about the living conditions in the camp and the state of his mental health. Here, he complained about the cramped living conditions, the indifferent attitude of the Swedish authorities, and the lack of opportunities for skilled and well-educated migrants in Sweden. By this point, journalists had visited the refugees' accommodation in Öreby a few times and had conducted interviews with the residents, the Syrians, and the volunteers. The vast majority of these stories reported in the local newspaper were very positive, focusing on the good work being undertaken within this particular village, the huge amount of donations the volunteers were able to collect, the impromptu language lessons, and how successfully local events had turned out, such as the annual Children's Day or National Day that twenty or thirty Syrian people who lived in the village had attended.

These articles fitted with the much broader frames of representation of refugees and migrants within the Swedish press. In the local newspaper, for example, the stories of the Syrian refugees themselves tended to follow a very prescribed pattern and distinct habitus: the new arrival would talk mostly about their lives and jobs in Syria before they were forced to leave (usually emphasizing that they were from a middle-class background, with a skilled, white-collar job) before talking about their difficult journey to Sweden and their families left back at home. In all these personal stories, (referred to as sob stories or *snyftartiklar* on the right-wing and anti-immigration blogs), the refugees spoke of their gratefulness at being allowed to stay in Sweden and talked about their hope for a bright future.

Despite the generally positive stories, however, journalists were, on the whole, regarded with suspicion by both the refugees and the volunteers in Öreby. This stemmed in part from photographers taking pictures of the newly arrived Syrians within a few weeks of arrival, despite their protestations and their requests to remain anonymous as they feared they were still wanted by the Assad regime in Syria and that their families could be at risk if it was known that they were in Sweden. Therefore, Rifat's interview with the British newspaper was not only seen by the volunteers as an affront to Sweden's hospitality and their efforts in particular to welcome him but also seen by some of the other Syrians as a slight betrayal and, at the very least, extremely unnecessary. Though Swedes and Syrians alike regarded Migrationsverket as somewhat inadequate, criticizing it was only permissible for the Swedes. The worthy Syrian was one who understood the huge workload of the agency and was patient and grateful in dealing with it.

Deviance from the role of worthy guest and its repercussions also manifested itself in practices around the designation of donated clothes. If a refugee was not extremely careful in the way donations were accepted or was perceived as complaining about a faulty or inadequate item received, this was immediately interpreted in terms of the ungrateful refugees against the generous Swedes. Within about two months of the first refugees being settled in Öreby, Bodil decided to clear her two garages of all the donated goods and designate the top floor of the activity centre for storage of clothes and goods that people had contributed. A lot of time was spent up here sorting clothes into what could and could not be used, by gender and by size. Anybody could then knock on the door of the activity centre, at any time, and go and take clothes that they needed.

This set-up worked extremely well for the first few weeks. Most times, when a new family arrived in the village, Bodil would take the mother upstairs to pick out a few items of winter clothing for the children and perhaps some warm shoes. On the whole, the Syrians were forthright in asserting their gratitude to the volunteers and would pass along some comment on how pretty, warm, or good quality the clothes were. However, problems began to arise around the end of summer and beginning of autumn: with donations beginning to wane, the supply of clothes started to dwindle. It was around this time that a new arrival, Ahmed, knocked on the door of the activity centre to return a jacket to Bodil that he had selected from among the donated clothes the previous week. He claimed that the jacket did not fit very well and asked if there were any more he could look at upstairs. Bodil agreed that he could look, but only if she supervised, as she was suspicious that he might take other items that he didn't really need. After looking through the clothes, Ahmed complained that there was nothing there that was suitable. This lack of gratitude irritated Bodil, and the hospitality and generosity of the donors began to be framed in nationalistic terms: "These are the clothes that Swedish people have kindly donated," she explained to Ahmed. "We're not all rich, you know. Some people have given up their clothes because they think you need them more than they do." Ahmed, somewhat impatiently, said that he understood but asked Bodil to keep him in mind if any new jackets were donated that she thought might fit. After Ahmed left, Bodil told Annika that she doubted there was anything wrong with the jacket Ahmed had, and that she suspected he was after a designer or branded jacket since two or three of the other young men had been happy to dig out Nike and Hugo Boss jackets over the last few weeks.

Within many studies of refugee camps and the practices associated with them, the worthy guest and good refugee is one who does not complain and accepts what is given. Drawing on Maussian conceptions of hospitality and his notion of "the gift," the recipient of the gift is placed in the temporary and conditional social world of the gift giver, generating elements of patronage and debt in which the recipient is robbed of any agency.[8] In the context of Öreby, the need for refugees to accept their lot and behave in a manner that was deemed fair game by the volunteers was conceived, on the whole, in nationalistic standards. In pushing the boundaries of what it meant to be a worthy guest, Nivine and Omar, Rifat, and Ahmed were all insulting either the imagined Swedish way or the generous Swedish people. However, as we discuss through the vignettes below, similar requirements of behaviour demanded from the refugees – for example, the need to be visibly suffering and vocal in articulating their experiences – were framed through much more subtle nationalistic stories. For instance, the need to educate Swedish children on the horrors of war so that Sweden could continue to act as a safe haven for refugees was strictly, though politely, enforced. And similarly, having a good time at an event not orchestrated by the benevolent hosts was conceived of, ever so delicately, as taking advantage of the good nature of the Swedish people.

"Be Needy": The Requirement for the Right Type of Suffering

The fifty-year anniversary of a walking trail from Öreby to the next village took place at the height of the Swedish summer, in mid-June, and was celebrated with the organizing of a special group walk of the trail, which took place on a sunny Saturday morning. By this stage, the refugees, still mainly Syrian, had lived in the village for about three months. I had been asked by the president of the local Residents' Association to translate posters advertising the event into Arabic. There was a great deal of buzz and excitement around the event on the day. Though due to begin at 11 a.m., a few dozen people had already gathered at the meeting point, a recycling station in Öreby's main car park, by a quarter past ten, when I arrived. The weather was already in the low twenties, a group of teenagers had taken to blaring Katy Perry songs from an old-fashioned looking ghetto-blaster they had brought along, and everybody was generally in good spirits. Most of the Friends of Syria group had come along for the walk, gathered together in a large group with their families and some other neighbours. Along the length of the 5-kilometre trail, small food stalls had been set up selling locally produced, artisanal produce like fresh bread and honey. At the finish line of the trail, in the next village along, some children's fun-fair games and a small bouncy castle had been erected, which seemed to be the favoured topic of discussion between a few of the grandparents and their grandchildren at the event.

I chatted briefly to Lasse, president of Öreby Residents' Association, who was standing with his two teenage sons and their huge Labrador dog: "I hope that you've managed to convince our Syrians to come along today," he warmly pronounced. Lasse was always friendly and welcoming in his dealings with me, never regarding me with anything like the same level of suspicion that some of the other villagers viewed me with. Likewise, I found him extremely genuine and gentle. "A few people have said they'd turn up," I assured him.

Sure enough, at around five minutes to eleven, a small family from Damascus whom I had met the previous week, Tariq, Sandra, and their two-year old daughter, as well as a young family of five from Latakia whom I had only met briefly a few days previously, arrived at the meeting point, warmly greeting me in Arabic and asking to be introduced to the rest of the group. Tariq and Sandra, both somewhat proficient English speakers, began to chat away with Lasse, commenting on the beautiful weather, which they had not expected when they planned to move from Syria. Lasse responded in Swedish (he was not a confident English speaker) that they were all most welcome at the event, and that Swedish summers were typically glorious. Though slightly awkward, the atmosphere was relaxed and pleasant, and Sandra used some of her newly acquired Swedish vocabulary to thank Lasse and agree that everything was "very pleasant."

As the trail walk officially commenced, signalled by a gunshot and waving of the Swedish flag by an elderly gentleman dressed in a traditional folk costume, the first few families began to stroll along the marked itinerary, with some of the children rushing ahead. The group of Syrians who had come to join the walk, and who by now had attracted a great deal of interest from a few of the Swedish families, also began to mill along the length of the trail as I began to play a sort of unofficial interpreter role (though this role became increasingly redundant as everybody gradually gained more confident in expressing themselves in English). "Please tell them that they are most welcome here in Öreby and that we're glad that we can provide them with somewhere they can feel safe," a tall, dark-haired man dressed in full hiking gear proclaimed. A middle-aged woman whom I had met a few times in the local library, presumably a friend of the gentleman with the trekking outfit, pointed to her three children and asked me if I could ask the Syrian people to explain what life is like in a war zone. She explained that her children had learned about refugees in school and had seen footage of the war in Syria, and it would be beneficial for them to hear about the situation from "real" refugees and why it's so important for Sweden to help them.

Tariq proceeded to explain, in English, that he was from Damascus, which hadn't suffered that badly from bombings or anything like that (at that point in time), but that he was related to members of the Free Syrian Army and was thus wanted by the Assad regime. "You are not free in Syria to say whatever you want to say. It is extremely difficult to live your life in this way. You even have to be careful what you utter in front of the children in case they repeat something at school. So you can imagine the difficulty in living a normal life under these circumstances." Tariq was sombre and serious.

The mother of three, and a few of her friends who had gathered around, let out a collective "*Usch*" to express their disapproval and discomfort at the thought of living life in such fear, and translated for the children that "in Syria, people are not free to say what they want about the government." The children aged between about six and twelve were quiet and seemed a little perplexed, but stayed politely silent, listening to what was being relayed to them. After strolling along for another few minutes, the woman continued pressing Tariq: "What was life like in Damascus though? You must have been hungry and cold in the wintertime." The children's mother proceeded with the conversation, speaking slowly and loudly in English, though apparently for the benefit of her two older children than Tariq and Sandra.

Tariq seemed somewhat bemused by the question. "To be honest, Damascus is a beautiful city. There are some fantastic concerts, great restaurants and nightlife. When we left, it was pretty much business as usual there. People gradually stopped going out at nighttime, sure, because of the hassle of checkpoints. We had everything there though: satellite TV, high-speed Internet, and food from all over the world. Materially, things were good there for us. That is why it was harder to give it all up." The middle-aged woman and her husband seemed a little exasperated that the narrative of life in Syria did not conform to their imagining of life in that city. "We saw footage on YouTube and on the news of all the terrible injuries that people have suffered from. They showed bombs going off everywhere and snipers on top of buildings." Tariq conceded that in many other cities, especially Dera'a, Homs, and Hama, which at that time had been most severely affected, this was indeed the case. He said that he had heard from friends in Aleppo that their city too had been very badly damaged. Then Sandra interjected, "But we are here now in beautiful Sweden, and the Swedish people have been so kind to us. And we hear that you need more computer engineers and English teachers, which is good news for us because that's what we have to offer." Though this was clearly an attempt by Tariq and Sandra to steer the conversation in a different direction, the Swedish family, and the group that had gathered around us, seemed reluctant to let the discussion proceed in this way. "It looked really bad for those people in the refugee camps last winter as well though, didn't it? *Usch*. I could barely look at the news. Some children didn't even have coats or shoes and were living in the most basic tents. I was heartbroken to look at their little faces, poor things," said a second lady, seemingly ever so slightly aggrieved at Tariq and Sandra's inability to empathize with their fellow country folk. At this point, Tariq, a man with a rather dry sense of humour and apparently not in the mood to be reminded of the situation for many Syrian people by a group of Swedes at a local festival, put an end to the conversation altogether: (laughing)"Well, I'm glad we remembered to pack Leila's [Sandra and Tariq's daughter] little fur jacket. She'd have killed me if we left that behind! Never mind the regime!" Still laughing, he picked up his daughter, threw her in the air, and then playfully bit her belly, pretending to be a dog. Leila squealed in delight.

The small group that had gathered gave an awkward sort of laugh and turned their attention to the family from Latakia, quizzing them on whether Latakia had been similarly fortunate in escaping the worst of the war so far. The group were then extremely attentive in listening to Ibrahim, the father-of-five, explain that, although Latakia was lucky at the beginning of the war in escaping the shelling and bombing, things there had recently deteriorated rapidly. Over the remaining kilometres of the walk, Ibrahim gave a detailed account of the way in which life in Latakia had suddenly transformed from being a relatively safe and protected part of the country (where President Assad has a palace used as a coastal retreat) to one that was now the scene of terrible violence. "I have seen things that you could not possibly imagine, only in your worst nightmares," Ibrahim explained to the group. He narrated how, in recent months, the Jihadi group Jabhat al-Nusra had made significant advances toward the city, and vicious fighting had begun just outside the city between forces loyal to Assad and Islamist groups. He described the terror of hearing shellings and bombings in the nearby hills, not knowing when they would reach the city.

The Swedish group listened patiently, occasionally muttering exclamations of horror or discomfort. By this time, Lasse had wandered back to join Tariq, Sandra, Leila, and myself, who were subtly, though seemingly not intentionally, being ignored by the larger group listening to Ibrahim's narrative. Quickly sensing the dark mood and attempting to lift everybody's spirits, Lasse intervened in Swedish: "Come on, everybody, this is supposed to be a happy, festive day! It's taken me weeks to organize! Why don't we all go and try some of these delicious cakes over here." After some nods and murmurs of agreement from the larger group, Lasse was eventually, however, politely ignored as the group moved more closely around the Latakian family, discussing in broken English a report that they had heard about the al-Nusra front executing a young boy in Aleppo for making a harmless joke about Allah.

After the walk and back in their small apartment, Tariq brought up the subject of the interest from the villagers about life in Syria. He confided that he was not at all comfortable talking about the situation back home, explaining that his entire family were still there with little chance of getting out. All of the family savings had been used to help Tariq, Sandra, and Leila leave and build a new life in Europe. "I hope they did not think I was being rude."

Though the Öreby dwellers were well meaning, this vignette illustrates the desire of some of them to seek some sort of gratitude, or at least compensation, albeit indirectly, for their generosity in welcoming the Syrians into their village. When Tariq and Sandra attempted to present themselves as equals, with qualities of their own to bring to Sweden, the pair was quickly ignored in favour of the more interesting, apparently needier, refugees who were perceived to have suffered more. Once again, we see here the appropriation of the national myth of moral exceptionalism shifting somewhat to mean for many of the people on the walk not only humanitarianism but also hospitality. It was Sweden and not Öreby, Skåne, or Europe that was invoked by the villagers as the entity that provided a safe haven for the Syrian people. However, this was articulated by some as though it were a gift bestowed upon them. The hierarchy between the Swedish people on the walk and the Syrians was not permitted to be breached, and even attempts by fellow Öreby-dweller Lasse to create a more equal and solidarist atmosphere was rejected. The refugees were required, in this instance, to educate the children about refugee life by going into great detail about the horror of the civil war in their particular experience. It was the villagers, however, who set the agenda as to what particular horrors should be discussed, with the more spectacular stories of overt violence and atrocities favoured over the more subtle accounts of an all-pervasive unease and self-discipline.

In reflecting back on the idea of a governmentality of righteousness, the re-appropriation and re-implanting of the national myth of moral exceptionalism and solidarity as humanitarianism and hospitality can be seen to fit nicely within the wiggle room and metis of this so-called conduct of conduct. As discussed, each actor operating within the governmentality of righteousness has access to a wide axes of practices. In this instance, the villagers on the walk who politely obliged the Latakian family to regale them with stories of suffering and to educate their children on the horrors of war (and presumably the importance of granting protection to people fleeing war) were in no way going against what it means to be a good or decent citizen. Neither were they through their actions attempting to redefine what decency looks like or embodies. We are not engaging here with a type of counter-conduct. The refusal by some of the villagers on the walk to engage with Tariq and Sandra as equals by recognizing the skills that they had to offer and respecting their right not to talk about the life they escaped in Syria, though seemingly going against an idea of solidarity as bound up with the national myth, was nonetheless in keeping with accepted standards of etiquette and decorum.

The desire that the refugees be visibly suffering or obviously needy was a common theme, expressed quite frequently in the first few months of refugees being resettled in Öreby (though this narrative was quickly replaced by one stressing the importance of the stoic refugee, as I discuss below). Nonetheless, as a researcher, volunteer, and translator, my first encounter with the phenomenon manifested itself within the first few days of my arrival in discussions among the volunteers regarding the apparent lack of suffering among the new arrivals. To be a worthy guest, refugees were obliged to be visibly suffering upon their arrival at Öreby. Anger could then be directed at Migrationsverket for settling the Syrians in the apartments in such a careless, clinical manner and failing to provide them with little more than the very basic articles they would need to live adequately.

With the first few families, discourse was along the lines of how remarkable the families appeared to be since a few of the volunteers mentioned how they had expected them to be a lot more mentally damaged and in need of much more medical attention than they actually required. It appeared that a few of the people in the village were somewhat disappointed that these new arrivals seemed to be functioning fairly well, keeping themselves to themselves, not breaking down in tears on the few occasions that the English-speaking Syrians would be obliged to relate stories of being shot at or of bombs going off outside front doors. Within a few days, this seeming admiration at the hardiness of the refugees became a sort of distrust and skepticism of their stories. For example, Bodil would often throw out a comment to some of the other volunteers about how surprised she was that the children especially didn't appear to be as mentally scarred as she expected. This became a deeper distrust whereby Bodil would get annoyed at the children playing outside or some of the families cooking barbecues and playing music: "I don't believe for a second half the stories they're telling me."

This skepticism of some refugees' stories reached its climax during Ramadan, which in 2013 took place at the height of the Swedish summer, with the communal grassy area transformed into a lively meeting place. Goran, a neighbour who lived a few doors away from the apartments where the Syrians were housed, knocked on the door of the activity centre to talk to Bodil about how nice it was that the Syrians seemed to be enjoying themselves, commending the volunteers on a job well done for helping the Syrians to feel so relaxed in their new homes. However, after sensing Bodil's disdain, Goran ventured that he "was not so sure that I would really be in the mood to celebrate if I had just fled from a war zone and half my family are left behind." This utterance was the first instance I witnessed that pushed the idea of decency into somewhat new territory. And it indicated the turn of events that was to come in the following weeks and months: the rendering public of what was until then said only behind closed doors, and the hatching of a new discourse through microphysics and tiny practices. This counter-conduct and the mechanisms through which a new terrain of acceptable behaviour toward the refugees was carved out is the subject of the next chapter. At this point in time, however, Goran's remark was a testing of the water. His admission opened the gates to talk about the refugees' actions in more negative terms. Goran made clear to Bodil that although we were all doing great work in helping to settle the refugees, we had to be careful not to let them take advantage of the kindness of the Swedish people, and let them "run amok."

Adnan the Flying Doctor and the Importance of Stoicism

As stated previously, the desire in Öreby that a refugee be visibly suffering was short-lived. Over time, notions of what it was to be a worthy guest or a good refugee also changed. As the Syrians who first arrived in Öreby gradually obtained residency permits and the all-important *personummer*, there was an expectation that they would now pull themselves together somewhat and take advantage of the opportunities that Sweden as a nation offered them. Any behaviour deviating from this stoicism was held in disregard by the volunteers. Similarly, the few who excelled in playing by all the rules were showered with praise and held up as exemplars to the rest.

Adnan was the embodiment of such expectations and rewards. Having technically completed an entire medicine degree in Aleppo, Adnan was obliged to flee the country before his official graduation or even collecting his transcripts and certificate. In Sweden, Adnan complained of not being able to contact the university in Aleppo for them to send his qualification (he had heard from friends in Syria that the university was still technically up and running, but they told him of recurring power cuts and of both phone lines and the Internet being regularly down). After a few weeks of trying to get in touch with his old department of medicine, Adnan was informed that they would be unable to issue him with his degree as it was impossible to access any of the examination records on their internal system. Frustrated, but persistent, Adnan spoke to the admissions department of Lund University, the closest university to Öreby with a Faculty of Medicine, and inquired about the options of resitting final year exams in Sweden before, he hoped, undertaking more specialist training or of possibly repeating the final year of his medicine program. However, he was disappointed to find out that the university would not accept transfer of any credits from his Syrian degree to Sweden; he would be obliged to retake the entire degree from the very start.

Though temporarily aggrieved, Adnan's stoicism impressed the volunteers as he regaled us with the latest twists and turns of his story. After a few weeks of persistently contacting everybody he could think of in the Faculty of Medicine at Lund University, and even further afield at the University of Gothenburg, with no luck regarding transfer of credits or validation of his past studies, Adnan decided that, instead of redoing an entire medical degree, he would postpone his career as a doctor (at least until he was able to collect his transcripts from Aleppo) and follow his other passion: flying. He would train as a pilot. He rationalized that he would become bored pretty quickly if he were forced to sit through an entire medical degree program again, and fancied his chances within the field of aviation. This announcement astounded the volunteers. Not only did this young Syrian man have the strength and determination to train as a doctor in the first place but also he was willing to now start again from scratch and work just as hard to become a pilot. It would only be a slight exaggeration to say that all of the volunteers were somewhat in awe of Adnan. The fact that he was an extremely handsome and charming young man, tall and doe-eyed with dark, curly hair, also added to his appeal. All five of the female volunteers flirted with Adnan, called him the "flying doctor" who would be able to attract any woman he wanted, and jokingly swooned whenever he left the activity centre. Only Åsa, an older woman in her sixties, would pretend to tut disapprovingly at our behaviour, before agreeing that Adnan would be an ideal son-in-law.

This treatment of Adnan demonstrates the value that the volunteers placed on the idea of stoicism and resilience among the refugees. After a few months in Öreby, the Syrians were now expected to demonstrate a capacity to overcome any adversity they may have faced in Sweden and be able to simply get on in creating a life for themselves. This contradicted somewhat the requirement for the refugees to be visibly suffering; however, this need to be obviously distressed and traumatized by the process of fleeing one's home was a temporary prerequisite. It was quickly replaced by the need for the refugee to legitimize the humanitarianism and hospitality of Sweden by quickly and without fuss taking advantage of everything that the Swedish state provided and re-establish their life.[9] Whenever any of the volunteers expressed dismay at the perceived failure of the Syrians to display fortitude and resilience, Monnika would reassure them that they shouldn't worry, that these Syrians were the strong ones as they had already garnered enough mental and physical strength to make the difficult journey from Syria to Sweden to start a new life. "The ones who make it all the way here are the ones who won't have a problem making a new life for themselves," she would often say. "They're the tough ones." In this manner, those affected by the war in Syria were defined, a priori, into those who fled and would be deemed successful – the tough, hardy individuals who were brave enough to make the decision to leave and simply made the best out of it – and those who stayed behind, eternally classified as a victim.

As happened with Rifat, who complained openly about his mental health to a newspaper, any indication of depression among the refugees was taboo in the view of the volunteers. None of the volunteers was trained in psychotherapy or mental health issues, although it is true that Bodil, in particular, did a wonderful job and was highly valued among the refugees for her patience and capacity in listening to their very traumatic stories and in empathizing with how stressed and impotent they felt with regard to their loved ones left behind. Whenever this depression manifested itself in anything more concrete than talking to Bodil, as was the case with Rifat, such behaviour was quickly demonized and sanctioned as it clearly went against the ideal of the stoic, enduring refugee. For example, the two attempted suicides that took place during my time in Öreby were the subject of much condemnation. "What's the point of fleeing a war zone only to try to kill yourself once you're in a safe and happy place with the possibility of a good life?" Bodil once asked Adnan after a newly arrived Yazidi man tried to cut his wrists one evening in the church graveyard. The actions of these suicidal refugees were deemed not only ungrateful and unwarranted but also dangerous to the "well-being of the children" (a point I return to in the next chapter). "You know that little Johan was cycling past on his bicycle and saw the man bleeding in the graveyard. What kind of effect would that have on a nine-year-old boy?" Bodil complained to Adnan.

Aside from demonstrating the required stoicism and resilience, Adnan's behaviour and attitude also made him an exemplar of the correct way to integrate and enter society, a role in which Adnan thrived, using his assigned morally superior status to ingratiate himself further with the volunteers. For example, the young medical student would often exclaim his exasperation with his fellow countrymen in the village, showing annoyance at the perceived lack of effort the other Syrians were making in adjusting to their new lives and at what he felt was a general negativity. For him, the living allowances provided by Migrationsverket were very generous: he was able to save around €70 per month. And with his residence permit having been granted, he was excited to start Swedish for Immigrants (SFI) lessons in the nearest town. "These people that you have taken in here in Öreby are trash," he would often tell the volunteers at the activity centre. Adnan was concerned that we were getting the wrong impression of Syrian people from our encounters with the Syrians who were settled in the village. Adnan would accuse them of being fraudsters and manipulating the Swedish state. "Most of these people haven't even come from the war in Syria. Believe me, they have businesses in Greece or Turkey and have only come here to milk your welfare system." He assured us that the majority of people in Syria were his "type." Those who came to Sweden, specifically those who settled in Öreby, were "low class" or "vulgar." The religiosity of some of the other refugees would annoy Adnan as well; he saw their Friday visits to the mosques as irritating and would complain to Bodil that they were merely trying to be problematic and should make more effort to integrate into Sweden.

Often Adnan would pass along gossip he had heard from around the camp. He would talk about how some of the more low-class Syrians were mocking the Swedish volunteers and laughing about how gullible they were. "You should not be so naive as to trust these people" – though he never identified anyone in particular in making these accusations. He would also talk about how he saw someone from the camp stealing, the most striking instance being a coat from a department store in town. "These people have a lot of money; they are just stealing because they are greedy and think that society owes them something." He told us that we didn't understand the mentality of these kind of "Middle Eastern people," as being European we were more used to fair play. We were often urged to "watch out" for ourselves and our belongings. Interestingly, it was a Syrian who, in this way, was first to openly articulate the skepticism and annoyance that had built up in reaction to the refugees being placed in the village. In wanting so much to be integrated and to be accepted – and perhaps foreseeing the eventual backlash against the refugees – Adnan propagated the stereotype of most Syrians being undeserving in order to position himself as an exception.[10]

After only a few months of SFI, Adnan began to communicate with the volunteers exclusively in Swedish, not English. Extremely pleased and flattered by Adnan's progress, the volunteers openly used him an example to the other young men his age about how easy it was to progress in Sweden if one simply knuckled down and applied oneself. Adnan's progress also vindicated the advisory and hands-on approach adopted by the volunteers, giving Bodil in particular a renewed energy to offer advice more assertively to the younger Syrians. Sweden's decision to offer permanent residence to all Syrians in September 2013 gave the volunteers more confidence in demanding certain standards. This decision generated mixed responses among the volunteers and within the village. Though of course relieved that there was no chance that the Syrians would be obliged to return in the future (though this was generally not a concern among the Syrian refugees in Sweden who had mostly been granted five-year residencies at that point), the idea of Sweden being once again morally exceptional also manifested itself with the country being seen as a soft touch, leading to the practices around the worthy guest, both on the part of the volunteers and of the refugees, becoming accentuated somewhat.

CONCLUSION

The title of this chapter, "Seeing Like a Good Citizen," is a nod to James C. Scott's work *Seeing Like a State*. And as Scott did in his analysis of how large-scale schemes to improve the human condition have failed, I have insisted on examining the tiny practices of metis enacted by people operating within a specifically local context, mobilizing distinctly practical operations that never make their nature explicit (cf. Detienne and Vernant 1991). Grounding my analysis additionally in the work of Michel Foucault, I have labelled the type of power relations within which these people operate as a particular type of governmentality – not an abstract governmentality of capitalism or neo-liberalism, or with a focus on the market, but a very particular governmentality of righteousness linked to a national myth of moral exceptionalism with which all good citizens identify.

This chapter began with the story of the people of Öreby, the villagers, the volunteers, and the refugees themselves and the myriad micropractices enacted under the broad banners of righteousness and decency. In viewing governmentality here as a tangible, ethnographic object, it discussed the sociology of power inherent within this framework, at the level of micropractices. As we saw, the types of conduct of conduct of oneself and others ensured that all of the refugees were provided with a materially high standard of living, with onstage posturing ensuring that nobody stepped too far outside of acceptable behaviour, at least within polite company. Therefore, biopolitics in this sense was far from catastrophic. We do not have the image of bare life within the camp, or of people seen only in terms of their capacity to live or die. What we have is a state of play linked with much earlier forms of pastoral power and a caring biopolitics, invoking ideas of secular redemption and the sacralization of life.

However, what we saw at play in Öreby was not an enactment of a sterile, rational type of solidarity as per the national myth – an ideal type, similar to what Tomlinson (2011) talks about when he refers to "a vision of a technocratic Enlightenment Universalism … populated by orderly, rational, cooperative, moral individuals" – but clearly something quite different. The villagers of Öreby demanded reciprocation for their generosity and kindness. They were quite clear that they would not engage with the Syrians as equals but as recipients of the benevolence of the good Swedes, a subjectivity articulated sometimes against imagined racists of nearby villages, sometimes against the cold bureaucracy of state institutions, but always against the uncaring and right-wing fellow EU member states: Denmark, the United Kingdom, or the southern, Mediterranean nations. This chapter pointed out that, along with demanding that all the refugees play by all the rules of what it supposedly meant to be deserving, there were the first signs – the testing of the waters by some villagers – of what was to come: the hatching of a new discourse of skepticism and hostility toward the Syrians that, at this point, was still only snatched bits of conversation and ambiguous, fleeting statements.

As the next chapter demonstrates, to view these tiny practices of metis as having minimal significance would be an extreme error. It is interesting how these micropractices of hierarchization and obligation for reciprocity at a very local level, though undoubtedly well meant, were connected to a wider array of social and political forces that added up to a type of social change. As we continue with the story of Öreby and the Syrian refugees, we see how these practices of conduct had as their corollary tiny acts of counter-conduct, pushing at the very limits of what it means to be decent. Likewise, this very public transcript of benevolence was linked to a symbiotic hidden transcript of marginalization and exclusion. As we conclude the story of Öreby, in September 2014 just after the Swedish general election, we see a crystallization of the "in" and "out" groups, accelerated by various moral panics (Cohen 1980), which allowed the Syrian refugees to be legitimately articulated as scroungers, violent, dangerous, unworthy, and ultimately dispensable. Thus, practices of violence were inherently linked to practices of integration, welcoming was linked to rejecting, and solidarity was linked to security.

4

Limits of the Governmentality of Righteousness

Counter-conduct and Moral Panic

Thus far we have shown how the particular governmentality of righteousness enabled by the Swedish national myth of moral exceptionalism enables a "repertoire of available practices" for the so-called good citizen. In its manifestations in everyday life, its effects are plural and varied. These practices, as we saw in the previous chapter, can reinforce and utilize this myth in generating a worthy guest, one who enjoys the benefits of the decent as opposed to the bare life but who also is required to play by all the rules of hospitality. In the terminology of James C. Scott, they can hence form a type of public transcript whereby, as long as nobody steps outside their assigned roles, a particular performance of decency is enabled. Anything that openly challenges this manifestation of moral superiority is disciplined and sanctioned. As we have examined in the previous chapters, the idea of a type of metis, or practical knowledge, has shown that there is quite a bit of wiggle room for the good citizen to manoeuvre in while remaining comfortably within the cherished narrative of solidarity and moral exceptionalism.

This chapter argues that, within these effects, wiggle room, and repertoire of actions available for the decent citizen, these practices can also, however, *evade* this myth somewhat. They can perhaps go ever so slightly against the grain of the cherished narrative (or possibly only *appear* to go against the grain) and enable some more open manifestations of exclusion. Here, the governmentality of righteousness can be seen to have reached its very outermost limits. This chapter conceptualizes these types of practices, in Foucauldian terms, as a type of counter-conduct (Foucault 2007; Davidson 2011), pushed up against the very boundaries of the practices of a good citizen in the Swedish case. It examines the way in which this counter-conduct, through various mechanisms, ultimately adopted enough uniformity to alter social relations completely.

Progressing in five parts, this chapter looks firstly at what is meant by and what is at stake when we discuss counter-conduct, focusing on its seemingly symbiotic, though never passive, relation to conduct. We then go back to reflect on the changing dynamics in the field – in the village of Öreby – between February 2013 and September 2014. We look at the way in which the behaviour of the Migration Board engendered a sense of powerlessness in the village, leading to asylum becoming a strictly policed taboo in the village. We then discuss the way in which this taboo was evaded and re-implanted at a banal, covert, and seemingly insignificant level, what I label a hidden transcript of marginalization and exclusion, particularly around the governing of the movement of village children and notions of gender equality. In shifting the focus to the Friends of Syria volunteer group, and their role as intermediaries between the refugees and disgruntled villagers, we look at the way in which a type of "compassion fatigue," albeit a seemingly ironic one, altered the area of acceptable conduct toward the refugees, exaggerating and exacerbating the social forces at play needed to underpin a more overt manifestation of violence. The final section looks at how, through the mechanism of several moral panics, relations between the villagers and the Syrian refugees became increasingly disbanded.

COUNTER-CONDUCT: ETHICAL, POLITICAL, EMBODIED, AND ORGANIZED

As we have examined in the previous chapters, the collective subjectivities brought about by the governmentality of righteousness enabled the refugees in Öreby to live decent life. A veneer of solidarity ensured cordial relations within the village, and facilities at the camp were quite comfortable, albeit cramped, in comparison with conditions for refugees in other EU states. What I have called a public transcript of solidarity enabled at least an outward impression of camaraderie and a functional relationship between many of the villagers and the newly arrived refugees. As described by the local head teacher, "They say *hej*, we say *hej* back, and everything seems to be working fine."

However, we have discussed how tiny, exclusionary practices manifested themselves in the appropriation of solidarity by the volunteers as humanitarianism or hospitality, whereby refugees are required to be visibly damaged, are forbidden to criticize their conditions, and are seen to be "mending their ways." In addition, we discussed how this certainty in one's rightness enabled a collective type of projection, where racism was deemed the province of somewhere else, other countries, or, when in Sweden, only in imaginary hillbilly villages populated by ignorant old men. This chapter thus goes on to examine practices of counter-conduct enacted by the villagers of Öreby that pushed the very limits of the governmentality of righteousness and what it meant to be a good citizen. It look at how this counter-conduct generated new ways to be a seemingly decent and generous citizen, while enabling practices of marginalization far beyond the worthy guest phenomenon.

Firstly, however, it is necessary to briefly discuss what is meant by, and what is at stake, when we talk about counter-conduct as opposed to conduct. Within the *Security, Territory, Population* series of lectures, Foucault goes into great depth on this notion of what he calls "counter-conduct" (2007, 191), a more accurate term for the author than "dissidence," "revolt," "disobedience," "misconduct," or "insubordination but that nonetheless embodies facets of these terms. In the introduction to the English translation of the course, Arnold I. Davidson gives a succinct analysis of Foucault's notion of counter-conduct, what he considers to be "one of the richest and most brilliant moments on the entire course" (2007, xix). Davidson has subsequently developed a great deal on this notion and offered a very theoretically sophisticated fleshing out of the term, which he considers a "new philosophical concept," both politically and ethically. It is useful to draw upon this rich concept in this chapter to illuminate the day-to-day practices of the Öreby-dwellers that seemed to go ever so slightly against the grain of righteousness and solidarity while at the same time nonetheless reinforcing and re-appropriating these ideas.

Firstly, in focusing on "conduct," Davidson explains why Foucault chose the term as the most apt translation of the Greek expression *oikonomia psuchon* and the Latin regimen *animarum*, which was in order to take advantage of the "double dimension" of conduct (2007, xix): the action of conducting an individual, "conduction" as a relation between individuals, and the manner in which an individual conducts himself or herself (2007, xix). "Conduct is the activity of conducting (*conduire*), of conduction (*la conduction*) if you like, but it is equally the way in which one conducts oneself (*se conduit*), lets oneself be conducted (*se laisse conduire*), and finally, in which one behaves (*se comporter*) under the influence of a conduct as the action of conducting or of conduction (*conduction*)" (Davidson 2007, 193).

For Davidson, *Security, Territory, Population* provides what he calls the "conceptual hinge" needed to enable us to link together the political and ethical dimensions of Foucault's thought (2011, 26). The most interesting element for Davidson, however, is that these techniques of power, historically contiguous as they are, both take as the object of their techniques and practices the *conduct* of human beings, with pastoral power locating these actions in religious institutions and governmentality within political apparatuses (Davidson 2011, 26).

To counter-conduct then, we remember that resistance for Foucault is, of course, never in a position of exteriority in relation to power (Foucault 1986). Likewise, the practices of counter-conduct that Foucault examines are never completely outside the conduct levied by the Christian pastorate (Davidson 2011, 26). For Foucault, counter-conduct is thus presented in terms of a detailed historical analysis at a particular disjunction in time, not as a particular theoretical framework. Foucault presents a number of practices that signify the development of counter-conduct movements in the Middle Ages against Christianity in its pastoral form: namely, eschatological beliefs, the use of Scripture, mysticism, asceticism, and the formation of communities (Foucault, 2007, 214). These practices effectively bypassed the pastorate as the only means to communicate with God, negating the need for a shepherd as an intermediary. Christianity, he argues, was never an ascetic religion, with the Christian pastorate requiring obedience at all times. Mysticism, Foucault thus argues, entitles the first major revolt in the West, whereby a direct connection between God and the soul can be achieved (Davidson 2011, 29).

As Davidson (2011) so articulately points out, these resistances to conduct also have a "double dimension." Counter-conduct is conceived as "a struggle against the procedures for conducting others, but also simultaneously generating a sphere where an individual can conduct themselves" (2007, 197). A crucial point to note is Foucault's insistence on these processes of counter-conduct occurring *not* as a type of reaction to the development of the pastorate but instead noting the existence of "an immediate and founding correlation between conduct and counter-conduct" (2007, 196): "Conduct and counter-conduct share a series of elements that can be utilized and re-utilised, reimplanted, reinserted, taken up in the direction of reinforcing a certain mode of conduct or of creating and re-creating a type of counter-conduct" (Davidson 2011).

Foucault was at pains to state that counter-conduct should by no means be seen as some sort of passive underside to conduct, simply the antithesis or reverse of conduct. Instead, counter-conduct is creative; it generates and activates something new, a whole new way of being and acting (Davidson 2011). Furthermore, he was also clear to ensure that counter-conduct should not be reduced to the juridical sphere. Davidson writes extensively on masturbation as a form of historical counter-conduct before the practice became pathologized, psychologized, and normalized, most notably a woman masturbating in a confessional booth as a form of religious counter-conduct (Davidson 2011, 36).

We have seen, therefore, that counter-conduct is never in a position of exteriority to conduct. It is both individual and present in everyday practices, but also sometimes organized and collective. It is creative, productive, and against the grain, but also largely invisibilized. It concerns not only how one engages with others but also how one views oneself and how one shapes an area for oneself to act.

Therefore, through this lens of counter-conduct, this chapter examines the types of everyday practices in Öreby that appropriated righteousness and solidarity and generated something new. Firstly, it examines how, through mundane banal practices, a hidden transcript of exclusion of the refugees was enabled around the ideas of an orientalized, hyper-masculinized collective image of the Arab men as a threat that could not be articulated aloud and of the perceived "damaged" refugee children as a threat to the well-being of the Swedish children. It investigates how a perceived sense of powerlessness on the part of the villagers exacerbated the sense of taboo around the refugees and the mechanism of the moral panic that enabled this hidden marginalization to become more overt.

A HIDDEN TRANSCRIPT OF RESISTANCE: EXCLUSION AND MARGINALIZATION

The Meeting: Engendering a Sense of Powerlessness in the Village

Going back to the very beginning of the story and the initial meeting in the school in Öreby when Migrationsverket came to discuss any issues the locals may have had regarding the resettlement of the refugees, despite pretensions to the contrary, Migrationsverket gave the people of Öreby no choice as to whether or not the refugees would be settled there, when they would arrive, and how many would be placed there. In addition, despite promising a follow-up meeting later in the spring, no such meeting materialized. In this respect, the notion that the people of Öreby had no actual say in their sudden obligation toward showing solidarity is an important one that goes some way in helping to illuminate the power relations in the interactions between the Syrians and the Öreby-dwellers.

The dynamics of that first meeting in which initial resistance was voiced to the resettlement of the Syrian refugees thus took place in an atmosphere of perceived equality. According to some of the meeting attendees, Migrationsverket had promised that they would "consult" the residents about plans to resettle refugees there, and many thought that there would be some sort of negotiation or compromise. Therefore, in this initial meeting the public transcript of complete solidarity with (up until this point "imagined") refugees was permitted to lapse somewhat. Within this meeting, the villagers articulated their resistance to the resettlement of the refugees along three main lines: the possibility of their house prices falling; the general law and order of the village due to "damaged" people; and, more explicitly, drawing on orientalist imageries, framing the refugees as a threat to the women and children of the village.

With the realization that the placement of the refugees in Öreby was something that they would be obliged to live with, rather than something that they were in discussions about, objections to the resettlement of the refugees were no longer voiced or articulated in formal settings, for example, the various village events (which took place roughly once or twice a month), such as the Spring Festival or Children's Day. Instead, these forums became a terrain through which the villagers could perform the role of decency to each other, as discussed in chapter 3. Thus the meeting at the school was the only occasion of such vocal resistance to the housing of the refugees in Öreby. Indeed, many of those people present at the meeting later denied being present or raising any objections, dismissing the resistance to the resettlement of the refugees as "ignorant people," or "people who were simply a bit scared of the unknown." With the villagers unable to influence the Migrationsverket's decision to place refugees in Öreby, power relations reverted to maintaining a certain ideal of respectability, and as we examined in the previous chapter, all the taboos and obligations enabled by the national myth were brought back into play.

The Policing of the Taboo

My position in terms of access to what was perceived to be taboo – only voiced behind closed doors – and what was acceptable to be voiced in polite company changed throughout the course of my fieldwork as I became better acquainted with many of the villagers and formed close friendships with the volunteers. My ethnographic studies into the relations between the people of Öreby and the newly arrived Syrians, as discussed in chapter 1, took the form of both a "deep hanging out" (Madison 2005) and more structured, formal interviews. As I previously stated, at the very beginning of my fieldwork, there was a marked unease among people I spoke to about the resettlement of the Syrians in Öreby. Many people were quite reluctant to talk to me at first, saying a few lines about how they were angry to hear about the resettlement of the Syrians by reading it in the local newspaper but then correcting themselves with some sort of platitude such as "but now they're here, we see they're just like us," or with a description about how the new arrivals just seem to keep themselves to themselves, so there's not much to worry about.

After tracking down everybody that had been at the meeting and organizing interviews with about two dozen or so people by phone or e-mail, the most interesting manifestation of the "policing of the taboo" came in the home of an elderly couple, Gun and Birger, when I knocked on their door a few days after arriving. The couple lived on the street parallel to where the refugees had been settled. Gun had agreed to talk to me about their feelings toward the new arrivals and how things were progressing in the village. After inviting me in and offering a cup of coffee, Gun proceeded to tell me about her anger at Migrationsverket for "dumping" the Syrians there without any consultation. For Gun, they would have been much better placed in Malmo or even Gothenburg, where there was more nightlife and they could be closer to the Arab diaspora and closer to libraries and Swedish for Immigrants classes to make learning Swedish easier. Gun then went on to mention, in a more hushed and somewhat conspiratorial tone, a few of the "bad habits" of the newcomers that she found annoying: rubbish bags not being thrown in the correct area and children playing outside until late at night.

Upon overhearing the interview, Birger came down the stairs and interrupted what his wife was saying: "What Gun means is that it will take a while for the newcomers to settle in, but we don't have anything against them being here." After Birger's intervention, Gun tried to once again state her grievances, however, her husband then proceeded to speak over his wife, explaining that it was time to start making the dinner, and hurried me out the door. Irritated at her husband's rude intervention, Gun corrected herself, asserting that she wasn't saying anything nasty against the Syrians, just telling me some of the things that people had been a bit annoyed about, at which point Birger loudly "shushed" his wife, mumbled something inaudible, and closed the door in my face.

This vignette, though isolated in the extent to which it demonstrates the policing of the taboo in the village around the refugee resettlement, nonetheless exemplifies the power relations embedded in the quotidian conduct of conduct in everyday life in Öreby. As discussed in the previous chapter, with any discussion on the refugees, or asylum policy itself, being rendered taboo, the day-to-day realm became one of governing conduct. Therefore, counter-conduct embodied practices that were sometimes hidden (what I call a hidden transcript of exclusion) or justified by righteous indignation.

The Development of the Hidden Transcript

In chapter 1, I introduced Scott's notion of a hidden transcript of resistance and then drew links to the Foucauldian concept of counter-conduct and de Certeau's "tactics." For Scott, however, such resistance can appear from the outside as *acceptance* of a dominating relation of power and works, almost paradoxically, by maintaining the illusion of a placid surface, while slyly making use of fleeting, seized opportunities that push the limits of what is permitted (Scott 1990, 196). We saw that such a notion of resistance mirrors that of de Certeau's tactics, which refer to the wide array of practices that the more uniform, regulatory concept of a "strategy" has *not* been able to domesticate, and although not themselves subversive, have a symbolic value that undermines strategic control (Buchanan 2000, 89). In the story of Öreby, the taboo around speaking about the refugees in polite company saw a hidden transcript of exclusion and marginalization of the refugees develop around very specific topics, demonstrating the way in which the performance of solidarity, discussed in the previous chapter, only went so far.

The most prominent example of the existence of this transcript was around the governing of the movement of village children. Here, the performance of solidarity and openness was evaded somewhat regarding the areas in which the Swedish children, particularly girls, were allowed to interact and play with the Syrian children. In February 2013, when the first handful of Syrian families arrived in the village, we remember that some parents began explicitly voicing their concerns about the safety of their children. They made particular reference to their teenage daughters and fear of sexual harassment, citing that Arab men were from societies that were used to seeing women as objects – a world apart from Sweden with its gender equality. For example, in the meeting in the local school three weeks before the arrival of the first refugees, a mother of three girls angrily stated to the Migrationsverket representative that they were responsible for the fact that she would no longer feel at ease allowing her girls to walk unsupervised around the village at night or to take the bus into town on their own.

Throughout the subsequent months, though some parents in the village described that meeting as "hysterical" to both Friends of Syria volunteers and me, the management of Swedish children's movement in the areas where the Syrian children lived and played was strictly controlled. However, the issues raised in the meeting were consciously downplayed: "Yes, we see now that they are just normal families like us, and we say '*Hej*' to them as they go past on their bikes." That said, entrance into the area where the Syrians congregated was still a taboo issue. Reluctance to permit the children to go and play in the grassy area that backed onto the Syrians' houses was framed in slightly more banal terms: their children were of course allowed to be "friends" with the Syrian children at school, but they didn't want their children picking up the bad habits of the newcomers, "tearing around" the village on their bikes or messing about with lighters or toy guns, which some had claimed to have witnessed the Syrian children doing. During Ramadan, which took place in 2013 in the height of summer, the issue of village children mixing with the Syrian children on the grassy area reached a climax when the refugee children were permitted to stay outside and play until nearly midnight.

Interesting to note is that the performance of the good citizen was never abandoned entirely; it simply came into conflict with another role: that of the good parent. To divert from the public transcript of complete solidarity with the refugees was thus permitted to a certain extent, with a person's reputation for decency still kept intact. However, resistance to the activities of the refugees was to be framed with very specific reference to the children if one was still to be seen as good. For example, during the four weeks of Ramadan, the four Swedish families who lived next door to the area in which the Syrian families were housed moved out of their houses into the town 10 kilometres away. This was carefully articulated as being for their "children's well-being," or in one case, with no explanation at all; a family of four simply disappeared one morning without notifying any of the neighbours.

With the exception of Bodil's two children, ten-year-old Anton and thirteen-year-old Emma, Swedish and Syrian children were only permitted to interact within the supervised settings of the school (during school time) or the football club, a joint activity for girls and boys up to the age of fifteen in the local sports club every Saturday. During training, Syrian parents congregated along a far end of the football field and Swedish parents separately along the length of the pitch. After the game, most of the local parents left immediately and ensured that their children were quickly shepherded away into cars. Bodil encouraged her children to play with the Syrian children as she felt it nurtured intercultural awareness and was hopeful that they might pick up some of the Arabic language. Furthermore, though her comments were veiled in the politest of terms, Bodil also complained of fellow parents discouraging their children from playing with Anton or Emma, especially when two or three of their Syrian friends were over.

In this respect, the particular imagined threat to the Swedish children was not only from the Syrian adults but also from the Syrian children. As time passed, and I became a familiar face in the village, some of the parents confessed that they conceived the Syrian children as being somewhat "deviant." They were spoken of as being damaged and mentally scarred from the civil war, and thus dangerous.

As mentioned earlier, what was said at the initial meeting came to me by way of second-hand accounts from various attendees. However, most people recounted a number of objections based on the notion of the Syrians somehow being a threat to the children in terms of their personal safety from the new war-torn children, their schooling due to the resources that would need to be employed to integrate the new arrivals in the system (despite reassurances from the head that there would be two additional "*modersmål*" teachers deployed to educate the children in their native language), and their susceptibility to picking up the bad habits of these new arrivals. The phrase "run amok" ("*gröper amok*") was voiced on a number of occasions referring to the imagined havoc that these new children would cause.

Gender (In)equality: Mending the Deficient Syrians

Going back to the initial meeting at the school once again, which could be envisaged as the closest point in which the hidden and public transcripts could be seen as one and the same, we also saw that, closely related to notions of the children's safety, were allusions to the threat that Syrian men were thought to pose to the women and girls in Öreby. From what others have said about the meeting, these imagined threats on the part of the villagers were only hinted at, with nobody directly saying that the men were potential rapists or criminals. Instead, allusions were made to disturbance in the "general harmony" of the village, wherein everybody respected everybody else. Some raised fears that incidents of harassment would increase, while others just voiced a general unease around men from this foreign culture now hanging around their streets and shops.

It was around the issue of gender equality, however, that the most marked agitation developed, notably among the volunteers themselves. All five women who had set up the Friends of Syria described themselves as feminists and were very proud of this. Annika, for example, would often voice her concern about the younger generation of women in Sweden gradually eroding the hard-won rights that her generation achieved in the 1970s by emulating footballers' wives and reality TV stars. Though the volunteers never openly said anything about the behaviour of the Syrian men, a type of unspoken agreement existed among the volunteers (including the one male volunteer, Benny) to "emancipate" the Arab women from their patriarchal mindset.

As intermediaries between the village and the refugees, Bodil and the Friends of Syria were also often the recipients of the grumbles and complaints of their neighbours, and thus took on the role of helping the Syrians to integrate and enter society. However, any attempt aimed at directly enforcing the Syrian men to "mend their ways" was deemed taboo. The Friends of Syria volunteers were aware that speaking about the Arab men as fanatical and potentially violent was in bad taste. Though acceptable to articulate this behind closed doors, to speak this way publicly was particularly unsavoury and an action relegated in their imagination to the realm of the far right. For example, Åsa, the volunteer in charge of running the weekly Swedish-language classes, would often utter the platitude that "sexism and racism are two sides of the same coin." In this way the public transcript of decency and complete solidarity could be upheld. Nonetheless, the Friends of Syria, to accommodate the unease of the wider community, took upon themselves the role to "do something" to help the new arrivals adjust to Swedish life, particularly with regard to the notions of gender equality and the upbringing of children.

The first manifestation of this need for the group to assist the refugees seemed sweet-natured and innocent, taking the form of a PowerPoint guide to life in Sweden. Bodil and her husband compiled the guide, with input from the other members of the group. Mirroring the anxieties expressed at the initial meeting, the group felt that emphasizing the prohibition of sexual harassment should feature quite prominently. After discussing the format of the guide, the group decided that a PowerPoint presentation shown in the homes of the new arrivals would be most efficient, to counter the chance that people might not actually read a printed leaflet. The group talked me through the slideshow: "The first couple are pointing out where Sweden is on the map, emphasizing that Sweden has been at peace for two hundred years." They quickly skipped over the slides about sunrise and sunset times in the summer and winter, and climate and wildlife throughout the country. I was touched at the thought and effort that had gone into putting the presentation together. Then the next slide simply showed a cartoon of a woman's hand grabbing a man's bottom, with a large red X alongside. "We thought we wouldn't have any text on this one, but just explain that, in Sweden, nobody is allowed to touch anybody else without their permission." When I enquired why the cartoon didn't show a male character seemingly harassing a female, as this was their main concern, Åsa explained that this cartoon would emphasize their point even more strongly. "You see, by using this picture, we show the men that Sweden is a gender-equal country as well as telling them that they can't go around groping anybody they want. And there's no danger of offending them by presuming that they're all perverts."

The next slide was also a cartoon; however, this time a woman was hitting a child.

Monnika explained to me that children's rights in Sweden were most important and that not hitting children is something that needed to be explained to all foreigners. Åsa interjected: "It's not that we think all Arabs are violent or anything like that. I mean, even you as a British person probably think it's strange that parents don't hit their children here," and proceeded to tell me a story about a holiday in Brighton with her children fifteen years ago where she saw a young mum thump her seven-year-old son on a bus, to the horror of her two sons. "We just don't want this sort of thing to become normal again in Sweden." In keeping with the imperative for the new arrivals to mend their ways, it was made clear to the refugees what decency looked like in a Swedish context. However, the volunteers were careful to ensure that no offence should be taken on the part of the Syrian men and that the presentation and content never strayed into territory that would be deemed in bad taste.

As the refugees began to settle in the village, one method used by the volunteers to avoid more open or direct criticism of the perceived patriarchy or sexism of the Syrian refugees – which would risk being viewed as indecent – was to articulate disapproval as though it was not completely serious, but more of a joke or lighthearted teasing that could be easily laughed off. This type of interaction was especially prominent in dealings between the volunteers and the older Syrian men and fathers. For example, Bodil would proclaim to the father of every new family that arrived that "Sweden is the opposite of your culture. Here, women are legally allowed to take four husbands and men are only allowed one wife," before quickly adding that she was "just joking." This teasing took every form, from trying to shock the Syrian men into dramatically altering their perceived norms of expectations of dress for their wives – "Don't be surprised come summertime when your wife will be in a bikini! You're not in Aleppo now." – to gently mocking the men for what the volunteers perceived to be a lack of domestic skills – "A Swedish woman would never let a man get away with that!" This type of advice, though having serious intent behind it, was always given playfully and, as such, was easily disowned in the (rare) case of a challenge or offence being taken on the part of the Syrian men.

The group viewed the Syrian women as more passive than the men and thus a somewhat safer target, so dispensing direct advice to them was seem as a more legitimate aim.¹ In addition to the Swedish lessons and general drop-in sessions held in the activity centre, the volunteers also held cooking classes every Tuesday, with two or three members of the group showing the new arrivals how to make simple Swedish recipes like cinnamon buns and pancakes. The rationale behind organizing this event was precisely to attract the women, to facilitate an arena in which to get to know the "real" person in the absence of the perceived influence of their husband, and to create a separate form of female solidarity.

The first few cooking lessons were deemed very successful, attended by around twenty or so of the women. The volunteers spoke to the women in English, but took care to teach them simple Swedish words as they went along. "They will never integrate and get a job if they can't even say basic sentences," explained Bodil, the chief volunteer. She encouraged the women to leave their children at home during these classes, citing the need for the women to have some well-deserved time to themselves, but also promoting the ideal of a more gender-equal style of parenting: "Besides, now that you're living in Sweden, it's time that your husbands did some child care for a change."

After about five or six weeks, however, most of the Syrian women stopped attending the cooking classes, with only a couple from Georgia as well as three Ugandan women making the weekly visit. This was a source of mild irritation to the Friends of Syria group, who saw their time as wasted if the Syrian women would not even make the effort to get to know the Swedish culture and simply "locked themselves away." With the absence of any Syrians, conversations at Tuesday's cooking classes were centred around their perceived deficiencies: they were seen to be "stuck in their ways" and weak-willed, unable to "stand up to their husbands" about the changes needed to integrate in Sweden.

The line between what was permitted to say in public and what was to remain taboo was most ambiguous with regard to the ideas of children's well-being and gender equality. It was clear that referring to the Syrian men as hypermasculinized or perverted was the realm of the far right and not that of the good citizen. The volunteers would often criticize those they viewed as "bigoted" and positioned those whom they imagined to be anti–gender equality firmly among the "dregs" and "folk devils" of the neo-Nazis or those belonging to the far right. Day-to-day practices, however, tended to somewhat evade this discourse, go ever so slightly against its grain, and generate an area of conduct in which marginalization of the Syrians was deemed legitimate. The second half of the chapter goes on to investigate exactly how these seemingly insignificant practices of counter-conduct served to influence broader social and political change. It examines how, through the mechanism of moral panics, more overt exclusion and suspicion of Syrian refugees was normalized.

BREAKING THE SILENCE AROUND THE TABOO: MORAL PANICS AS A MICROPHYSICS OF OUTRAGE

Thus far we have examined the multiplicity of ways in which the morally exceptional national myth was appropriated at an anthropological level by people who saw themselves as decent citizens, claiming to be proud of their country's humanitarian record and stance toward refugees. By never openly criticizing or voicing objection to the resettlement of the refugees, the volunteers and residents of the village reinforced, but also utilized, the national myth to retain a sense of their own moral superiority. In this respect, a public transcript was firmly in place, giving the appearance of a tranquil, placid surface in which everybody accepts the prevailing norms. All the volunteers acknowledged these hidden practices and the unease around the Syrians. They reasoned, however, that as long as nobody actually said anything out loud to the Syrians, or tried to hurt them, then this unease would perhaps lessen with the passing of time. Stories of *flykting*förläggningar (refugee camps) being vandalized in other villages or towns reinforced this idea that everything was well in Öreby.

Though a marked unease around the resettlement of the refugees was present in the village, any resistance to their resettlement, aside from the initial meeting, was forced into a more hidden realm if one was to maintain a decent image. The only terrain where it became acceptable to let this public transcript lapse somewhat, while still maintaining the good citizen image, was around concerns about the perceived gender inequality and parenting practices of the new arrivals. Though allowed to be voiced in the initial meeting, now any allusion to the Arab men as violent or fanatical voiced openly in the public domain would immediately render the speaker a "dreg" (Gullestad 2002) or, at best, un-Swedish. As long as the refugees played by all the rules of being a worthy guest – accepted the advice of the volunteers on how to be more gender equal and raise their children – this public transcript of complete acceptance was maintained, and talk of violent, lustful, or risky men was kept somewhat hidden.

However, to see these tiny, almost insignificant micropractices of exclusion and hierarchization around gender equality and good parenting as the whole story, as having only minimal implications or a limited reach, would be an extreme error. As analysts of social action, we are interested in how these tiny practices of counter-conduct go on to inform a more far-reaching phenomenon, adding up to a type of social change (Neumann 2002). The unease that was markedly present within the village regarding the issue of the refugees did not disappear because of the projects of the Friends of Syria or because it was not acceptable to be voiced openly after the initial meeting.

One could conceptualize this hidden transcript of unease within the village and the micro-biopolitical practices of hierarchization, marginalization, and stigmatization of the Syrian refugees by the volunteers as the concealed base of the iceberg. As discussed below, through various mechanisms, it enabled the more public articulation of the Syrians as a threat and open voicing of the controversy over the perception of Arab hypermasculinity and tendency toward violence. In articulating the shared unease about the Arab men as dangerous, we also see how moves toward an "us and them" position become more acceptable within the public domain.

The First Moral Panic: The Shooting of the Man in Jämtland

While driving to Öreby one morning in November, I heard the news of a young Somali man being shot dead by police the previous night in a small village further north in the country. The report was very brief, with the newsreader stating that the man was brandishing a knife and waving it around the small block of flats where a few refugee families had been housed. The man was said to have been drinking alcohol and running toward the police when he was shot.

When I arrived at the activity centre, it was much busier than usual, with thirty or so people milling around in the lounge and kitchen. Bodil explained that she had called a meeting to discuss what had happened last night and what the implications might be. The atmosphere was a little tense, and Bodil seemed tired, a little irritated, and short-tempered. However, as usual, she put on a happy, energetic face for everybody.

Bodil explained to the Syrians that a few people had phoned her in the morning or approached her at the school gate to talk about the incident in Jämtland. People were worried that something similar could happen in Öreby, reasoning that damaged people straight out of a war zone were capable of anything. Despite refugees having lived in Öreby for about eight or nine months by this point, with no violent incidents whatsoever, the actions of a refugee hundreds of kilometres north had once again legitimized speaking of the refugees as potentially very dangerous, with some sort of "action" needed to ensure that Öreby stayed free of this sort of trouble. However, this was the first time that Bodil had conveyed this general unease to the refugees themselves, positioning herself as one of the villagers, instead of taking the usual role as an intermediary. "I just want to tell you all that you have to behave yourselves. This is what happens in Sweden if you don't behave yourself. It is a good country, but if you come here, you have to respect our rules." Bodil's speech to those gathered was short and to the point, directed at everybody there.

Adnan's protestations that this man was Somali – and thus, in his reasoning, completely uncivilized and backwards, as opposed to Syrians who were cultured and peaceful people – was gently dismissed by Bodil. True, he may be from another country, but he was also a "guest" in Sweden whom the good people of Jämtland had been so kind as to protect. When the meeting finished, everyone left except for Adnan, a young Georgian couple, Bodil, and me. Talk around the kitchen table once again reverted to the police shooting. Adnan was astounded at the shoot-to-kill policy of the Swedish police, stating plainly to Bodil that the exact details around this incident were unclear and admonishing her for being so quick to tell everybody to "behave" themselves, when in actual fact it could be the Swedish police that need to "behave."

This was the first time that there was a firm and neatly demarcated line between the people of Öreby, with Bodil firmly embedded, and everybody else. As a foreigner, I too was prevented from criticizing the actions of the Swedish police and was, for the first time, placed in the "out" group of the now-polarized dynamic of Swede versus foreigner that had taken place.[2] Later on, when Bodil walked me to the bus stop, she expressed her surprise that I would take "the side" of the refugees under such circumstances.

This vignette of the police shooting and the subsequent reaction in Öreby is extremely telling. The Somali man in Jämtland had most spectacularly broken the rules of being a worthy guest by wielding a knife. Therefore, within the collective imagination of the Öreby-dwellers, the stakes of the game had changed somewhat. And this perceived change altered the power dynamics in Öreby and rendered sayable what was taboo only the day before. The danger to the people in the village, previously only imagined, was now thought to be more concrete and likely. This frenzy over the Somali man in Jämtland, the way the incident appeared to have arisen from nowhere – but was in fact underpinned by wider social and political forces: the base of the iceberg – can be viewed as a moral panic of sorts. This concept – though somewhat problematic in our case study, as we will see – best illuminates the mechanism through which a certain arrangement of specific relations of power can enable a momentary eruption of frenzy in which social relations become momentarily disbanded. It is also best placed to help illuminate how this type of frenzy, usually fleeting but often bringing about a change in how a society views itself, is in fact engrained in and enabled by much wider social forces.

So what is a moral panic? How can the term help us to understand the story of Öreby? For Cohen, this state of affairs occurs every now and then when a "condition, episode, person or group of persons emerges to become defined as a threat to societal values and interests" (Cohen 1980, 1). In Cohen's groundbreaking study of the framing of Mods and Rockers in the late 1960s, these moral panics are defined and presented first and foremost by the mass media. Newspaper editors, clergymen, and politicians denounce what they see as morally unacceptable behaviour and various "experts" are wheeled out to decipher the roots of the problem and put forward solutions. Football hooligans, recreational drugs, single mothers, and pedophile priests have all, at one time or another, been the subject of such panics. Emerging quickly into the limelight and then often disappearing just as quickly, they sometimes nonetheless enable more long-term changes in social policy (Cohen 1980).

However, Cohen is clear that in labelling a phenomenon a moral panic does not imply that something does not exist or that the reaction is grounded in fantasy or hysteria (1980, vii). Instead, the label denotes an element of exaggeration, both in the object of the panic's significance and magnitude, both in "itself" and compared with other, more serious societal problems (1980). Crucial to our understanding of the story of Öreby is the importance Cohen places on *rumours* for the creation of new social rules and the designation of deviance. Cohen sees rumours arising as a means of reducing ambiguity over a given situation, as in a group setting where one encounters narratives that reinforce one's own outlook (Cohen 1980, 36).[3]

Cohen admits that he has faced a great deal of criticism for his ambiguous use of the term "panic" in talking about certain types of phenomenon due to its connotations of an irrational mob, of frenzied, out-of-control behaviour, and of crowds fleeing from an imminent danger. Some critics argued such an analogy was inappropriate as Cohen was more accurately speaking of collective delusions and urban myths. For Cohen, however, the concept of panic is one that he refuses to downgrade to mere metaphor (1980, xxxiii). He points to the two elements of moral panic that permit the phenomenon to retain its notion of panic, and which also enable us to borrow the term as a lens through which to view the incident in Öreby: first, volatility and, second, disproportionality.

In terms of volatility, a moral panic is never permanent. This is an extremely important point for Cohen, as a permanent moral panic is oxymoronic. Panics come to an end because they simply run out of steam or resonate as part of a cyclical sequence, the "danger" fizzles out, or the media's exaggeration of the danger is recognized as overt by the general public. However, despite Cohen's insistence on the novelty of the moral panic – his assertion that it cannot be downgraded to the "dull sociological rubric of collective behaviour" or "part of the human condition" (1980, xxxviii) – he is unambiguous that *such an episode does not appear out of the blue* and, hence, must resonate with wider social angst.

Cohen is clear that in contemporary times, anomalies must still remain within the format of the spasmodic and transitory (i.e., newsworthy, while at the same time being represented as some kind of long-term unease. Moral panics and their accompanying folk devils, though often fizzling away and disappearing from view, can nonetheless enable more far-reaching social controls within society, which can remain in place long after the initial panic has subsided. Interestingly, though seemingly paradoxically, Cohen points to the example of for-profit detention centres for asylum seekers in the UK: "The fragmented and the integrated belong together: moral panics have their own internal trajectory – a *microphysics of outrage* – which however, is initiated and sustained by wider social and political forces" (Cohen 1980, xxxix, emphasis added).

Cohen is quite forceful, however, in arguing that the narrative of refugees "flooding our country" by the British tabloid press and government is a crucially different type of moral panic, if a moral panic at all (Cohen 1980, xxxiii). In discussing the now somewhat infamous rhetoric of the *Daily Mail* in its representation of refugees and asylum seekers, Cohen considers this campaign of vilification "too deliberate and ugly to be seen as a mere moral panic." The other crucial element of a moral panic is the disproportionality of its response to the phenomenon in question. This, for Cohen, goes way beyond ideas of risk, proportionality, or statistical reasoning. One cannot label something a moral panic simply by exaggerating numbers or probability. Instead, questions of symbolism come into play; representation is based on emotion and cannot be converted into sets of statistics (Cohen 1980, xxxv). However, Cohen does recognize the criticism that a sociologist's shout of disproportionality invokes some sort of fictitious "universal measuring rod" for gauging the action/reaction gap and hides an inherent political bias in deciding which panics to expose (Cohen 1980, xxxvi).

The moral panic caused by the media report of the shooting of the man in Jämtland created the conditions for a *seemingly* "exceptional" moment. Here, the Syrian men were told, in no uncertain terms, that they were deemed deviant, risky, and abnormal, and would have to behave if they did not want to be shot dead. Here, violence was explicit and crude. Though the episode with the Somali man did not take place in Öreby, or anywhere near it, the subsequent moral panic allowed Bodil to publicly voice what people had being saying more or less privately in phone calls or in conversations at the school gate. In his book *Domination and the Arts of Resistance*, Scott would call this moment the "first public declaration of the hidden transcript." As discussed in chapter 2, however, Scott's conceptualization of resistance as progressive and emancipatory leads him to discuss this breakthrough of the hidden to the public transcript in terms of restoring a "sense of respect and personhood" of the person making the declaration (Scott 1990, 210). He also points to the change in the social atmosphere when an entire group of people "suddenly find their voice is no longer stifled" (Scott 1990, 210). With respect to Bodil's admonishment of the refugees in Öreby, however, the opening of this new sphere of acceptable counter-conduct shifted dynamics, perhaps only ever so slightly, so that the refugees, particularly the Syrians, were now deemed a legitimate target for more open suspicion and hostility. That the panic fizzled out within a few days and was largely forgotten did not negate the fact that social forces had shifted, broadening the area for counter-conduct.

Compassion Fatigue: Suspicion and Doubt among the Volunteers

The role of the volunteers was crucial in negotiating acceptable practices toward the refugees. During the initial period of refugee resettlement, this was limited to practices that encouraged refugees to mend their ways; with the passing of a year and a half and resettlement of about forty more refugees, many of them non-Syrian, regarding the Syrians as suspicious and dishonest became an acceptable mode of conduct. Rumours of the Syrian refugees "playing the Swedish system" began among the volunteers themselves, most notably with Åsa about two months after the Jämtland incident and emanating from blogs and forums that her husband had come across on the Internet. These rumours quickly escalated both within the group and, gradually, outside the group to other villagers.

It all started when Åsa, who came to the activity centre every Wednesday afternoon to run informal Swedish lessons, confided in Benny and me that she believed one of the Syrian families among the first to arrive in the village from Dera'a, with seven children, had Italian citizenship and a house and business in Italy. "I have been speaking to them quite a lot. The husband is always going back and forth somewhere, apparently to Malmo, but it all seems a bit suspicious to me." Åsa's evidence for this suspicion, besides the father's intermittent absences from the camp, were the mother's unwillingness to even attempt to learn any Swedish, despite having lived in the country for about nine months. She also pointed to inconsistencies in their stories about when exactly they left Syria and the route they had taken. "My husband found a blog from insiders at Migrationsverket. Apparently half of these Syrians already have residency permits for other countries, but just turn up here after mysteriously losing all their papers because Sweden is 'better.' You know how it is. No investigation into the backgrounds of these Syrians is carried out." The assertions of Adnan (the medical student from Aleppo) later that week that the family was "trashy" and "no good" and that the villagers shouldn't be so trusting established as fact the deceitful motives of the family. The links to Italy were never made explicit within these rumours, but the mother in the family had mentioned a few times having a brother-in-law in Milan who had helped them with the money needed to leave Syria.

After Åsa had written down the name of the blog for the others, talk of cheating and deception among the Syrian refugees in Sweden became a major topic of conversation within the group. According to Bodil, the subject was also a big talking point among some of the parents she spoke to and was apparently raised in one of the meetings of the Residents' Association. Bodil explained the rationale behind their fears: "First I started off feeling sorry for them, then I became suspicious, but now I'm pretty angry to be honest, having found out about the level of deception." The blog contained alleged stories of disgruntled members of Migrationsverket claiming that since the decision to grant permanent residency to every Syrian arriving at the border, many of the newly arrived Syrians were not Syrian at all, had permanent residency in another country (usually a Gulf state), or planned to move to another country after obtaining their documentation. The blog talked about ungrateful Syrians in the north of the country moving away after complaining about the weather and boredom.

Every new Syrian arriving in Öreby became subject to a greater level of scrutiny by the volunteers regarding their background, with judgments passed on whether or not they should have been legitimately granted immediate asylum – with an increasing number of families being judged unworthy. Monnika, a teacher in the local primary school, was particularly suspicious of one family that claimed to be from Kurdish Syria but did not understand any Syrian Arabic at all: "All the other Kurds from Syria understand all the others when they speak Arabic. They must be from somewhere else altogether – Turkey or Iraq – and lying to us. That's the only explanation." In this way, the mere presence of Syrians (never refugees of other nationalities) aggravated the group of volunteers and some of the villagers more widely. The Syrians came to be framed as taking advantage of the good nature of the Swedish people and to be spoken about as conniving, manipulative, and shrewd.

Tied up with the discourse on Syrians milking the system was irritation that other refugees were not entitled to the same level of treatment. This grated very much on the volunteers and non-Syrian refugees within the camp, with the Syrians and their automatic right to permanent residency seen to be depriving others of their need for refuge in the country.

The bitterness toward the Syrians was exacerbated when Adrianne and Biktor, the Georgian couple who were now parents of a newborn baby, were not granted asylum and were obliged to return to Georgia. The effect of this decision upon the community was extensive, as by this time the group had become very attached to the young family. Adrianne and Biktor were two of the very few asylum seekers and refugees in Öreby who, with their fluent English and tertiary education (Adrianne also had a master's degree in linguistics), had been able to befriend a couple of the people in the village beyond the group of volunteers. The Swedish class in which Adrianne announced the bad news became a session of consoling the visibly upset pair, with tempers quickly rising.

Close to tears, the couple told Monnika, Åsa, and me about the letter they received that morning. A young group of three Damascan brothers who had been in the village for a few months, Adnan, and a newly arrived Iraqi pharmacist and his teacher-wife listened with great interest. Clearly very distressed, Adrianne turned to the Syrians; "I hope that you appreciate how lucky you are to be Syrian. *Your Syrian lives are clearly worth more than ours.*"

Slightly embarrassed at the emotional display, the Damascan brothers, along with the Iraqis, told Adrianne and Biktor how sorry they were to hear the news and, along with the couple, left for their respective apartments. Adnan, however, stayed in the activity centre with Bodil, Monnika, and me. "I'm sorry, but Sweden is killing itself sending people like Adrianne and Biktor home and letting all these thousands of Syrians stay. They have so much to give your country. What can people like Samira [a young woman from Dera'a] and her seven brats offer you? You are crazy people."

The perceived preferential treatment received by the Syrians from Migrationsverket at a more day-to-day level also became a source of complaint among the non-Syrian refugees. Behdad, an Iranian veterinary science student who had befriended Adnan and the glamorous Aleppan couple, Omar and Nivine, frequently complained about the behaviour of the Syrian men with whom he shared a house: their playing of loud music, smoking inside, and leaving the kitchen and bathroom dirty. "I've asked Migrationsverket to move me about ten times, but they would never do anything to upset their precious Syrians!"

In this way, the treatment of the Syrians – their entitlement to automatic permanent residency and family reunification – was framed as upsetting Swedish notions of human rights fair play, in which all people are of equal worth: "*Alla manniskor har lika värde.*" Syrians were viewed as positioning themselves as, de facto, more worthy than the others, despite their individual circumstances. Automatic permanent asylum given to a Syrian, it was rationalized, meant that even more needy Iraqis, Eritreans, or Afghans were obliged to be sent home.

The Compassion Fatigue Thesis: Solidarity as Irony?

Luc Boltanski poses a similar question to my own when he asks: "Why is it so difficult nowadays to become indignant and to make accusations or, in another sense, to become emotional and feel sympathy – or at least to believe for any length of time, without falling into uncertainty, in the validity of one's own indignation or one's own sympathy?" (Boltanski 2000, 12).

The move of the volunteers away from attempting to encourage the refugees to mend their ways toward more open suspicion and hostility, particularly toward the Syrians, I argue, contributed toward the creation of a new area of conduct in which more overt practices of hostility were enabled. The fact that the volunteers themselves were now openly labelling the Syrians as dishonest added to the legitimacy of the criticism of Swedish asylum policy. These people worked day in and day out with the refugees and were thus perceived by many to be best placed to criticize notions of solidarity and the moral exceptionalism of Sweden.

In examining how the kindness and good intentions of the volunteers progressed into open disdain and skepticism, the much-maligned thesis of "compassion fatigue" can be seen to offer a simple, though certainly undertheorized, lens through which to view this seeming transformation. The concept, when used in relation to the media, embodies connotations of overload, a psychological theory that signifies a sheer quantity and intensity of stimuli that surpasses our mental capability to pay attention. Also implicit, however, are ideas of normalization and routinization, which suggest that once exceptional images of suffering, as a result of sheer accreditation, come to be accepted as normal, and lastly "numbing," the mind becomes desensitized to endless horror images or atrocity statistics (Cohen 2001). As Cohen points out, the fatigue element refers not simply to a reduced *emotional* capacity to feel empathy but also a weakened *moral* sensitivity, and what some label an "intellectual fatigue," incorporating delicate practices of collective rationalization

(Cohen presents the clichés of a certain class of people, for example, who wonder why on earth they should be sending money to Burundi when all that happens is they kill the volunteers who are there trying to help). Compassion fatigue points to a very real acceptance of the "meta-image of chaos" and the idea that "we" have absolutely no chance of solving these problems, even if "we" tried. Though the doctrine is usually talked about in reference to how the media and humanitarian agencies are obliged to frame certain events and atrocities in order to keep the audience's attention (Moeller 1999), a number of studies have used the term to look at how people close to suffering seem unable to cope with too much revelation and practice strategies of avoidance (Cohen 2001).

As a volunteer myself, I was certainly not immune to feelings of fatigue, despite being at the activity centre for a far shorter time than the others and spending long periods away from Sweden. I sometimes found myself becoming numbed to the tales of some of the most recent arrivals from Syria, their desperate situations and the state of the country they left behind. I would switch off feelings of guilt and shame, which often left me drifting into a sort of nihilistic state of mind and feeling as though my presence in Öreby, my research, my career aspirations, and my privileged, middle-class and cosmopolitan existence were entirely pointless. I would seek out Adnan or some of the original, now long-term, middle-class Syrian residents to chat about old times in the more affluent parts of Damascus: the fancy restaurants in the old town, our favourite drinking haunts, or the joys of people-watching the glamorous and bejewelled characters that used to hang out at the Sheraton hotel swimming pool. They would tell me about a cool Lebanese restaurant they found in Malmo, update me on the progress of their plans to find Swedish girlfriends, and describe the antics of their eccentric Swedish for Immigrants teacher.

For the volunteers, too, distancing of the Syrians seemed to stem from their presence in Öreby simply having become boring and banal because they no longer made the volunteers feel good about themselves. Working with the refugees no longer enabled feelings of righteousness among the volunteers and those surrounding them. The Syrian refugees were no longer viewed as exciting, exotic victims but as problematic. They had become merely an annoyance. Stories of leaking dinghies in the Mediterranean, wives and children left behind in Turkey or Lebanon, and great treks on foot through Europe became a sort of background noise to the everyday goings-on at the activity centre. There were no "new" stories to arouse interest or sympathy.

The main weakness of the compassion fatigue thesis in this case is that it is firmly rooted within an Arendtian "politics of pity" narrative. How long can someone feel pity for distant, or even not-so-distant, sufferers? Luc Boltanski (2000) is one of the main proponents of pity forming a basis for social solidarity, whereby Western morality and ideas of justice are inextricably bound up with the idea of pity. Relying on the language of guilt, this solidarity of pity discourse, for Boltanski, has nonetheless enabled a dominant discourse that relies on grand emotions at a distance (Boltanski 2000). Though pity is certainly a feature in Swedish refugee discourse, in public discourse, feelings of guilt and shame toward refugees are not aroused as much as those of pride and virtue toward Sweden's morally exceptional policy. Therefore, we cannot say that Swedish solidarity toward refugees is entirely a solidarity of pity.

On the other hand, Lilie Chouliaraki's (2011, 2013) notion of a "solidarity of irony" perhaps offers a more accurate theoretical framework to examine this particular occurrence of so-called compassion fatigue. Unlike a solidarity of pity, a solidarity of irony is focused more on "us" than "them." It wonders whether "we" can save the world through feel-good acts of altruistic voyeurism. Unlike pity, irony privileges the short term, a low-intensity form of agency and what she calls a "playful consumerism" (Chouliaraki 2013). Solidarity in this sense embodies, for example, wearing a "cool" armband or framing famines in sub-Saharan Africa in terms of our experiences of crash diets. In this respect, an element of pleasure of the self is also brought into play, thus rendering a straightforward notion of compassion fatigue blurred and somewhat problematized.

For the volunteers, working with the refugees no longer brought about feelings of righteousness, sympathy, and indignation. Social forces had changed so that it was now the volunteers one was supposed to feel sorry for, to sympathize with for all the work they were obliged to take on because of the Swedish asylum policy and for the time they were missing out on with their own families. Feelings of indignation were fostered and encouraged, but with a different target. The Syrians were people who could not be trusted, whom it was legitimate to be suspicious of. They were turning up in Sweden simply to take advantage of the good and kind nature of the Swedish people. The final section of this chapter examines how the rumours started by the volunteers as the result of an ironic sort of compassion fatigue laid the foundations for another, much broader moral panic that, although it eventually disappeared, disbanded social relations to a much greater extent.

The Second Moral Panic: Scrounging Off the System and Selling Passports

Amid this atmosphere of suspicion and marginalization, the rumour that Syrian refugees were selling on their passports within the camp became prominent. As Bodil and Monnika became more disillusioned with volunteering – feeling less appreciated and increasingly lonely – Bodil began not only reading but also posting on anti-immigration Internet blogs and forums. Here, the idea of Syrians with permanent residency (PUT) selling their passports to other Arabs in southern Europe for a few hundred euros came to enter the discourse of the Friends of Syria. Bodil claimed that she suspected one man, who had been settled in Öreby around a month earlier, was planning to sell his passport on to somebody in the United Arab Emirates. Adnan, the medical student, had suspected the man's plans from questions he had been asking some of the more-established Syrian residents about possibilities of acquiring a replacement passport with a residency permit in the case of him losing the original. From what Bodil had then gone on to read in the blogs, this was in fact "common practice," with passports with a PUT paper selling for about €500 apiece.

Compounded by the distrust and suspicion that had been building around the notion of the Syrians milking the system, this new accusation of certain people abusing the Swedish asylum system and the good nature of the Swedish people became a sort of final straw for the volunteers. They made a collective decision that something needed to be done to make sure that everybody woke up to the way in which Sweden and the Swedish people were being exploited.

GOING TO THE PRESS
The TV report on the local news about conditions in Öreby resulted from this general unease that had, at this point, become quite a tangible entity in the village, especially among the volunteers themselves. Reporters from the local newspaper were something of a continuous, though sporadic, presence in Öreby. From the very

beginning, journalists had visited Öreby to report on all the good work and generosity taking place there, publishing stories of the manner in which locals had "stepped up to the plate" (the Swedish expression *"ställde upp"* emphasizes more the importance of broader actions, rather than simply donating goods) and had come together to support the new arrivals. The newspaper had then, every few months, run stories of the volunteers, with in-depth interviews about their backgrounds, their motives for helping the new arrivals, and life in the village.

The local press, with their glowing reports of how wonderful life was for the refugees in Öreby, and how kind and generous the villagers and volunteers had been, was now seen by the volunteers as reinforcing the idea that there were no problems in Öreby, or with Swedish asylum policy in general. They were accused of glossing over many of the issues that the volunteers had pointed out to them: the cramped living conditions, the supposed widespread drug use, and the day-to-day "untidiness" of the place.

Bodil's idea to invite television reporters from the local news channel to show them what life was "really like" in Öreby and what sorts of dodgy activities the Syrian people were actually engaged in was greeted positively by the group. Aside from the hysteria around Syrians milking the system, there seemed a need to reveal to the rest of the country exactly how burdensome the workload had become and how their family lives were suffering, and to convey a more general message about the "unspoken" consequences of Sweden's asylum policy, especially for people in Skåne, where the majority of refugees lived. On the day the TV crew came to Öreby, I was back home in London for a few days and returned three or four days after the filming had taken place. Samira, with her youngest baby, was the first person I ran into, struggling with her shopping as she got off the bus. I took a few of her carrier bags and walked the ten minutes it took to get to her house. "The fucking bitch Bodil has been letting TV reporters into our apartments when we're not here!" Samira spat out the words. "You have to tell them [Friends of Syria] we're not like a human fucking zoo." When I reached the activity centre, Åsa and Bodil were sitting at the kitchen table with Adnan. Bodil seemed to be boiling over with rage and, without even saying hello, proceeded to tell me everything that had happened while I had been gone: "Samira reported me to the police! She accused me of breaking into people's houses!

I had to spend all day on Thursday down at the police station!" Adnan explained to me that it had all been a misunderstanding. Samira had thought that her next-door neighbours, a family from Hama, had not given their permission to allow the cameras into their home, whereas Bodil insisted that they had. Apparently the family from Hama had been telling one thing to Samira, and the opposite to the volunteers.

Other Syrians in the village, however, were also extremely angry with the volunteers. Even the three Damascan brothers, who at this point were very close to Monnika, Bodil, and Åsa, accused Bodil of speaking badly of them to the TV crew, though they did not reveal the details of what had been so offended them. Upon asking Bodil a few days later exactly what she had said or done to upset so many people, she backtracked, claiming she was just presenting the reality of life in Öreby to the TV crew: how overburdened the volunteers were and how cramped and dirty the living conditions were.

As it transpired, the thirty-second report, shown on the local news the following week, did not feature any stories of Syrians milking the system but instead presented the volunteers as kind, though overworked, villagers trying to do what they could in the face of widespread global violence and unrest. In this respect, the attempt by the group to make public the now not-so-hidden transcript of marginalization, suspicion, and hostility on a much broader scale could be seen to have failed. Instead of achieving the desired outcome – to show the rest of Sweden how naive and trusting they were in the face of these sneaky scroungers – inviting the TV crew to Öreby merely succeeded in completely disbanding social relations between the Friends of Syria and the Syrians themselves. At this point, it was only Adnan who would still come to the activity centre to drink coffee and practise Swedish with the volunteers.

Samira's outburst – that "we aren't like a human fucking zoo" – demonstrates the way in which this microphysicis of outrage is entirely relational: a process of distancing is at play on the part of both the volunteers and the Syrians. As I stated in chapter 1, though I was not party to the hidden transcript of the Syrians to the same extent as I was to that of the volunteers, this does not mean that undercurrents of anger and rage were not present. Samira's articulation indicates the hidden transcript of the Syrians (or some of the Syrians) breaking through into the public realm, with the invitation of television cameras into their houses seen as a final straw.

This disbanding of social relations, the microphysics of outrage and open hostility, can be seen as a truly dynamic phenomenon: the less friendly the Friends of Syria became, the less accommodating and amiable the Syrians became. If the volunteers dared to voice their hidden transcript, then the Syrians likewise dared to voice theirs.

In looking back at Cohen's thesis, we note that moral panics begin first and foremost as rumours, which circulate through a certain group or population, encouraging a frenzy. What is crucial, however, is the role that social, as opposed to mainstream, media played in driving this particular panic in Öreby. In contemporary times, we could say that the "agents" of moral panics have become more democratized. Agendas need not be set by newspaper editors or the clergy. In Sweden, as we have seen, where criticizing asylum policy is somewhat taboo, "revelations" on social media were sometimes seen to be more truthful and more accurate than the mainstream press, which was accused of political correctness or driving a certain agenda. Disclosures on certain far-right websites from "insiders" working in various governmental agencies relating to migration and asylum – Migrationsverket, *Arbetsförmedlingen* (Swedish Public Employment Service), and Försäkringskassan (Swedish Social Insurance Agency) – were given the status of whistleblowers, courageous individuals not afraid to go against the grain and speak truth to power.

VOTING FOR THE SWEDEN DEMOCRATS: CONFESSIONS OF THE VOLUNTEERS

I hadn't visited Öreby, the refugees, and the Friends of Syria in about three months, but had kept in contact with the group, especially Bodil, at regular intervals. Throughout the summer of 2014, she updated me on the news in the village: Adnan had been accepted to study medicine again at Lund University and had given up on the aviation idea; Tariq and Sandra had finished the Swedish for Immigrants course and had moved to a new apartment in Malmo; and Ibrahim's eldest daughter, Sarah, had a Swedish boyfriend with whom she seemed to be deeply in love, somewhat to Ibrahim's disdain. Monnika e-mailed pictures of a trip they all took to the beach during Sweden's most extreme heat wave in ninety years; the school allowed her husband to borrow the school bus to take twenty of the refugees, along with the volunteers, on a much-appreciated day out. It seemed as though the incident with the TV crew, if not forgotten, had at least been forgiven by the Syrians and life seemed to be, at least from my perspective back home in the UK, working pretty well. I was extremely touched to hear that everybody was missing me, and planned a short, one-week trip back to Öreby at the end of the summer to drop in and hang out. I missed everybody and, arriving back at the village after such a long absence, its slow pace and its perfectly cultivated exterior felt warm, welcoming, and comfortable.

My visit coincided with the 2014 general election in Sweden, and the village was covered in posters and placards from political parties. However, nobody spoke much about the election, with the exception of one conversation around the kitchen table involving Bodil, Åsa, and a newly arrived English teacher from Iraq, Sarah. Sarah was interested in the success of the Feminist Initiative party, which was on course to enter parliament for the first time, and Åsa and Bodil debated whether or not a vote for this party could be a wasted vote.

The following day, when I arrived at the activity centre, Bodil confided that in Sunday's general election she would be voting for the anti-immigration Sweden Democrats party, but hadn't wanted to say anything in front of Sarah. She was almost eager to tell me, like a sort of confession, and launched straight into the topic as soon as we were alone together in the kitchen. She gave her reasons for confiding in me: "I know you probably think it's really bad, and you'll judge me, but I'm telling you because you're writing about it and I think it's important for people to know how it really is in Sweden. We just can't cope with these numbers. It's crazy. It's our schools and elderly care that suffers and these people [the refugees] aren't even grateful. You've seen how snowed under we are here." She urged me not to tell anybody else, especially not the other volunteers, for fear of being labelled a racist.

The "confession" did not come as a surprise as all of the volunteers had been echoing the discourse of the far-right party for the past few months. I told her that I understood her rationale and would not judge her decision, but urged her to take some time off, perhaps take a holiday, and that maybe she would feel differently after a break. A few days later, when I told Åsa and Monnika that I heard it had been tough going in Öreby, they too confided that they felt forced to vote for the Sweden Democrats: "Bloody Reinfeldt [then prime minister] tells us to open our bloody hearts to the immigrants [referring to a speech made in August 2014, during the election campaign]. He doesn't have a bloody clue in his mansion in Stockholm. Why should we have to suffer?" They too spoke of the topic being taboo and not being allowed to openly discuss the perceived problems they were facing in the village: "Of course you can't even talk about with anybody because they'll call you a racist. But we're the ones who have to work with them week in, week out. Everyone else round here can just shut their doors and pretend it's not happening."

It was insinuated, however, that many people felt the same way. Öreby had already done its fair share, but could not be expected to carry on like this. As an outsider, it seemed I provided an outlet for these feelings of dissonance. Being from a country in which public discourse is openly hostile to migrants, I was deemed to be a safe person to whom to confess. Though I had been and worked in the village over a period of many months, I was never deemed to be one of them.

I returned to Öreby the day after the election. As it was early on a Monday morning, there wasn't much activity, most of the older children were in school, and it was too wet and windy for the younger ones to be out and about. I brought up the topic of the election results, and the surprise result of the Sweden Democrats, set to take around 14 per cent of the vote, exceeding all previous expectations and predictions. The three women seemed triumphant, as though they had somehow gotten their revenge on the system, but quickly changed the subject. Upon returning home to London and more in-depth analysis of the election results, I was rather unsurprised that what the volunteers themselves had labelled the far-right party had received 27 per cent of the vote within the village of Öreby, one of the highest proportions in the entire country, and a huge 16 per cent increase on the 2010 vote. Later that week I received a text message from Faisal, the eldest of the Damascan brothers, which mentioned the result: "I am shocked! They [the Öreby folk] are two-faced people, kind to your face only but evil behind your back. It's better in Malmo but there is still no future for us here." His subsequent text messages went on to talk about his plans to come to London, wondering whether I could help arrange work for him and his brothers, or at least somewhere to live. I assured him that I would do what I could, but that the situation for Syrians in the UK was much worse and advised him that they'd be much better off staying in Sweden.

With the disbanding of social relations, Bodil criticizing the prime minister, and the admission of all of the volunteers to voting for the Sweden Democrats, we have seen the way in which the microphysics of outrage has opened up the possibility to speak about and act toward the refugees in completely new ways. However, this new way of thinking was not generated by party politics, a resistance against a perceived out-of-touch elite, or the manifestation of a rural versus urban divide. These are simply the visible manifestations of the microphysics of outrage we have discussed in this chapter. Far from embracing a far-right ideology, Bodil and the other volunteers still considered themselves decent people, a world apart from other ignorant, racist people who would support the anti-immigration party. No, as opposed to those others, Bodil and the volunteers voted for the party for noble reasons, and as such could still maintain that they were good and righteous.

CONCLUSION

This chapter has focused on practices of counter-conduct within the Swedish governmentality of righteousness, practices that, in Davidson's (2011) words, utilized and re-utilized, reinserted, re-implanted, and, most importantly, re-created what it means to be a good citizen in terms of Swedish asylum policy. There was no official, organized resistance to the resettlement of the refugees in Öreby; on the contrary, surface relations were largely cordial and tranquil. However, we have seen how these practices of counter-conduct actually serve to push at the very limits of this governmentality, generating something that is innovative and new: a means of marginalization, hierarchization, and suspicion of the refugees going way beyond asking them to mend their ways or be visibly suffering, as we spoke about in the previous chapter.

Borrowing anthropological terminology from James C. Scott, that of the hidden transcript, we saw how a day-to-day type of counter-conduct was conceived around the governing of the movement of village children and around the behaviour toward the Arab men, who were deemed exotic, violent, and dangerous. Exacerbated and exaggerated by a sort of compassion fatigue on the part of the volunteers, albeit one that focused more on the diminishing of their own feelings of righteousness rather than a numbing to the suffering of the refugees themselves, we saw how the possibility of what Cohen calls a microphysics of outrage developed. Moral panics around alleged violent behaviour of a Somali refugee hundreds of miles away and rumours of Syrians milking the Swedish system generated a collective hysteria that, though quickly cooling off, nonetheless served to shift what was considered acceptable behaviour in relation to the refugees.

The existence of these moral panics, and their subsequent repercussions, demonstrate the *coexistence* of hidden and public transcripts, as well as the coexistence and continuum of practices of benevolence and practices of violence. This hysteria did not come out of the blue, and was only enabled by the much wider social and political forces that underpinned it, forces that re-inscribe Sweden and Swedish people as morally exceptional, and all the baggage that this entails. With one in four votes in the village, including those of the volunteers, going to the anti-immigration party they had once deemed "frightening," it is clear that not only governments, political parties, or even the media deem certain groups as a societal threat. As we have seen, individuals, groups, and communities are seemingly just as capable of acting as so-called authorized speakers in the name of their security, even when it goes completely against the grain of what it means to be decent.

The word "limits" in the title of this chapter refers to the contestation of a certain way of thinking and the hatching of something new. The strength of the taboo whereby nobody decent criticizes asylum policy within polite company is now undermined. This is how the hidden transcript becomes public and the whole notion of righteousness is changed, not by evolution or a gradual development, but by the capacity that each element within this particular framework is now read differently, through a different mode of thinking. What emerges, therefore, is something new. Not an alternative meta-narrative, one that rejects Sweden's moral superpowerfulness, but simply microphysics, these tiny practices of conduct and counter-conduct that carve out new terrain of acceptable behaviour. The next chapter discusses these broader theoretical issues, opening up a dialogue between anthropology and problematizations of security, and putting forward the concepts of reflexivity, metis, and solidarity (and its appropriations) as major interventions toward an anthropological rethinking of CSS.

5

Anthropological Rethinking of Critical Security Studies

Reflexivity, Metis, and Solidarity

The previous two chapters discussed the way in which a small, rural Swedish community housing over one hundred refugees ultimately took the matter of security into their own hands. While seemingly going against more official national discourses of solidarity, they simultaneously kept all notions of decency firmly intact. As opposed to a moment of exception (Wæver 1993; Agamben 1998), or even a governmentality of unease (Bigo 2002), and moving beyond the biopolitical hierarchization spoken about by many within the anthropology of humanitarianism in terms of the hatching of a new way of thinking (Agier 2002, 2011; Pandolfi 2003, 2008; Fassin 2010, 2012), I have described how these practices of marginalization were undertaken by actors operating in what I have labelled a governmentality of righteousness. This set of relations is built on nationalist narratives connecting Sweden's decision to grant asylum to all Syrians arriving at the border with a cherished myth linked to a particular historical period tied to the formation of the modern nation state.

The purpose of this final chapter is to reflect upon the more conceptual questions brought to the fore and to examine the three main ways this book aims to rethink CSS along more anthropological lines. Firstly, I argue that the role of reflexivity is crucial in this project of shifting ontological primacy and generating a meaningful dialogue between the two disciplines of IR and anthropology. The book proposes a Scott-based approach to examining the appropriation of humanitarianism, generosity, and solidarity as a form of security, based on his conceptions of both public and hidden transcripts and practices of metis. Absolutely crucial regarding the use of such an anthropological framework is that the focus is not on ethnography as a method, as discussed in chapter 1. I argue that it is in focusing on the reciprocal positioning of the hidden and public transcripts, and on my relation to my objects of study and the effect of my presence on what we label practices of metis, that brings the importance of reflexivity to the forefront of any possible dialogue between IR and anthropology. I argue that reflecting on the configuring of my own role and power position within my research was absolutely crucial in how I have told the story of the people of Öreby and the resettled refugees. The ways in which my role as a British translator and volunteer shaped the narrative was critical in the writing of my anthropology. Therefore, instead of attempting to build some kind of overarching, meta-narrative, an anthropological approach to studying security practices should attempt to build traces and connections, which are themselves written into the story.

Metis is then the focus of the second section of the chapter, wherein I argue that any study of processes of (in)securitization must not simply be a study of security as top-down coercion. As well as destabilizing Copenhagen's insistence on security as speech acts and examining the far right solely through party politics and spokespersons, a focus on metis is also argued as being the most productive manner through which IR and anthropology can open a dialogue on problematizing security.

Thirdly, and relatedly, the chapter looks at the role the idea of solidarity played in generating security practices. How was it possible that what appeared as the contrary of security could, nonetheless, be appropriated as a form of security? This final section argues that the re-utilization of solidarity was absolutely central for enabling the refugees to be deemed undeserving, undesirable, and dangerous. The conduct and counter-conduct, the microphysics of outrage, and the dramatic, seemingly exceptional moral panics could be conceptualized as part of the baggage that re-implants solidarity as a moral obligation. Far from a rational solidarity, as within the Swedish national myth, we have a very local understanding of a *free gift* of sorts. The section reflects on the anthropological literature on humanitarianism that has discussed the way in which humanitarian practices can actually serve to biopolitically hierarchize human life, and argues that, in light of my project's findings, this type of managing and hierarchization should simply be seen as the concealed base of the iceberg, the tip of which sees the sacrifice of an unwanted group in the name of protection.

REFLEXIVITY

The story of the refugees in Öreby presented here is the story that I chose to tell. Its narrative and the connections that I made are some of many that I could have chosen, but decided not to. Altogether, I spent nineteen months in Öreby working with the grassroots NGO, the Friends of Syria, and with the refugees. These nineteen months were some of the happiest I had experienced in recent times, especially at the beginning. I formed close friendships with some of the group – Åsa, Monnika, and especially Bodil. I also became very fond of some of the Syrians living in Öreby – Nivine, Omar, and, of course, Adnan. I had lived in Damascus in 2008 and 2009, studying Arabic in the university and hanging out, night after night, in trendy restaurants and drinking haunts of the Christian Quarter in the Old Town. In 2008, the city was awarded "Arab City of Culture," with regular concerts in the citadel and spontaneous gatherings and sing-songs on the streets of *Bab Touma*, where young people gathered with a *shwarma* and a beer and strummed guitars and tapped on drums to the latest rock songs. That summer also saw one of the country's most ferocious heat waves, with temperatures soaring into the low-fifties Celsius; several friendships were forged when local Damascenes approached me, the pasty, fair-haired northern European woman, to ask how I was coping with the extreme weather. That was also the year that I came to adore Damascus and the people living there. In my memories, the place was entwined with being young, free, and happy, without responsibilities or worries.

Therefore, the arrival of Syrian refugees in Sweden reignited this spark of pleasant recollections, however naive, simplistic, and orientalist. Syrian people in Sweden, how wonderful! The Swedes should recognize their privilege in hosting such charming and cultured people. If the refugees settled in Öreby were from elsewhere, I am quite certain that, though I would have been sympathetic to their plight, I perhaps wouldn't have cared quite as much. Maybe I would have been more understanding of the villagers' initial complaints. Who knows? But in my mind, Syrian people were like me and, as such, deserved a very warm welcome. To be sure, I wanted the Syrian refugees to succeed in Sweden simply by virtue of them being Syrian. It was only after several months when I got to know refugees from Iran, Georgia, and Uganda who had been placed in Öreby that I felt the same kind of empathy with them.

There are many ways of narrating the story of the Syrians in Öreby. Like the Swedish news report that decided to portray everyday life in Öreby in terms of the hard-working and underappreciated volunteers, doing all they could in the face of the worst refugee crisis since the Balkan War, or the foreign newspaper that chose to give a voice to Rifat to speak about his depression and boredom in small town Sweden. None of these narrations could be seen as any less true than an alternative telling.

Crucial to the anthropological approach that I adopted, therefore, was the importance placed on the notion of reflexivity. It was absolutely essential for me to constantly question my own position – with regard to the volunteers and the refugees, the effect of my presence, my Britishness, my very close friendship with Bodil, my ability to find common ground with many of the younger people from Damascus and Aleppo – a position that was never static and manifested itself differently in every situation. And certainly, the uncritical importing of ethnographic methods into IR has failed to pay sufficient attention to recent debates in critical anthropology regarding the role of the researcher. However, placing the notion of reflexivity at the forefront of any analysis permits an incorporation of the hierarchies of power and disparate power relations between the people being studied, and crucially between the research subjects and myself as a researcher, and accounts for these relations in interpretations of the way in which people behave.

Understanding that different people would approach the situation in Öreby, or the wider issue of the situation of refugees and asylum seekers in Europe, differently is to also understand that the very way in which any research question on the issue could be structured and framed would also vary considerably. As Yanow (2006, 78) forcefully argued, knowing and understanding are intersubjective processes and a presumed isolated independence of an individual response ignores how all analyses are contextualized, formed, and constrained by different characteristics of academic practice. Thus, as the meaning of acts can only be understood through interpretation, the first step to being "scientific" would be to realize my own commitments and prejudices.

As my experiences were naturally a direct result of the disparate power relations between myself and the other members of the group, the residents of the village, and the refugees, recognizing the power dynamics or different situations and reflecting on how my presence altered people's behaviour brought strength to my research question and collection of data. Though from a similar social class, ethnicity, and background as the volunteers in the Friends of Syria group, I was of course seen as a foreigner, with constant references invoked regarding refugee relations "in my country." Acting as a translator between the tiny, makeshift organization, the other villagers, and the refugees shrouded me in a little bit of mystique as few of the refugees spoke fluent English and no village residents or members of the organization spoke any Arabic. To deny the oppressive effect on others of this kind of professional "knowledge" would be at best naive. For sure, many people thought of me as some sort of expert on refugee integration, though I presented myself as nothing of the sort.

In utilizing an anthropological framework and viewing the governmentality of righteousness as an ethnographic object, one becomes acutely aware of how these power relations play a role in the production of knowledge. At the beginning of my fieldwork, I became instantly conscious that I was, to some extent, part of a sort of machinery of governance whereby the residents felt obliged in many instances to perform the role of the good, welcoming Swede toward the new Syrian residents, or to demonstrate their tolerance more generally, for my approval. As a foreigner from the United Kingdom, this was expressly articulated to me on several occasions, as already mentioned. Therefore, in many respects, my ethnography acted as a situated intervention between governing and resistance, strategies and tactics, and conduct and counter-conduct. Though in many regards, as a researcher, I could access a hidden transcript or that which would not have been openly said around, for example, the other members of the grassroots social organization, the villagers, or the refugees themselves, I was conscious that a great deal of the performance of publicly welcoming the Syrians was at least in part played out for my benefit as well as for the benefit of fellow residents.

Of course, one could have viewed the villagers and the Friends of Syria as insincere and hypocritical from the outset. One could argue that the organization of the grassroots group was simply self-indulgent, a way in which the relatively middle-class, well-educated folk could relieve their guilt by treating the refugees as some sort of "pets," a way for the volunteers and wider community to give meaning to their lives without recognizing the refugees as fellow humans with all the same rights and responsibilities. For me, however, this would not only be a complete misreading and misunderstanding of the dynamics at play in Öreby but would also render meaningless the refugees' own interpretations of the actions of the Friends of Syria and Örebydwellers. We remember that the group was very much appreciated and respected by the Syrian refugees in general, and the people of Öreby were viewed as very kind and good people. Bodil was held in extremely high regard, being labelled a gift from God and a guardian angel by some of the Syrians who were first to arrive in the village.

There is no meta-narrative or overarching theory as to how the Syrians in Öreby came to be seen as undesirable and dispensable. The manner in which they came to be conceived of as threatening, requiring that some sort of action be taken to protect the Örebydwellers, was very much a process and a journey. And as I was a key player in the development of that journey, problematizing my position at every node and juncture is essential if we are to have an honest discussion.

BEING IN BETWEEN: BUILDING TRACES INSTEAD OF META-NARRATIVES

To reiterate briefly from an earlier chapter: I initially placed myself in the role of "in between" – I was first and foremost a translator and interpreter in Öreby. I conveyed grumbles and complaints between the villagers and the Syrians, but also passed on the grievances of the Syrian refugees to the Friends of Syria group. I was good friends with the women in the NGO but also formed bonds with some of the refugees – Nivine, Adnan, Sandra, and Tariq especially. As a British person, from a country whose political discourse is much more openly hostile toward refugees, the volunteers saw me as a "safe" person to whom they could confess. I was sympathetic to their workload. I was interested in what they were doing. For example, I was privy to Bodil's admission that she had started to write for the far-right anti-immigration blog. All of the volunteers also confessed to me first, before confiding in each other, that they had voted for the Sweden Democrats. I was seen, for whatever reason, as somebody who would be more understanding and less judgmental. And perhaps I was less disapproving. I had witnessed all the hard work they had taken upon themselves and was sympathetic to the fact that they had much less time to spend with their husbands and children because of the sheer numbers of refugees who had been placed in Öreby, with very little in the way of official support.

As someone who had lived in Syria, albeit briefly, I was also seen as a friendly ear by some of the refugees. My time in Damascus meant that it was easy for me to find common ground with some of the refugees. During the first half of 2013 relatively few Syrians were arriving on Sweden's border, nothing like the numbers seen during the so-called refugee crisis of subsequent years. Those who had made the journey at that time were also much more likely to be highly educated, middle class, and quite young, meaning that it was very easy to strike up conversations and relatively likely that there would be some common interests. Nivine and Omar, for example, were not hesitant to complain to me about how slow paced and quiet they found life in Öreby to be, an observation they were far too polite to relay to any of the other volunteers. Similarly, Rifat, Ahmed, and Tariq felt comfortable enough around me to pass comment on how they had felt about villagers' remarks or actions, which they would not be so rude as to report to any other members of the Friends of Syria.

I also had the benefit of being able to leave my fieldwork for periods of time. Unlike everybody else, I did not live in Öreby but instead was about a twenty-minute bus journey away. I also travelled back home to the UK fairly frequently or attended conferences and seminars in different parts of Europe or North America. It was only when I was away from Öreby that I was able to examine what was going on there with a fresh eye and conceive of my own role in the events.

As my fieldwork progressed, however, many friends and colleagues outside of Sweden commented that I had moved further and further away from this role of in between, which was reflected in the narration of the story of Öreby in the previous two chapters. I became bound up with the work of the volunteer group and their practices. As friendships with the volunteers became increasingly stronger, what I had access to also increased over the course of my fieldwork. I thus started to see the Friends of Syria and the villagers as my objects of study. And this caused many of the Syrian voices to be marginalized somewhat. "But what of the hidden transcript of the Syrian people?" I would frequently be asked. "What are the Syrians feelings about the Swedish self-perceptions of righteousness?"

As I set out in chapter 1, it would be disingenuous to claim that I had the same kind of access to the Syrian people as I did to the members of the Friends of Syria. Though I strove to place myself in between and managed to build good relationships, I am quite sure that I was never privy to the darkest depths of the hidden transcript of some of the Syrian refugees. Indeed, for the Syrians there was much more at stake in forming an open friendship with me and discussing their feelings about life in Sweden. Though some people complained of being bored, the Syrians were there to make a new life for themselves, so most people remained very polite and perhaps somewhat guarded. This was not the case for my relationships with members of the Friends of Syria. As intermediaries between the refugees and the villagers, they positioned themselves as having nothing to hide and were thus much more forthcoming about their feelings toward the refugees.

Not having an anthropology background, I was also perhaps ill-prepared for the emotional exhaustion that fieldwork would bring and the moral ambiguity of many of the situations I found myself in, as well as the continuous questioning on my own standpoint (see also Eckl 2008). As I became good friends with the members of the Friends of Syria, I became much more sympathetic to how they viewed the situation in Öreby, and felt sorry for the workload they had taken upon themselves. When chatting about the group to other Swedish friends or family, or back home in the UK, I found myself defending the behaviour of some members of the group – the disciplining of Omar and Nivine's brashness, the desire for some kind of gratitude from the refugees, and even the echoing of the Sweden Democrats' rhetoric that the Syrians would be better helped in the overseas refugee camps instead of being encouraged to come to Sweden. I cared very much for my new friends in Öreby, and wanted them to be happy and fulfilled again in their volunteer work. I wanted them to be appreciated by the refugees and to be reassured that they were good, kind people. "They're just so nice!" I would find myself explaining to friends and colleagues. Perhaps they were right and Sweden can't shoulder such a burden, practically single-handedly, I would rationalize. If they felt that the Sweden Democrats were the only ones speaking up for them in a climate where nobody felt they could criticize Sweden's asylum policy, then who was I to say that they were wrong? Sometimes the moral ambiguity I found myself in was suffocating, stressful, and completely destabilizing.

As described in the previous chapter, only after the complete breakdown of social relations in the village; after the various moral panics that saw a TV crew being invited to film the "real" goings on in Öreby and some of the group members writing what they regarded as the "truth" about the Syrian refugees in Sweden; and ultimately, after the volunteers (and 27 per cent of the residents of Öreby) decided to vote for the anti-immigration Sweden Democrats in the general election, did the extent of the disdain of many of the Syrian people for both the volunteers and the villagers become obvious. To wit: Samira's articulation that we "are not a human fucking zoo," Adnan's anger at the police shooting in Jämtland, and Faisal's disgust at the increasing popularity of the far-right party in Oreby. In these instances, the hidden transcript became public.[1] Within these various ruptures, a line of separation was drawn between the volunteers and me. I was reminded that I was a foreigner, that I did not understand the pressure that Sweden was under. As Britain had taken so few of the refugees, I was naive about how cunning, manipulative, and unscrupulous the refugees could actually be. For me, though the atmosphere was often rather tense in Öreby, the various moral panics and the complete disbanding of social relations came as somewhat of a shock. I was never in any doubt as to the motivations of the Friends of Syria. I never regarded them as self-satisfied or smug.

I was thus too embedded in the day-to-day goings-on in Öreby. My presence undoubtedly changed certain dynamics and altered the turn of events. Everybody in Öreby – the volunteers, the refugees, and the wider village community – knew that I was there to loosely research the issue of the Syrian people in Öreby. Everybody knew that they were being watched and written about, and adjusted their behaviour accordingly.

The telling of the story of the Syrians in Öreby in not supposed to be an objective, fly-on-the-wall account of what happened in the village between February 2013 and September 2014, and I have not tried to portray it as such. Hence, an ethnographic approach, treating governmentality as an anthropological object and using the work of Scott to explore the wiggle room for actors operating within this governmentality, is best placed to capture the messiness of the everyday practices on Öreby, the reciprocal positioning of the hidden and public transcripts, and my relation as a researcher to the processes and practices that eventually came to render the Syrian people undesirable.

Though Scott has traditionally been charged with "attempting to produce an innocent knowledge outside the constraints of theory" (Vrasti 2013), the use of Scott's framework not only encourages creativity and flexibility in the process of data gathering but also enables the systematic "writing in" of the researcher to all stages of the research process and enables reflexivity at each point. Going further than analyzing everyday life and its links to political practices or official discourses, this Scott-inspired ethnography, by drawing on the way in which my engagement as researcher shapes my data, very much strengthens the research question and problematization.

Building on this argument by Yanow (2006) and, therefore, what is necessary for an interdisciplinary dialogue between political anthropology and IR on security, is to write in a way that captures the messiness of the security landscape, while still remaining convincing. More important than attempting to build a grand, overarching narrative is to build traces, where the story of how I make various connections becomes part of the story itself (cf. Levi-Strauss 1965).

Therefore, in turning to metis in the following section, it is important to bear in mind that these practices of metis are not simply what I observed during my fieldwork. Metis is also the relation that I have to my objects of study, my embeddedness in the day-to-day happenings, and the tiny acts of (counter) conduct that occurred as a result of my being there. For this reason I argue that the most meaningful dialogue between IR and anthropology on questions of security comes through the concrete study of the everyday practices of actors, these tiny acts of metis, which destabilizes both the idea of a pre-defined, demarcated security terrain or apparatus and the notion of security as decisionist politics and audiences. Putting metis at the forefront of my study not only disrupts Copenhagen's insistence on the speech act as the securitization process but also offers a more damning critique of the "critical anthropology of security" school of thought and those that uncritically use ethnography as a method through which to study pre-defined "securityscapes" (Albro 2011; Gusterson 2004). Against these authors, I argue that the most important offering anthropology can give to IR on studies of security is not a tradition of holism (cf. Albro 2011), but one of relationism. Against holism, even the most traditional anthropological context, that of the village, can be seen not as an object to be explained but as an explicitly partial and always "contingent window into complexity" (Candea 2007, 167). Nicholas De Genova (2005, 1, emphasis added) captures it best when he speaks of anthropology not of examining a "thing called society," but instead looking at "how social life comes to appear so *thinglike*," and "how people immersed in those processes seek to make sense of them." Mick Dillon and Julian Reid (1999, 9), who authored the term "relationism," mean by it "that nothing is without being in relation, and that everything is – in the ways that it is – in terms and in virtue of relationality."

Therefore, instead of aiming for some sort of synthesis, the use of metis allows for the positioning of myself in a situated intervention between the Swedish people and the Syrians, between conduct and counter-conduct, and between the hidden and public transcripts. Central to this intervention is accounting for the irregular, constantly shifting dynamics at play and, of course, the fundamentally contested nature of the terrain depending on one's angle of vision.

METIS

There is no doubt that *mētis* is a type of intelligence and of thought, a way of knowing; it implies a complex but very coherent body of mental attitudes and intellectual behaviour which combine flair, wisdom, forethought, subtlety of mind, deception, resourcefulness, vigilance, opportunism, various skills, and experience acquired over the years. It is applied to situations which are transient, shifting, disconcerting and ambiguous, situations which do not lend themselves to precise measurement, exact calculation or rigorous logic.

Marcel Detienne and Jean-Pierre Vernant 1991

Chapter 4 saw us discuss the limits to the governmentality of righteousness and examine everyday practices of counter-conduct by the villagers of Öreby, which completely destabilized and thus liberated and reconceptualized what it meant to be a decent or righteous citizen. Fuelled and accelerated by various moral panics, this very mundane counter-conduct generated something new and innovative: a shift in what was now deemed acceptable behaviour toward the refugees. As we saw, this shift was not due to a sudden rupture or an abrupt, open manifestation of collective resistance by the Öreby-dwellers against the newly arrived refugees. This new terrain of acceptable behaviour, though seemingly exceptional, was carved out through tiny, subtle everyday practices that went only ever so slightly against the grain of decency, but added up to a social change.

In September 2014, we also saw how one in four people in Öreby, including most of the volunteers with the Friends of Syria, voted for the far-right party they themselves once considered abhorrent. Two members of the group even began writing posts, on the real stories behind the Syrian refugees in Sweden, for an anti-immigration blog aligned with the party. As I wrote at the end of the previous chapter, these people did not suddenly come to identify themselves as anti-immigration, let alone nationalists, racists, or neo-Nazis. They did not abruptly come to see themselves as having something in common with the much-demonized residents in Sjobo, 100 kilometres away – the "ignorant farmers" and "skinheads" – who, only a year and a half earlier, were still the subject of much condemnation and ridicule, a crucial folk devil used to keep the public transcript of complete solidarity intact. In fact, in Öreby, the complete opposite was the case. The villagers and the members of the Friends of Syria who voted for the far right maintained that they were not at all aligned with the far right. Some of the Friends of Syria still maintained that they found the party repugnant, despite voting for it. Unlike the imagined uneducated rural men of Sjobo who were filled with hatred and ignorance, the Öreby-dwellers were utterly convinced of their decency. Their practices, though pushing at the very boundaries, were still subsumed by a governmentality of righteousness – a type of counter-conduct, certainly, but never an action from outside, or diametrically against, what they conceived of as being righteous. Their actions were simply one of the many axes of practices available to the good citizen in their position, very much a tactic instead of a strategy.

For the Friends of Syria, voting for the far-right party was justified as the most noble action to take. They thought of themselves as protecting the well-being of the Syrians who had already arrived in Sweden against the hordes of imagined racists, who were sure to mobilize if Sweden continued on this so-called dangerous route of allowing so many refugees to settle. Bodil, for example, justified her act in terms of gatekeeping; in voting for the far-right party, she was shielding the refugees who were already settled in the village from the menace that her fellow Öreby-dwellers posed if the village were obliged to accept even more refugees. "We just cannot cope with the strain here in Öreby anymore," she would often tell me. "It is a suicidal policy on behalf of the government and I'm seriously worried about what's going to happen in the future for these people if Sweden just carries on like this." A new way of being good was thus brought into being. And done so through practical operations, which never "makes its nature explicit or justifies its procedures" (Detienne and Vernant 1991).

So, with an anthropological rethinking of security, the importance of metis comes into play in the construction of a group as dangerous and undesirable. Though originally conceptualized by Detienne and Vernant, anthropologist Michel de Certeau refers to the ancient Greek term *"mētis"* to illustrate a type of behaviour where the aim is "to obtain the maximum number of effects from the minimum force" (de Certeau, cited in Neumann, 2002, 633). James C. Scott also utilizes the concept of metis to talk about "a wide array of practical skills and acquired intelligence in responding to a constantly changing natural and human environment" (Scott, cited in Neumann, 2002, 634). The second way I propose to rethink CSS concerns this notion of metis. Here, I argue that any study of processes of (in)securitization should not be a study of top-down coercion, spokespersons, and audiences. I put forward the argument that the most productive dialogue between IR and anthropology on questions of security can take place, firstly and most importantly, through Scott and metis.

Metis as the Most Sophisticated Dialogue between IR and Anthropology on Questions of Security

In chapter 3, we reconceptualized Tilly's idea of the Swedish standard story of moral exceptionalism as a type of governmentality that I labelled a governmentality of righteousness. In using Tilly's notion of the standard story as a point of departure, we discussed how moral exceptionalism could not be seen as an elite narrative or ideology imposed on a passive population that uncritically reproduces the narrative. Through utilizing the Foucauldian notion of governmentality in relation to Tilly, the standard story is not only one that is actively performed by and embraced by members of the public but also one that has come to shape and normalize how citizens come to view themselves and others as moral beings. The decent citizen is brought into being by the governmentality of righteousness. As opposed to treating governmentality as a Weberian ideal type, I proposed viewing governmentality as an anthropological object. Instead of being viewed as an abstract concept, the governmentality of righteousness cannot be conceptualized outside of its concrete manifestations on the ground, through micropractices and microphysics.

The first and most important lesson in anthropologically rethinking CSS is to see the space and place where practices of security take place as not being predetermined or pre-defined; instead attention is paid to their emergence and contingency. This suggests a much more profound role for anthropology in the current debate by placing ontological primacy on ethnography as a way of knowing. As my project has shown, the day-to-day practices of metis within a small village in Sweden served to enact a security scene through the utilization and evasion of, and the wiggle room incorporated within, what I labelled a governmentality of righteousness. In stressing the roles of a collective, shared, though largely hidden, transcript, similar to what Appadurai points to when he discusses the processes of collective imagination in the construction of a –scape, my project points to a much more important role for anthropology regarding security questions. In asking what we mean by the "everyday," my project has emphasized the need to always examine questions of security and security terrains and apparatuses as relational. As Scott's idea of the hidden and public transcripts has shown, the examination of day-to-day practices only makes sense when one accepts their reciprocal positioning. We can then abandon questions of levels of analysis or brush off criticism that carrying out such in-depth, ethnographic fieldwork is not proper IR.

In mobilizing the work of James C. Scott and the idea of metis, my case study of a Swedish village in chapters 3 and 4 has shown the importance of the idea of appropriation and collective imagination in the construction of a group as threatening, in a very local context, both utilizing and evading grander nationalist and international myths. I then went on to demonstrate that the appropriation of discourses of not only humanitarianism or hospitality but also solidarity can construct the terrain of the security landscape, quite devoid of any official security discourses or practices. The exact importance played by solidarity is discussed later in this chapter. Important thus far, however, is that a critical anthropology of security has articulated its desire to show notions of security to be "contingent, contested and always cultural, *even within security apparatuses*" (Maguire, Frois, and Zurawski 2014, emphasis added). Again, anthropology here, despite all contestations to the contrary, has taken these technologies of security as given. In fact, this critical anthropology of security, in its insistence on demystifying security and moving beyond the nation state ends up mirroring a great deal of work already taking place in IR and css, what Diana Fox (2010) has called the "bread and butter" of many IR departments.

In arguing that security terrains or apparatuses should not be viewed as grand narratives, my case study has not only stressed the intersections between discourses of solidarity, humanitarianism, and security, which I discuss further in the final section, but also emphasized the importance of these everyday acts of appropriation, translation, and evasion. As Didier Bigo (2014a, 191) has so eloquently stated when discussing the importance of a critical anthropology of security, "processes of managing (in)security can transform everyday politics into a security scene." Therefore, in reflecting back on my first intervention, a far more important role is conceived for an anthropological way of knowing within CSS than many have envisaged. By not taking security scenes as a given – an a priori definition in the fields of IR, political science, or even criminology – and simply importing ethnographic methods into the mix, my project has demonstrated the way in which political anthropology is best suited to exploring the contradictions and continuities of how communities can constitute their security in a horizontal fashion and take the matter of security into their own hands.

Metis and Everyday Theories of (In)securitization

As chapter 1 noted, traditional scholarship on securitization of migration traditionally conceives of a securitizing act as an elitist phenomenon, situated within the professionals of politics, enabling a type of exceptional or panic politics. This type of framework, including some of the more sociological offshoots (cf. Balzacq 2016), which place far more significance on the role of the audience within these securitizing acts, resonates with much of the established literature on the far right, viewing the demonization of migration, for the most part, in terms of ideology. In this sense, power is conceived as top-down, restraining and shaping the behaviour of individuals. Within these explanations of the construction of migration as a threat are several assumptions. Firstly, those who come to accept that migrants and migration are a danger to their culture or values are usually somewhat quiescent. They are largely passive consumers of the speech act, or at the very least, as in Balzacq's more sociological re-conceptualization of ST, they are influenced by the speech act to the same extent that the enunciator is shaped by public opinion.

Secondly, the group is also largely conceived of as somehow disadvantaged. They are to some extent disenfranchised, or view themselves as disenfranchised, due in part to the uncertainties brought about by globalization or free-market capitalism. This is certainly the case in Sweden, as we saw in chapter 2, which looks at how various counter-insurgency practices and official rhetoric around radicalization and fundamentalism have beckoned the end of Swedish exceptionalism and moved Swedish citizens toward accepting the narrative about the need for the generation of a "New Sweden" (see, for example, Dahlstedt 2005; Dahlstedt 2008; Schierup and Ålund 2010). Beyond Sweden, the traditional tabloid narratives of the marginalized white working classes, under threat from not only immigrants, committing more crime and claiming welfare while simultaneously stealing jobs and undercutting wages, but also from a metropolitan, urban, liberal elite intent on destroying their way of life, is a familiar narrative. Lastly, these type of theories assume that the group in question is not directly coerced into accepting the status quo. There is an element of conditioning at play.

In the more IPS-inspired frameworks for (in)securitization through the routine or the everyday, scholarship moved away from what Vaughan-Williams and Stevens (2016) have called these "elitist" sites of exceptional security to take into account the cultural milieus in which (in)securitization moves take place. This has led to a much more sophisticated and robust conceptualization of security and everyday practices than simply speaking of audiences, as in Balzacq's (2016) approach. Huysmans (2014) recognizes the "double analytical status" of the realm of the everyday whereby we are able to capture *both* (in)securitizing practices as well as the negotiation and appropriation of these moves by certain groups. In this way, we can no longer say that far right is nothing to do with us – something external, objective, and "over there," neatly demarcated. We are instead obliged to acknowledge the subtle practices of normalization of this seemingly exceptional politics and how rather nice people, even people a bit like us, can own this type of politics.

A turn to metis pushes this theorization of the everyday even further by taking these tiny micropractices as our specific ontological point of departure, opening up the possibility to move *beyond* the dualisms of seeing the everyday in terms of just reproduction or contestation of pre-defined (in)security practices. An ethnographic way of knowing and of knowledge takes "everyday" to mean these very situated lived experiences of people and the various spins they put on things – the sets of relations in which they are embedded that make them, at certain points, feel insecure or threatened.

In conceiving of the everyday in terms of acts of metis, and placing ontological priority on these micropractices and all their complexities, a political anthropological reconfiguration of studying security has demonstrated that (in)securitization processes can not only be extremely far from top-down manipulation from political entrepreneurs claiming an easy fix to a complex problem, or even a distinct doxa that emerges within fields of professionals, but also be something very different. The story of Oreby has shown danger and threat constructed at a very local level through tiny practices – what Scott would perhaps label "resistance" – but where all images of decency are kept intact. What appears as the opposite of security – hospitality, humanitarianism, and solidarity – nevertheless looks like a form of security. Here, security is also about protection and welfare. Righteousness, in this instance, is a form of security. Through local forms of knowledge, embedded in local experiences, a security scene is created from something appearing traditionally at odds.

The final section examines the role played by solidarity within Swedish discourse in the generation of this security scene, not by looking at what the concept of solidarity *is* but instead what solidarity *does*. The manner in which solidarity is translated and appropriated in everyday practice and the way in which local forms of knowledge, through the described practices of metis, carves out a new terrain of acceptable behaviour in which the Syrian refugees are able to be legitimately articulated as a threat.

SOLIDARITY

In the foreword to her translation of Marcel Mauss's *The Gift* (*Essai sur le don*), Mary Douglas proposes the thesis that the theory of the gift is in fact a theory of human solidarity (Mary Douglas 1990, xv). With this tension and overlap between the idea of the gift and that of solidarity in mind, this section explores the much broader question of how solidarity, a concept that appears to be at polar opposites to any idea of security, actually came to look, to all intents and purposes, like security practices when played out in everyday life. It argues that the notion of solidarity within Swedish popular discourse becomes an empty signifier of sorts. Therefore, more important than what solidarity means is what solidarity does: the everyday practices it mobilizes and enables. Though conceived within Swedish political discourse in completely rational-choice terms, with the citizen perceived as being completely free from the bonds of moral obligation, solidarity in terms of relations with refugees in fact mobilizes a very specific type of gift economy. The position of Sweden as morally exceptional regarding refugee and asylum policy and the generation of the Swedish governable subject and righteous citizen enables notions of humanitarianism, generosity, and charity to be brought into being. Therefore, from a Weberian perspective, we have an instrumental "associative" style of solidarity based on individual choice, masking the expectations associated with more communal types of solidarity based on gratitude and obligations. It is this tension and overlap that enables the tiny practices of metis spoken about above to go ever so slightly against the grain of solidarity while maintaining all notions of decency and righteousness.

Because of Sweden's 2013 decision to grant permanent residency to all Syrians arriving in the country, as well as the strict interpretation of the term "solidarity" in the TFEU by Swedish political elites with regard to refugee policy, which prioritized resettlement from third countries over relocation of refugees within the EU (as a "burden sharing exercise"), I argue that a supposedly "pure," rationalist notion of solidarity stands in contradiction to the idea of Sweden as moral exemplar and to the functioning of the governmentality of righteousness. In its appropriation at an everyday level, therefore, the functioning of the governmentality of righteousness *requires* this element of moral supremacy. Instead of solidarity in its strictest sense, a gift economy is brought into being.

Day-to-day life in Oreby, as discussed in chapter 3, permitted open articulation of the expectations of the refugees to be worthy guests to some extent in polite company, something that was very much in keeping with the conduct of conduct of the decent citizen. Nevertheless, the decent citizen was one who never openly complained about Swedish asylum policy, thus generating a public and hidden transcript of behaviour: what is and is not acceptable to be voiced in polite company. As discussed in chapter 4, solidarity thus takes on a somewhat *ironic* element: it becomes about convincing oneself of one's generosity, decency, and righteousness. As long as the refugees play by all the rules of being a worthy guest, this performance is maintained. However, any perceived deviation from this role is deemed an affront to the good nature of the Swedish people and is heavily sanctioned. As we saw in the previous chapter, the arena of acceptable conduct toward the refugees is broadened, until they are legitimately able to be labelled a threat with all perceptions of decency on the part of the Swedish hosts able to be kept intact.

Moral Obligation or Rational Egoism? The Messiness of Solidarity in the Swedish Story

First to the abstract concept of solidarity: "As to the question which gave rise to this work, it is that of the relations between the individual personality and social solidarity. What explains the fact that, while becoming more autonomous, the individual becomes more closely dependent on society? How can he simultaneously be more personally developed and more socially dependent? For it is undeniable that these two developments, however contradictory they may seem, are equally in evidence. That is the problem which we have set ourselves. What has seemed to us to resolve this apparent antinomy is a transformation of social solidarity due to the steadily growing development of the division of labour" (Durkheim [1893] 1964, 37–8).

Emile Durkheim famously saw solidarity and the nature of social ties as the central problematique of the field of sociology. Departing from the thinking of his predecessors, such as Tönnies's distinction between pre-industrial so-called organic societies and more contemporary societies that are said to be characterized by a more instrumentalized and individualized type of "mechanical" solidarity, Durkheim instead reverses the concepts. For the scholar, "organic solidarity" is seen instead as a more accurate term through which to describe the types of bonds that characterize modern types of communities, grounded in individual difference instead of collectivized and shared norms and rooted in the division of labour of the nineteenth century. A relatively small-scale solidarity rooted in codes of conduct that are often based in religion and repressive law is replaced by mutual dependency and the conception of a completely rational individual who holds abstract, secular, and universal norms (Durkheim [1893] 1964). Weber too distinguishes between different types of solidarity and social relation: "communal" social relationships, often grounded in tradition and based on a general "feeling" of togetherness, and a much more instrumentalized "associative" relationship, based, for example, on market exchange. In the latter case, solidarity is tantamount to the pursuit of the collective interest of atomized, mutually dependent individuals (Weber [1922] 1947).

That said, these classical theorists, the founding fathers of social theory, both stress that, in reality, these different types of solidarity very much overlap and coexist in variable combinations. Organic solidarity does not exclude mechanical solidarity, in the same way that communal social relationships are not completely distinct from associative relationships. This pluralism of solidarity is a crucial observation for us in the telling of the Swedish story. Chapter 2 discussed the manner in which the oft-cited solidarity served as a defining feature of Sweden's national myth. This interpretation of solidarity is very much in keeping with more modern, rational-choice interpretations of the concept. We discussed how solidarity, in this instance, can be seen as "the humanitarian claim *par excellence* ... (The) imperative to act towards vulnerable others without the anticipation of reciprocation" (Chouliaraki 2011, 364, emphasis in original). As a value, solidarity here is thus supposed to transcend the hierarchical power relations and aspires instead to "a vision of a technocratic Enlightenment Universalism ... populated by orderly, rational, co-operative, moral individuals" (Tomlinson 2011). Solidarity as a concept, especially in the Swedish sense, thus operates outside the principles of quid pro quo, not requiring some kind of payback or counterbalance.

Since the inception of the discipline, anthropology too has provided illuminating insights into solidarity, but more along the lines of the idea of the gift and gratitude, their purpose in forming social bonds and relationships, and ideas of moral obligation and reciprocity. Malinowski, Mauss, and Levi-Strauss all provide visions and understandings of the notion of a "gift economy," a tradition that has spawned a great deal of scholarship, especially with regard to the notion of humanitarianism and charity, as we touched upon in chapter 2. Malinowski ([1922] 1950), in some of the most groundbreaking insights into gift-giving, proposed the importance of the capacity of a gift to "move," in that a fundamental characteristic of any gift is that it should be given and later reciprocated. In his pioneering work *Argonauts of the Western Pacific*, he talks in detail about the Kula, the ceremonial exchange of gifts by the inhabitants of the Trobriand Islands off the coast of New Guinea. Articles of exchange travel in opposite directions around the ring of islands in a closed circuit. Necklaces made from red shells travel clockwise, from person to person, while bracelets made from white shells simultaneously travel anticlockwise. What is crucial is that the gift continues to be kept in motion. Indeed, a person who held an item for what was deemed too long a time would earn a bad reputation. Therefore, it was the principle of give and take, not the objects themselves, that Malinowski saw as important.

Similarly, the work of Mauss ([1923] 1990) talks about the idea of the gift in terms of a cycle. In his study of the practices of the Maori, he sheds light on the notion of *hau*, the spirit of the gift. Within this cycle, the forest hunters offer some of their hunted game to the priests, who cook the birds upon a sacred fire. The priests, after eating part of the bird, then return their bones to the forest as the embodiment of the hau, with the hope that the forest would then produce a new profusion of birds to be hunted once again. For both Malinowski and Mauss, the principle of the gift cannot be separated from an expectation of reciprocation, or *do ut des* (I give for you to give in return). For Mauss especially, there is famously no such thing as a free gift; "generosity and self-interest are linked in giving" ([1923] 1990, 68). Writing some years later, Levi-Strauss builds on these insights to examine the notion of reciprocity in Western societies: for example, the giving of gifts at Christmas. As opposed to being an impartial object, gifts are "vehicles and instruments for realities of another order: influence, power, sympathy, status, emotion; and the skilful game of exchange consists of a complex totality of manoeuvres, conscious or unconscious, in order to gain security and to fortify one's self against risks incurred through alliances and rivalry" (Levi-Strauss 1965, 68).

The core tenet of much of the scholarship of those in the anthropology of humanitarianism has drawn attention to this great line of thinkers, this darker side of communal relations configured along the lines of a gift, or as Fassin (2012, 133) labels it, this "ambivalent hospitality." Drawing on Derrida (who in turn is critiquing Mauss), he traces linguistically the connection in Latin between guest, *hospes*, and enemy, *hostis*, both of which derive from the word meaning "stranger." As the author points out, however, *hostis* has not always had this negative connotation; initially it referred to a contractual relationship establishing reciprocity, which implied moral obligations and systems of exchange (Fassin 2012, 135). This confusion between hospitality and hostility, Fassin argues, is absolutely critical to any reflection on "foreignness" today. Within contemporary humanitarian governance, it is the very condition of the relation between the two parties, the giver and the receiver, that generates this profoundly unequal power relation. The goodwill of the agents is irrelevant as the sentiment of compassion generates the need for a counter-gift. The problem is not ethical, but purely sociological (Fassin 2012, 3).

The power relations in the humanitarian versus the assistance-receiver association results in the fundamentally unequal ordering of human lives between those who are granted full "biolegitimacy," in Fassin's words – the recognition of a biographical life in which individuals can themselves give meaning to their own existences – and those whose victimhood is reified and are defined merely by their biological lives (Fassin 2012, 254). As Pandolfi has observed, in labelling somebody a refugee or trauma victim, "past experiences and individual and collective histories are erased by new categories in which human beings are catalogued" (2008, 169). Therefore, humanitarianism as a "politics of life" has a "triple problematic" (Fassin 2007, 519). Firstly, it acts to "distinguish lives that can be risked," i.e., those of the humanitarian workers, and "lives that can be sacrificed," the populations whom these agents work amongst (Fassin 2007, 519). Secondly, it separates lives into those with higher value, the expatriate workers, from those who are granted only limited protection, the national staff. Instead of being limited to NGOS and interventions abroad (cf. Fassin and Pandolfi 2010), this type of humanitarian reason is now a general mode of governing populations *within* states, whereby it has now become part of "our making" of modern politics (Fassin 2010).

The Swedish narrative is testament to the murkiness of solidarity and requirements for a counter-gift. As sociologist Alvin W. Gouldner famously argued, "there is no gift that brings a higher return than the free gift ... For that which is truly given freely moves men deeply and makes them most indebted to their benefactors" (1973, 277). In the Swedish instance, as demonstrated in chapter 4, solidarity in terms of refugees and asylum seekers within the national myth – with demands made on the refugees to show visible suffering, to mend their ways, and to be constantly grateful – is certainly seen by the decent citizen as the embodiment of the free gift. This is especially the case since the unusual intertwining of solidarity as a national myth with the added relational element of the superlative – being ranked *the best* at solidarity – enables an ever more profoundly unequal exchange between the givers and the recipients.

In the case of the refugees in Sweden, it is the messiness and overlapping of these two ways of constructing social ties – solidarity as rational and egoist, and solidarity as reciprocity and exchange – that ultimately forms the basis of the moves toward the (in)securitization of the refugees. An understanding of this abnormalization of solidarity is crucial in illuminating how the sphere of conduct and counter-conduct, the practices of metis that pushed ever so slightly against the grain of decency, was able to be stretched and shaped to form the base of the iceberg, with the tip embodying the various moral panics that legitimately disbanded relations between the village and the refugees. As put forward in the third hypothesis of this book – that within the axes of practices subsumed within the governmentality of righteousness, within the wiggle room and metis of this specific conduct of conduct, solidarity is re-appropriated and re-implanted as humanitarianism, hospitality, and generosity, with all the baggage this embodies – this re-utilization of solidarity is absolutely central to everything that followed. The conduct and counter-conduct, the microphysics of outrage, and the dramatic, seemingly exceptional moral panics could all be conceptualized as part of this baggage, a result of the need for reciprocation and a counter-gift.

Solidarity Paradoxes in Swedish Political Discourse:
The Impetus for Reciprocation

We recall that in chapter 2 Swedish historians Trägårdh and Berggren (2015) made a controversial, though seemingly popular, intervention into the Swedish solidarity narrative by putting forward the hypothesis that the supposedly socialist- and consensus-orientated Swedes are in fact hyper-individualists, pursuing personal autonomy to a much greater extent than even citizens of the US. Based on data from the World Values Survey, which positions Sweden as the most secular-rational country in the world, as well as the nation that places the highest value on self-expression, the authors argue that the conjunction of the ideals of social solidarity with independence and economic equality have been institutionalized in what they call a "radical alliance" between the Swedish state and the individual, what they label "statist individualism." This has served to balance the "deep existential desire" for personal freedom and, simultaneously, social cohesion, "liberating" the individual from what they call unequal and patriarchal forms of community, such as the bonds to family, churches, and charities. The authors go further, placing at the heart of their model a deeply rooted conception they label a Swedish "theory of love," wherein authentic love is only possible between people who are truly independent and equal. Since Swedes fulfil these criteria, the authors hold relationships in Sweden to be more meaningful and more loving than those in other nations.

Though Trägårdh and Berggren base their argument on the social contract theory of Rousseau and make no explicit references to any sociological or anthropological theories of solidarity or gift-giving – neither Durkheim or Weber, nor Mauss and Levi-Strauss – the authors are clear that for them, within the Swedish story, solidarity is entirely removed from the moral economy of gift-giving. Hence, the authors conceive of Swedish solidarity as a purely rational and egoist form of solidarity. This formula of Swedish solidarity, according to the two authors, even goes so far as to speak of love in rational terms, invoking Lacan's ([1950] 1992, 248) well-known definition of love as "giving what you don't have." By its very nature, the act of giving or making love to someone must exist outside any notion of reciprocity or payback, with any expectation of reimbursement from either of the parties automatically annulling the meaning of love, and cementing it instead within a system of exchange. To love a person, by its very definition, cannot conceive of the act as a type of gift, something the recipient must be grateful for and indebted to the giver for.

Even within Swedish asylum and refugee policy, however, this notion of a completely rational notion of solidarity is disturbed somewhat, especially in relation to other European states. In chapter 2, we discussed the precise way that solidarity has been conceived within Swedish governmental discourse regarding an EU common asylum policy. Sweden interpreted solidarity within the external element of the EU's asylum policy in terms of resettlement of refugees from third countries in conjunction with the UNHCR. Sweden was one of the few member states to regularly resettle a quota of refugees within Sweden directly from camps in the neighbouring states of conflict zones, as opposed to other member states that conceived of solidarity in terms of intra-EU relocation. Of the other twelve states that offered some kind of resettlement program, many were accused of using earmarked quota spaces for refugees relocated from other EU member states as part of a burden-sharing exercise. As we saw, Sweden thus fashioned itself as a de facto spokesperson for resettlement over intra-EU relocation as the most effective means through which to protect some of the most vulnerable refugees, aiming to convince the member states that did not offer any type of resettlement program with the UNHCR to adopt one, and encouraging those states that did participate in the quota system to increase numbers (see Regeringen 2013).

This interpretation of solidarity, I argue, went some way in enabling the concept to be appropriated as generosity, hospitality, and humanitarianism, both within political discourse[2] and within the realm of everyday practices toward refugees. By interpreting solidarity in the manner that is seen as most effective in protecting vulnerable refugees – i.e., adopting the largest quota in conjunction with the UNHCR and reserving these spaces for refugees directly from third countries and not other EU member states – Sweden positioned itself as best at doing solidarity. Solidarity was thus defined only in terms of solidarity with refugees and third countries rather than in terms of the relationship with other member states, which deemed themselves overly burdened. Instead of transcending the type of hierarchies talked about in the Maussian-inspired studies of hospitality and humanitarianism discussed above, a mentality of ranking was produced. If Sweden was best at showing solidarity with refugees and did not petition for any sort of intra-EU burden-sharing mechanism to relieve the numbers of people being resettled in Sweden, then a relation of power is introduced: the impetus for reciprocation comes into being. This is evident in relation to other EU member states, wherein Sweden required recognition for being the "odd" country that was actually campaigning for more refugees (chapter 2), as well as in relation to the refugees themselves, who are required to be grateful that Sweden is best at performing solidarity. In light of the Swedish government announcing that it has been "obliged" to change this policy as a result of the refugee crisis of 2015 and asking the European Commission for refugees to be relocated from Sweden, this mentality of ranking was able to be maintained in the face of this apparent U-turn by rationalizing that Sweden had reached its limit while other European member states had not. The concluding chapter further discusses the implications of these developments.

This rationalization could also be seen to be the case with Sweden's unilateral offer granting all Syrian refugees arriving at the border permanent residency and the right to family reunification as of September 2013. Though Swedish political elites did not articulate this policy in any sort of humanitarian terms nor attempt to position Sweden as more generous than other EU member states, instead simply stating that the country was fulfilling its legal obligations, the fact that only Sweden made such an offer rendered the concept of solidarity somewhat murky in everyday practice. Similarly, the supposed reversal in this policy, with most Syrian refugees as of January 2016 being granted only temporary permits, could be seen as the logical conclusion of interpreting solidarity in the manner described. Other member states failed to do their part; they failed to show solidarity; therefore, Sweden was obliged to rescind its previous policy. Though it was considered a shame, it was seen as largely outside of their control. This logic is also discussed in the concluding chapter.

The whole notion of solidarity thus becomes self-contradictory in the context of Swedish refugee policy. The failure of other member states to interpret solidarity in the same manner as Sweden destabilizes the meaning of the concept. If other member states are deemed to not be pulling their weight in terms of obligations toward refugees, then they are not acting in proper solidarity with the refugees, third countries, or, indeed, Sweden, which is deemed to be shouldering a disproportionate level of responsibility. As discussed in chapter 4, the positioning of Sweden as moral exemplar in this regard is absolutely crucial for the functioning of the governmentality of righteousness. Returning to the first hypothesis of this book – that the Swedish national myth of moral exceptionalism, especially regarding Sweden's refugee and asylum policy, generates a particular type of subjectivity and plays a major part in the construction of governable subjects – we see that such a governmentality would not function as well if all the other EU member states adopted similar policies toward the Syrian refugees or interpreted solidarity in the same way. A question such as "Why is it only Sweden that is doing the right thing?" quickly enters popular imagination and is essential for the maintenance of a certain subjectivity. The notion of an element of ranking or hierarchy regarding morality is absolutely essential in this regard. In chapter 2, we saw how the notion of Sweden as morally exceptional was able to function as a national myth and standard story when contrasted to the idea of Denmark a morally inferior. If Denmark were to suddenly adopt similar policies to Sweden, likewise pressing other EU members to resettle larger quotas of refugees, the functioning of the governmentality of righteousness would be completely disrupted.[3]

Everyday Solidarity in Öreby: Gratitude and Raising Stakes

Returning to my fieldwork in Öreby, we recall that gratitude was a crucial expectation that the villagers and, to some extent, the volunteers with the Friends of Syria had of the refugees. Although it was never expressly articulated that the Syrian people should be grateful for being granted refugee status and permanent residency in Sweden – any such articulation would have gone very much against the accepted conduct of conduct within the village – the everyday practices and behaviour around the refugees conveyed this expectation and, as such, demands for the refugees to be worthy guests fit very much into how the polite person could be seen to act. The Syrians, as discussed in chapter 3, were expected to accept their lot, and it was deemed in very bad taste to complain about circumstances in Öreby, or even act in a way that gave the impression that life in the village was somehow not enough (as we saw from the reactions of the volunteers when Nivine and Omar bought the so-called flashy car or when Rifat gave an interview to the foreign press).

The re-appropriation of solidarity as a gift economy was most prominent in events that appeared to raise the stakes for the villagers, of which there were a number. We remember, for example, September 2013, when Sweden took the unilateral decision to grant permanent asylum to all Syrians arriving at its border (a move that, at the time of writing, no other EU member state has followed). By this time, refugees had been settled in Öreby for about seven months and many had already been granted five-year permits to stay.

Therefore, for the Friends of Syria, the granting of permanent asylum to all Syrians was somewhat hypothetical, largely an academic point far removed from the day-to-day goings-on in Öreby. It did not mean that a greater number of Syrians would be resettled in the village nor did it mean that those already there would remain for a longer period of time. After the Syrians had been officially granted residency and received their *personummer*, official guidelines obliged them to be removed from the care of Migrationsverket and placed under the welfare of *Arbetsförmedlingen*.[4]

Despite being largely theoretical, the move by the Swedish government nonetheless provoked a reaction among the volunteers. There was a palpable sense that the stakes had now changed. As discussed in chapter 2, this move suddenly propelled Sweden from a nation acting more or less like any other EU member state to one acting from a position of moral superpowerfulness. A much more conscious and considerate reawakening of the national myth emerged, with Sweden once again being hailed as the saviour of refugees, a position that, despite the nation receiving much greater numbers of refugees per capita that the majority of the other EU member states in the recent past, had not been a dominant narrative in the media since the days of the war in the former Yugoslavia, which saw Sweden take a record number of refugees.

With this changing of the stakes, the idea of the good person was more strongly re-implanted as a good Swedish citizen. The decision created a unifying move among the imagined good Swedes within the public transcript, with tolerance and benevolence no longer defined in terms of being a village or being against Migrationsverket's cold bureaucracy. Nor were there references to racists in other parts of the country. Instead, Sweden was vindicated by the volunteers as a beacon of progressiveness once again. It was now the UK and Denmark that needed to up their game and match the generous example Sweden had set.

Sweden's unilateral move, though articulated largely through a legalistic terminology of rational solidarity by political elites and not in terms of humanitarianism, was nonetheless interpreted by the volunteers as a generous move on the part of Sweden. As discussed in the previous chapter, the obligation of refugees to mend their ways around issues of gender equality and parenting became even more forceful. The Syrians were told to behave if they did not wish to be harmed by the Swedish police, or accused of milking the Swedish system for its generous benefits. It became far more acceptable to use Adnan, with his progress in the Swedish for Immigrants program and determination to study in Lund, as a poster child through which to pester the other Syrian refugees.

The move, however, as discussed in the previous chapter, formed a crucial part of the base of the microphysics of outrage that led to the moral panics and complete disbanding of social relations within the village. The Friends of Syria, armed with the knowledge that Sweden was now single-handedly saving the Syrians, became even more certain of their rightness and decency. This was articulated both to me, as a foreign researcher from a country with an appalling record on treatment of asylum seekers and refugees, and more notably to the refugees themselves, who were more forcefully obliged to play by all the rules of being a worthy guest.

As also discussed in the previous chapter, the stakes regarding the resettling of the Syrians in Öreby appeared to change as well after the Somali man was shot dead by police in Jämtland. Again, this changing of stakes was largely academic on the part of the villagers; the refugee who wielded the knife did so hundreds of miles away from Öreby. Nevertheless, the villagers, including the Friends of Syria, positioned themselves as now being at increased risk of violence thanks to their good nature. This allowed the broadening of the acceptable area of conduct toward the refugees. These incidents that supposedly raised the stakes thus enabled an even stronger hierarchization between those who were deemed desirable and those deemed less desirable. The decision to grant permanent asylum to all Syrians acted as a catalyst in the sorting of the good refugees – who attempted to mend their ways, be grateful to Sweden for its kindness, and perform the correct role of suffering while at the same time demonstrating stoicism and resilience – from the less willing refugees, who could be made an example of. At the same time, pity and sympathy could more forcefully be demonstrated toward the refugees of nationalities other than Syrian. As we saw in the previous chapter, the Georgian family were deemed completely just in complaining that the Swedish authorities viewed their lives as lesser than Syrian lives. Very quickly, the Syrians moved from being an object of care and assistance to being undesirable, threatening, and able to be "sacrificed in the name of protection" (Balzacq et al. 2010, 10).

A Solidarity-In(s)ecurity Iceberg: From Unworthy Guests to Folk Devils

The making of the refugees from deferent insiders to outsiders and threats moves one step beyond what many of the authors in the anthropology of humanitarianism have drawn attention to by accounting for the way in which the relations of power between the good Swedes and the refugees not only create a hierarchy, reify victimhood, and categorize human lives but also mark a shift in what is deemed acceptable conduct toward the refugees. For scholars from the field of anthropology writing on humanitarianism, the effects of these operations aimed at protecting civilians are somewhat multifarious. In highlighting the "aporia of humanitarian governmentality" (Fassin 2010), they bring forward the manifold of ways in which humanitarianism is inextricably linked to biopolitical categorization (cf. Pandolfi 2003; Redfield 2013; Ticktin 2006). For Ticktin (2006, 34), the effects are somewhat subtle, with the illness clause in France, obliging asylum seekers to employ ill health as a means of acquiring legal residency, constituting a form of "minimalist humanity." Similarly, for Fassin (2010), who focuses not on war or camps but on nearby suffering such as the poor and asylum seekers in France, biopolitics places more emphasis on decisions about the *type* of life people may or may not lead rather than simply the normalization of these lives along biological lines. For Pandolfi (2008, 170), however, the effects of this biopolitical-humanitarian intertwining are much more brutal and profound in that the "the person classified under one of these international categories [victim, refugee, trafficked woman, trauma victim] is an exportable, irrelevant entity."

It is the shifting dynamics between the refugee as a fellow human, however minimally this is construed, and the refugee as an "exportable, irrelevant entity" that this book has brought to light. We saw how the refugees in my case were not conceived of in a minimally biopolitical way but were, instead, provided with all the necessities for a seemingly decent life. More importantly, though they were ranked and hierarchized, sorted into worthy and unworthy, and marginalized through the many tiny biopolitical practices discussed in the previous two chapters, this marginalization was not the final story. Through what followed in Öreby, we saw how these tiny practices broadened the acceptable area of conduct toward the refugees. They enabled a public transcript of socially acceptable behaviour, but also a hidden transcript of practices taking place behind closed doors and away from polite company. In the same vein, an area of counter-conduct also developed, pushing at the very limits of what it meant to be a good citizen while simultaneously generating multiple new ways of being "good." The various moral panics spoken of in the previous chapter positioned the Syrian refugees as folk devils (Cohen 1980). As well as being undeserving and dispensable, the Syrians now saw their identity as refugees deemed public property, with their presence used to show society exactly "which roles should be avoided" (Cohen 1980, 3). Thus, a line could legitimately be drawn between those worthy of solidarity and those not. A new way of thinking was brought into being – albeit one whereby solidarity as a value need not be rejected given that an ironic reading of solidarity (cf. Chouliaraki 2011, 2013) ensured that the actors operating within this righteous governmentality could still feel good about themselves. They were honourable in their intentions, and thus righteous in their moves to turn against the undeserving refugees, (in) securitizing them as a folk devil and a problem to be dealt with.

At the end of my story, the people of Öreby no longer wanted the Syrians in their midst. Over a quarter of them voted for the anti-immigration party they had once vilified. The Friends of Syria group fizzled out; the activity centre closed; social relations between the villagers and the refugees completely disbanded. This is what solidarity did, in this case. So the move from solidarity to security is not as big as one might first imagine. The shift from victim to threat happening in the space of only nineteen months should no longer be seen as the result of seemingly spectacular or exceptional events, carried out by a minority of racist thugs divorced from the majority of social interactions around refugees in Sweden. These various moral panics should be conceived of as the tip of the iceberg, with the concealed base reaching down to the depths of solidarity in the Swedish story, its appropriations and re-appropriations.

CONCLUSION

This chapter has put forward the three propositions to ontologically and epistemologically rethink CSS along anthropological lines. Firstly, it has stressed the importance of reflexivity. I did not attempt to portray the interactions between the Swedes and refugees in Öreby with some sort of unchallenged authority. As stated in chapter 1, my project was not an attempt to garner attitudes toward refugees in Sweden or put forward some sort of policy recommendations to the Swedish government. Rather, I wanted to tell a story of how a new paradigm was brought into being; about how being good was reconfigured over time through various mechanisms and how the far right came to represent people who would never conceive of themselves as far right. In telling this story, I was careful to write myself in to each turn in the narrative. Central, too, were the temporalities of subject formations, whereby both the villagers and the Syrians constructed themselves differently at different points of time. This is the strength of a political-anthropological approach to theories of (in)security, realizing and recognizing one's own commitments in telling the story and being open and honest about them.

Secondly, my project put forward the importance of metis in reconfiguring theories of critical security along more political-anthropological lines. A focus on metis, appropriation, and local knowledge completely destabilizes political science's focus on speech acts and the spokesperson. By viewing the far right only in terms of ideology and audience, mainstream political science approaches provide an impoverished understanding of the far right and are unable to conceptualize the way it can come to represent good and decent people. Such an understanding is increasingly relevant in an era where anti-immigration parties are rising to prominence all over Europe, as I discuss in chapter 6. Furthermore, a focus on metis has provided a more profound voice for political anthropology in its dialogue with IR on questions of security than other anthropological approaches that uncritically allow political science to define the terms of engagement, thus ending up with analyses of security simply as pre-defined and already-enshrined security technologies.

Lastly, my project has built on the scholarship conducted within the anthropology of humanitarianism by examining the functioning of the humanitarian claim par excellence, that of complete solidarity. In highlighting how such a notion of solidarity with refugees jars with the mentality of ranking at play within the governmentality of righteousness, this book demonstrates the huge amount of wiggle room within which the good citizen can operate. By appropriating solidarity as a free gift, good citizens can carve out new social and political forces whereby the desire for reciprocity is inherently linked to the legitimate articulation of the Syrians as undeserving. My project has conceived of the (in)securitization of the refugees as an iceberg, the tip being the various moral panics that cast the refugees as disposable and the base extending all the way down to the tiny, snatched micropractices of hierarchization and obligation on the part of the Syrian refugees.

6

Conclusion
The Devil in the Anthropological Detail

"The E.U. is becoming more and more ungovernable," said Mark Leonard, director of the European Council on Foreign Relations, a research institute. "The stakes internationally are higher and higher, but politics is becoming more and more parochial." The scale of the trouble facing the European Union is hard to overstate. Across the Continent, populist, nationalist and far-right movements are upending traditional politics and promoting anti-Brussels sentiment. The effects of last year's huge wave of migration continue to roil Germany and many other countries. The bloc is struggling to maintain stability in the single currency zone. Most of all, Britain's vote in June to leave the European Union hangs over the entire European project, a reminder that decades of work in knitting together disparate nations can be reversed in a relative instant.

Kanter and Castle, *New York Times*, 20 October 2016

The idea of Europe in crisis – the rise in populism and xenophobia, and the surge in popularity of far-right parties – has risen to prominence since I finished my fieldwork. The above quote from the *New York Times* paints a grim picture of politics across Europe from an outsider's viewpoint, describing the biggest upsurge in nationalist politics since before the Second World War. Writing in the wake of the 2016 US presidential election, an election also characterized by the eventual victor courting the far-right vote and intensifying xenophobic rhetoric, the authors are some of many commentators warning of dark times ahead. I began my research in February 2013, less than two years after the beginning of the Syrian Civil War and when far fewer Syrians were arriving in Europe than nineteen months later toward the end of my fieldwork or in the subsequent few years during Europe's so-called refugee crisis. The situation in Sweden, and all over Europe, has certainly changed a great deal over this time. Now, when the government states that it has done its part, Sweden has nothing to be ashamed of in justifying the implementation of borders and the attempts to reduce refugee numbers as noble moves. The link between solidarity and security is made much more explicit.

This chapter links my experiences working with the Friends of Syria NGO at the very local level and the developments that have taken place at the national and, to an increasingly greater extent, European levels. Moving away from the Swedish story, it argues the broader case for studying processes of (in)securitization in a horizontal fashion, reiterating the importance of examining the precise mechanisms through which solidarity comes to be abnormalized, permitting boundaries to become crystallized between those who are deemed deserving and those deemed undeserving. The growing popularity throughout Europe of the far right and of increasingly hardline practices toward refugees, the implementation of borders and fences, and the paying off of authoritarian regimes to prevent departure of refugees are coming to represent not only a normal but also, in many cases, a decent response to the so-called crisis. In this context, the conclusion argues that the current situation requires a political-anthropological approach to studying these (in)securitizing practices as they evolve and become normalized, rather than a traditional political science approach that can only offer a post-facto analysis focused on political parties and spokespersons.

A SOLIDARITY–(IN)SECURITY CONTINUUM: THE LOGIC OF SOLIDARITY AS A FREE GIFT AND THE CRYSTALIZATION OF BOUNDARIES

In analyzing the mechanisms through which boundaries were crystallized and solidified, my fieldwork in the village of Öreby shed light on the myriad micropractices that manifested around interactions with the refugees. Those actions that went ever so slightly against the grain of the Swedish national myth, but could by no means be seen as a modality of resistance of counter-conduct to the enactment of moral exceptionalism, nonetheless served to hierarchize and stigmatize the refugees. An element of patronage and debt was always at play within these relations. Refugees were required to be worthy. They were prohibited from criticizing any element of their lives in Sweden, and they were expected to mend their ways and to clearly display their suffering when called upon, only to later be required to demonstrate hardiness and resilience. Never were the Syrian refugees allowed to present themselves as in any way equal to their Swedish hosts, and a marked unease would manifest itself whenever refugees stepped out of their place in this hierarchy. These fleeting articulations of skepticism or annoyance – the first indication of the wider moral panic and breakdown of social relations that would later follow – were largely masked by the then–public transcript that prohibited any open and obvious criticism of the refugees, enforced strict rules of etiquette, and prompted exuberant displays of onstage posturing.

Demonstrating how it was not through a competing meta-narrative or official, organised resistance that the refugees came to be seen as unworthy, undesirable, and, later, somewhat dispensable and able to be sacrificed (cf. Balzacq et al. 2010), chapter 4 explored the modalities of counter-conduct opened up within the governmentality of righteousness. Rather than conceptualized as a passive underside to the types of conduct discussed in chapter 4, this counter-conduct was seen to be creative, spontaneous, and cunning, generating myriad new ways of being good, righteous, and decent. It spoke about how the notion of the perfect citizen was not abandoned but came into tension with the idea of being a good parent or a right-thinking supporter of gender equality. It looked at the way in which this behaviour manifested itself initially through a type of hidden transcript whereby it was still viewed as taboo to outwardly and openly accuse the Syrians of being sexist or their children being deviant and dangerous. The hiddenness of this transcript, as in Scott's original thesis, maintained to the outsider the illusion of a tranquil surface and of everyday relations rubbing along nicely.

Through the mechanisms of various moral panics – momentary eruptions of frenzy, volatile and disproportionate – we saw how this hidden transcript of unease was able to become public. A *perceived* changing of the stakes in the resettlement of the refugees in Öreby (the moral panics came from the relations of power within Öreby and not from any external event) enabled more open suspicion and hostility toward the refugees. Rumours and assumed eyewitness accounts of the *real* goings-on in Öreby, as opposed to media representations and received wisdom, formed the base of microphysics of outrage, which allowed social relationships between refugees and volunteers to break down. The kindness and good intentions of the volunteers and, more broadly, the villagers progressed into open disdain and suspicion. There was no sudden change of opinion or moment of epiphany when the good Swedish people of Öreby decided to embrace an anti- instead of a pro-refugee sentiment. Likewise, the villagers did not get seduced by a right-wing ideology. The disbanding of relations was the final chapter in the appropriation and re-appropriation of the national myth of moral exceptionalism. Solidarity was seen as ironic, rooted in "us" and not "them." In what I have called an ironic compassion fatigue, elaborated on in chapter 4, the Syrians were no longer deemed exciting. Helping them no longer engendered feelings of righteousness, but rather annoyance and wariness. In the same vein, voting for the nationalistic Sweden Democrats, which only a few months earlier would have almost certainly been unthinkable for the volunteers, was now rationalized as a righteous move, justified in terms of protecting schools and the elderly, sometimes even justified as protecting the refugees already settled in Sweden from the throngs of imagined thugs and racists who would be sure to mobilize if Sweden's refugee policy continued along the same path.

THE EUROPEAN REFUGEE CRISIS OF 2015–16 AND RECENT DEVELOPMENTS

In response to Europe's so-called refugee crisis, different EU member states initially reacted in completely different ways, from Sweden's and Germany's solidarity approach to the more egoist responses of the UK, France, and Hungary, with Orbán's Hungarian government, as well as Austria's, Slovenia's, and Bulgaria's, erecting fences to try to prevent refugees from entering the country. However, even in the solidarist nations, a significant proportion of local populations were or became uneasy about the number of refugees arriving, leading to an increased call for more stringent measures. In March 2016, shortly after the crisis reached its peak, the EU, at that moment chaired by The Netherlands, reached an agreement with Turkey. It included the provision that in exchange for €6 billion and the promise of visa-free travel to Europe for Turkish nationals, Turkey would guard its borders to prevent refugees from travelling to Europe. The agreement further stipulated that all refugees arriving "illegally" in Europe from Turkey would be sent back there, the aim being to dramatically reduce the incentive for individual refugees to risk crossing to Europe (Carrera and Guild 2016). During the same time frame, far-right parties have also made gains in elections throughout the West, with many campaigns exploiting the so-called refugee crisis and invoking fear of terrorism or erosion of Western values as a rationale for closing borders or limiting migration. Despite the election of Macron in the French general election of 2017 and Merkel's re-election as German chancellor in 2017, the nationalist wave in Europe is far from over.

Schengenland and the Re-introduction of Border Controls

Article 25 of the consolidated version of the Schengen Borders Code (SBC)[1] provides EU member states the option to "exceptionally reintroduce temporary border controls at all or specific parts of its internal borders" within the Schengen area to be decreed as a matter of last resort. In response to the so-called refugee crisis, several member states situated along the most affected migratory routes have made use of this entitlement. From September 2015 onward, several member states invoked these mechanisms, reintroducing internal border controls for a limited period of time. Germany (European Commission 2015b), Austria (European Commission 2015c), and Slovenia (European Commission 2015d) in September 2015 and Sweden, France, Denmark, and Norway shortly afterward saw themselves reintroducing temporary border controls at certain internal borders in accordance with the SBC rules (Europa.eu 2016).

About a year after I returned home, the Swedish government undertook measures to drastically reduce the number of refugees arriving in the country; one of those was reinstating the southern border with Denmark. The ruling centre-left coalition, in talks with the centre-right opposition, also moved to reduce the living allowances that asylum seekers receive; rescinded its decision to grant permanent residency to all Syrians arriving at the border, with the majority of refugees now eligible for a temporary permit lasting between one and three years; made rules on family reunification much more stringent; and only accepted into the country the minimum number of refugees under EU law (see SVT 2015; *Guardian* 2015a). These policies, which would have been unthinkable only a few months previously, have been rationalized both in overt security terms and in the name of the state needing respite from the large numbers of refugees they receive (Regeringen 2015b). A new area of acceptable conduct, discourse, and behaviour toward refugees at the governmental level has been carved out, as was the case in Öreby just over one year previously. These moves, rationalized in terms of burden sharing, were also justified in much more overt security terms. In January 2016, Swedish prime minister Stefan Löfven stated that, "The government now considers that the current situation, with a large number of people entering the country in a relatively short time, poses a *serious threat to public order and national security*" (Löfven, cited in *The Guardian* 2016a, emphasis added). The announcement of the new measures in November also came very shortly after terrorist attacks in Paris by the Islamic State of Iraq and the Levant that killed 130 people. Migration and asylum policy minister Morgan Johansson linked the threat of terrorism with the movement of refugees and the justification of identification checks at the border in helping authorities prevent attacks.

The new discursive framework around refugees therefore much more clearly and explicitly links solidarity with security. As was the case in Öreby, the reification of refugees as victims has enabled them to also be viewed as damaged and deficient, unworthy, and inherently risky. With refugees now openly able to be articulated as threats, the hidden transcript has diminished and the public transcript has changed shape. All political parties in Sweden can now be seen to be "approaching the standpoint of the Sweden Democrats" (Tommy Moller, Department of Political Science, Stockholm, cited in Local 2015). As my research has demonstrated, however, the way in which this grand scheme to be moral exemplar broke down and the manner by which the far right came to represent people who see themselves as good and decent was not simply through the triumph of a competing meta-narrative but also through a series of very diffuse and low-key operations. In different parts of Europe, some more affected by the refugee crisis than others, similar dynamics were taking place.

Germany

August 2015, the height of the so-called crisis, saw German chancellor Angela Merkel's government challenge Sweden's position as Europe's moral superpower with regard to Syrian refugees by offering sanctuary to any Syrian who turned up at the border, regardless of whether they had previously sought asylum in another safe country, and stating that there would be no upper limit to the number of refugees Germany could take. With this move, Germany propelled itself directly into competition with Sweden in the humanitarian stakes, and Merkel's declaration, "We can do this!" (*Wir Schaffen das*) came to define her third term as chancellor. Germany and Sweden were jointly praised by António Guterres, United Nations High Commissioner for Refugees, who urged other member states to adhere to their "clear, legal duty" in accepting refugees and arguing that it was "not sustainable" for only two nations to take the majority of refugees on the continent (Svenska Dagbladet 2015).

Within this discursive frame, Swedish prime minister Stefan Löfven stood alongside Angela Merkel against the restrictive policy of the other EU member states, and the two politicians were at the forefront of lobbying for a forced refugee quota system to be implemented at a European level. Echoing Sweden's long-standing approach to forced refugee quotas within the EU, the government reiterated their "ten point plan" on how EU refugee policy should be reformed:

> The EU must establish a permanent and obligatory redistribution mechanism in the event of disasters. The EU must continue to prioritise the saving of lives. All EU Member States must take their responsibility to maintain the EU's external border and live up to the asylum rules. The EU's asylum and border agencies must be strengthened. The EU must continue to combat the people smugglers. The EU must ensure the efficient and humane return of refugees and agree on a returnee programme.
>
> The EU must quickly agree on a system of safe countries of origin. The EU must drastically increase the number of quota refugees to approximately 100,000. The European Commission must propose more legal routes into the EU. The EU needs a more active foreign and aid policy to help people on the ground. (Regeringen 2015a)

At a press conference detailing these proposals in September 2015, the two politicians articulated their policy "as a question of values," with Merkel stating that Sweden and Germany shared the same view on the refugee crisis (Sverige-Radio 2015). However, in September 2015, one month after Merkel's offer to grant asylum to all Syrians arriving, Germany introduced temporary controls on its border with Austria to cope with the large numbers of refugees it was receiving.

The government also introduced a number of legislative policies in the form of two separate asylum "packages." The first, which came into force in January 2016, included measures such as higher requirements for granting right of residence, lower requirements for deportation imprisonment, the denial of residence for asylum seekers denied refugee status in third safe countries, and the ability to access foreigner's mobile phones to prove their identity (Deutscher Bundestag 2016). The second package proposed the tightening of family reunification rules for people with only subsidiary status and the re-classification of Morocco, Tunisia, and Algeria as safe states, creating a higher threshold for asylum applicants from these three states (Deutscher Bundestag 2016).

Through the end of 2015 and into 2016, there was also a great deal of hostility toward refugees and resistance to Merkel's *Wir Schaffen Das* approach, particularly in former East Germany (Sueddeutsche 2016). Hundreds of arson attacks targeted refugee shelters and a sharp increase in xenophobic-fuelled hate crime was reported. The sexual crimes on New Year's Eve 2015 in Cologne (further discussed below), as well as various terrorist attacks, particularly the attack on a Christmas market in Berlin a year later, saw a great deal of political discourse speak of societal chaos and massive criticism of Merkel's handling of the situation (Reuters 2016a).

Though Merkel won a fourth term as chancellor in the German elections of September 2017, many commentators attributed her loss of authority and the reduction in seats for her conservative Christian Democratic Union of German party (and sister Christian Social Union party in Bavaria) at least in part to resistance regarding her handling of the crisis. These elections simultaneously saw the election into parliament for the first time of the anti-immigration AfD party, which gained the third largest proportion of votes, mainly in eastern and southern regions of the country (FT 2016).

Austria

The situation in Austria perhaps best demonstrates the seemingly paradoxical co-existence between solidarity and exclusion and the ease with which one can give way to the other. Only a few days after 31 August 2015, when Angela Merkel joined Sweden in competing for humanitarian superpower status by declaring that Germany, too, would grant residency to all Syrian refugees arriving at the border, Austria received approximately 15,000 refugees in less than twenty-four hours. The "refugees welcome" movement in Austria mobilized extremely well, and a great number of volunteers and activists gathered to collect and distribute donations, to great media attention. Simultaneously, official state institutions were criticized for their poor handling of the situation and inadequate preparation.

However, this movement to welcome refugees was simultaneously criticized, particularly on social media platforms, and used as a point of departure by right-wing and anti-immigration groups and political parties to launch attacks on the ruling Social Democratic and Green parties' official welcoming policy of refugees into Austria. As early as October 2015, the Freedom Party of Austria campaigned in regional elections on an anti-immigration platform (Kurier 2016). However, It was the general election of October 2017 that saw anti-immigration rhetoric ratcheted up by both the centre-right Austrian People's Party and the far-right Freedom Party, with the leader of the former, Sebastian Kurz, articulating "political Islam" as a threat to Austria throughout the campaign. Both parties increased their voter share by about 13 per cent and, at the time of writing, are likely to form the next government on a mandate for change, reversing the taboo in Austrian politics of mainstream parties working with the Freedom Party (*Telegraph* 2017).

United Kingdom

Even though asylum applications increased in the UK, especially from 2013 to 2015, the country has not been as impacted by the refugee and migration crisis as other EU member states, and the most recent numbers of applications from 2016 actually declined. In the first quarter of 2016, for example (January to March 2016), first-time asylum applications for the UK had dropped by 14 per cent compared to the previous quarter (from 11,695 to 10,065), and the second quarter saw another drop, to 9,765, in first-time asylum applications (European Commission 2016).

Nonetheless, the vote in a popular referendum in June 2016 for the UK to leave the EU can at least partly be attributed to the way the refugee crisis played out in popular imagination and the ways it was linked to issues of national security and terrorism within the Leave campaign, particularly the notion of "taking back control" of borders. The referendum bill was proposed in a political climate that had for a long time been hostile to immigration, both from outside the EU and in the exercise of freedom of movement by

EU nationals. Discourses of immigration were traditionally linked to job security of British nationals and the idea of wage suppression brought about by large-scale unskilled migration. Then–prime minister David Cameron had already proposed several policies in the Conservative Party manifesto of 2015, aside from the Brexit referendum, which could be seen as restrictive toward migration and foreigners: for example, the Immigration Act 2016, which introduced disciplinary measures such as criminal charges for undocumented migrants and those employing or renting accommodation to them as well as promises to the electorate to reduce net migration to the tens of thousands (BBC 2015).

An examination of opinion polls shows that, although there was an initial upswing in support of receiving more refugees immediately after the peak of the so-called crisis in the summer of 2015, this also coincided with an increased support for Brexit in the polls (Business Insider 2015). By the time of the referendum, Vote Leave (supported by Eurosceptic members of the Conservative Party, Labour Party, and UK Independence Party) was openly campaigning on a platform of less immigration. Two weeks before the vote, Leave.EU (supported by the UK Independence Party and funded by Arron Banks) revealed a giant poster of a long queue of mostly male refugees taken the previous year at the Croatia-Slovenia border above the words: "BREAKING POINT: We must break free of the EU and take back our borders."

Although it is impossible to determine the role the refugee crisis played in the Brexit decision, it does demonstrate the way in which the topic of immigration can shape the broader political agenda. The outcome of the Brexit referendum and the policy initiatives of the centre-right government show how a traditionally multicultural and multiracial society like the UK, with a long history of migration, is increasingly adopting more nationalist and isolationist politics.

The Netherlands

The situation in The Netherlands in response to the refugee crisis, as in Germany, Austria, and Sweden, initially saw a great deal of goodwill extended toward those fleeing war. When the crisis reached its peak in September 2015, about 27,000 people signed up to a plan offering spare bedrooms to refugees. Many people also offered to volunteer in other ways, and clothing was collected on such a large scale that organizations collecting items for refugees were obliged to call a halt to donations due to their inability to process the sheer quantity given (Kanne and Klein Kranenburg 2015). In addition, an online survey revealed that 70 per cent of the Dutch population would not object to a refugee centre in their local town, as long as careful procedures were followed by the authorities (*Guardian* 2016b). Nearly half of the respondents said that The Netherlands should always welcome immigrants in search of safety.

However, the end of 2015 also saw several protests, some turning to riots, in Dutch towns regarding government proposals to house refugees and build large-scale refugees' centres. To be clear, most of these protests were directed at the government handling of the situation, poor communication between government and local communities, and decisions to resettle thousands of refugees in small villages (*Guardian* 2016b).

Right-wing parties, however, also gained in popularity during this time, particularly after the incidents in which a sexual crime involving migrants or terrorist incidents took place. For example, on 31 December 2015, about one hundred women in Cologne, as well as other German cities, reported being sexually assaulted and mugged by large groups of men of Arab or North African appearance (*Independent* 2016a). Groups of these drunk and aggressive men were said to have surrounded the women in large groups before closing in to assault them or steal their belongings. Both police and the media were accused of deliberately under-reporting the events so as not to incite anti-immigrant sentiment (*Independent* 2016a). These types of incidents saw an increase in support for Geert Wilders's far-right Party for Freedom in Holland, tied to discourses about how Arabs' views on sexuality and the position of women in society were a threat to Dutch values (NRC 2016).

The Dutch general election of March 2017, about one year after the controversial EU-Turkey deal to prevent refugees from leaving Turkey, saw Mark Rutte from the centre-right People's Party for Freedom and Democracy re-elected as prime minister. This was portrayed as a defeat for populism in that Wilders's Party for Freedom was denied a much-feared majority.

However, in a bid to combat the nativism of the Party for Freedom, both Rutte and the leader of the other centre-right party moved to the right, also engaging in nativist politics, and simultaneously presented themselves as defending so-called Dutch and Christian values against the threat of Islam. Christian Democratic Appeal party leader

Sybrand Buma and Prime Minister Rutte argued on a platform of upholding traditions like Easter eggs and Christmas trees as well as defending the controversial Christmas character Black Pete (Zwarte Piet). Furthermore, Rutte suggested that those with immigrant roots were merely "probationary" as opposed to "real" Dutch people and called on them to "act normal" or "sod off" (*Guardian* 2017a).

THEORETICAL IMPLICATIONS OF MY RESEARCH

Appraising the Nice Guys: The Importance of Critique

Sweden has certainly done far more than any other European nation in sheltering refugees, and has been doing so for many decades. Sweden was a beacon of hope and protection for many people fleeing wars in Vietnam, Chile, Yugoslavia, Iran, and Iraq. The country had taken in a far greater number of refugees per capita long before Aylan Kurdi's body washed up on a Turkish beach and the topic of refugees became "sexy," with Germany competing for capital in having the most moral refugee policy. To take the position of criticizing Swedish policy and everyday practice toward refugees and asylum seekers is to stand on somewhat shaky ground. However, we must also realize that "one cannot stay put in moving sands" (Bauman 1998, 78). To be sure, neither am I am trying to diminish the significance of rationalities of solidarity and their role in providing refugees with not merely a bare life but indeed a decent life. I do not take for granted that the status of an individual as a victim can mobilize compassion and empathy. It is important, however, to be able to understand the political and sociological as opposed to the ethical implications of such a form of governmentality and to open a space for critique, even in these best-case examples. This involves an examination of the limits of the functioning of this type of governmentality, the manner in which solidarity is appropriated as generosity, and the very fragile relationship between a seeming acceptance of the refugees and the complete disbanding of social relations – moves that took place in the story of Öreby and, as we have seen, in the Swedish and, increasingly, European stories.

Certainly, throughout the course of my project, many commentators branded my book a bit "mean"; questioned why I was focusing my attention on Sweden instead of Texas, Greece, or the like; and asked what was really so wrong with generosity, hospitality, and humanitarianism. Would I prefer malevolence, hostility, and open rejection? My response is that this kind of anti-intellectual approach suffocates critique and misunderstands the role of the anthropological rethinking of CSS that I'm proposing. I have never argued that I think the Swedish approach to migration and asylum is hypocritical or that Swedish people are secretly bad or racist. As discussed in the previous chapter, there is no position from which I could exercise objective judgments on individuals; besides which, this would be a highly irrelevant undertaking. Instead, I am interested in the power relations that constructed these subjectivities, in objectivizing these practices of metis and appropriation, and in examining their implications. At times, this may place some of my conclusions in morally and normative ambiguous territory, with this re-humanizing of the far right also legitimizing them and their policies. What I have hoped to show with this book is that relying on people's sense of goodwill – through hospitality, humanitarianism, or the abnormalization of solidarity – is an extremely slippery situation in which to ground refugee and asylum policy. In this instance, the feeling that one has already given too much, one has already done more than their fair share, and thus rendering it legitimate to say "enough is enough," is completely rational. It is no longer about absolute refugee numbers and an ability to cope, but about the perception that nobody else has stepped up – so why should we? It is about the increased disciplinization and categorization of refugees into deserving or undeserving, which comes from the perceived changing of stakes and the idea that as long as "we" are good, right, and want all to be well, then any action "we" take is beyond reproach.

In this way, appraising the nice guys can tell us a great deal more about the normalization of hostility and xenophobia toward migration and refugees than any study of more overt racist or ultra-conservative politics or political acts.

Forgetting Audience, Forgetting Speech Acts: The Gravitas of Political Practices

In January 2016, Prime Minister Löfven of Sweden called refugees entering Sweden a "serious threat to public order and national security" (cited in *Guardian* 2016a). At this (very late) stage in the story, one could therefore point to an all-important speech act – an enunciator situated within the political elite articulating the refugees as a threat to Swedish security – as what political science approaches to the securitization of migration would take as their point of departure. Nonetheless, a focus on speech acts, spokespersons, and political parties would have bypassed all the important elements of how refugees in the Swedish story came to be seen as unworthy and unwelcome. The ontological and epistemological rethinking that I have argued for, which examines the multifarious range of practices and processes that led to this new way of thinking, produces a much richer and more subtle account of the way in which open articulation of the refugees as threatening is now deemed acceptable. It illuminates how taboos are enacted and then disrupted, not through a sudden rupture or through an audience suddenly becoming seduced by an ultra-regressive ideology, but through everyday politics that metamorphose into a scene of security. Instead of a retrospective study of incidences of securitization, a political-anthropological approach enables the evolving process of migration, integration, and rejection to be studied from the beginning of the story, as it unfolds.

Therefore, for securitization approaches that focus only on elite narratives, discourses of humanitarianism and solidarity would still be viewed in opposition to the securitization of refugees and asylum. The Swedish story, despite recent developments, would still most likely be ignored in favour of Denmark's more spectacular centred and official practices.[2] The securitization of migration would still be deemed an ultra-regressive move and could not be conceptualized as decent and righteous, linked to notions of protection and solidarity.

In working within IPS and its shift toward examining the gravitas of security practices far removed from any realm of elites and the cultural milieus in which security knowledge takes shape (cf. Bigo 2002, 2007; Huysmans 2014; Leander 2015; Basaran 2015), my book has argued to move from speech acts or fields of professionals to an anthropology of security by placing ontological primacy on the everyday derived from liveable lives and the ethnographic knowledge stemming from engagement with these lives. In making this possible, the book has put forward the conceptual apparatus of public and hidden transcripts combined with interstitial work that takes place between everyday micro experiences and practices of metis on the one hand and national normative and identity repertoires that take the form of a governmentality of righteousness on the other hand.

Would my project have mattered if the far right did not make such large gains in Sweden, if the decision to grant permanent asylum to all Syrian refugees at the border had not been reversed, and had the border with Denmark not been reinstated? These are questions I am often asked. Do the contingent details only matter because of the bigger picture? It is true that I was in Sweden conducting my fieldwork at a time of change.

And though my book would perhaps still be interesting if the hidden transcript had not become public or the tiny acts of metis and appropriation did not reach the limits of righteousness, in the Foucauldian sense of the word, the conclusions reached would not have been as significant. That is not to say that my research on the everyday appropriations of moral exceptionalism should be seen as some sort of prologue to the more "pressing" matters of spectacular politics. It is just to say that, as analysts of social action, we are interested in the effects of the practices rather than the practices themselves – how these practices can challenge established norms and inform a more far-reaching phenomenon, and how change can be manifested through local and situated operations and techniques rather than at any official level (cf. Neumann 2002; de Certeau 1998). As I stated in chapter 1, when I embarked on this project, I did not expect to be engaging with the far right or those who identified with them. I did not imagine that such a grand scheme to be a moral exemplar would break down to such an extent. Though I could not have predicted these developments a priori or, at the time, pointed to exactly which practices would make a difference, recent changes in Sweden have demonstrated that reconfiguring CSS along more political-anthropological lines could herald some very rich and productive scholarship in understanding this type of phenomena. Indeed, Neumann (2012, 183) articulated the difference between the two fields: "Anthropologists focus on the constitutive, political scientists on the outcome … anthropologists focus on the preconditions for political order, and political scientists on how that order is maintained." Though a somewhat simplistic distinction, Neumann demonstrates the manner in which it is the "blossoming of political anthropology that keeps the classical study of politics alive" (Neumann 2012, 183).

As I stated in chapter 2, the idea of Swedish exceptionalism being consigned to the dustbin of history is an oft-repeated trope. I do not want to add to the literature heralding the end of an era, specifying the end, this time, as occurring now in the aftermath of the refugee crisis instead of in any of the previous years branded as the death of the humanitarian ideal. I do not know what the future holds for asylum policy in Europe or if the so-called wave of populism has now waned. However, my fieldwork has demonstrated the way in which this change in policy, shift in norms, and transformation of taboos is best studied from the point of view of the micropractices of actors far removed from official political circles – prejudices spreading horizontally instead of top-down and new ways of thinking being hatched through microphysics and tiny, seemingly unimportant actions or utterances. The devil, in this instance, is firmly in the anthropological detail.

To briefly reiterate, this book is not intended to inform policy or make recommendations to mainstream political parties on responding to the rising far right. Nor do I wish to advise governments or humanitarian organizations dealing with migration on how to better integrate refugees or how to respond to local resistance or unease over resettlement. These are important issues, but ones that are outside the scope of my study.

The more significant intervention of my book comes from the insistence on a focus on these everyday diffuse micropractices and all their complexity as a means of analyzing the rise of the far right. This approach offers rigorous empirical data and scale of analysis on what is usually addressed through the study of high politics or media. A side effect of the latter is that the far right is positioned as something external, objective, and nothing really to do with us. We can study and document these people, their strategies, and their electoral success, but they remain in a world far away from ours. In contrast, this anthropological approach aims to understand how these previously taboo behaviours and attitudes become normalized by a vast array of people and how we are all implicated in these sets of relations. In documenting the interplay between righteousness and the far right, an anthropological rethinking of CSS is one way of shedding light into this dark corner and helping us to see how becoming far right can happen to anyone.

Notes

PROLOGUE

1 I have not cited this website and have changed some details of the text of the blog to maintain the confidentiality and anonymity of my research subjects.
2 I qualify the term "refugee crisis" with the prefix "so-called" or set it in quotation marks on initial use to demonstrate that I'm critical about the wide use of this terminology. By mobilizing and thus reproducing the labelling of the situation in Europe as "crisis," a certain exceptionality would be invoked and the roots of this crisis obscured. As noted by Jeandesboz and Pallister-Wilkins, the mundane and routine practices of bureaucracies that construct the EU border as a hostile environment underpin the so-called crisis insofar as "crisis and routine are relational as stand as mutual conditions of possibility" (Jeandesboz and Pallister-Wilkins 2016, 2).

CHAPTER ONE

1 As Bigo and Mc Cluskey (2018) point out, there was a great deal of crossover and discussion between the so-called Copenhagen School and other constructivist approaches to security, namely what were labelled "Paris" and "Aberystwyth" schools.
2 Throughout the book, counter-conduct refers to the tiny practices of the Swedish villagers and volunteers that went ever so slightly against the grain of what it meant to stand in complete solidarity with refugees but permitted them to retain their image of righteousness. A Foucauldian term, counter-conduct is important because it is never in a position of exteriority to conduct, is productive and creative, and shapes a new arena in which one can act (hence a more accurate term than resistance or evasion). I

connect these tiny practices of counter-conduct with Scott's notion of a hidden transcript to demonstrate that it was through these very subtle and somewhat concealed acts of appropriation that a new acceptable arena for behaviour toward the refugees was carved out. I discuss the empirical manifestations of counter-conduct in chapter 4.

3 I use this term with particular reference to its Greek origin – *bios* (life) and *opsis* (sight) – to draw attention to the way in which my ethnography aims to provide some sort of cross-section of day-to-day social and political life at the level of micropractices, from my perspective.

4 I conducted the first ten months of fieldwork in one block visit. The remainder of the primary research was undertaken in nine two-to-three-week visits spread over nine months, until my final visit to Öreby in September 2014.

5 In terms of research ethics, my fieldwork complied with all requirements of the Ethical Approval Committee at King's College, London. All participants were provided with an information sheet detailing the nature of my project. In addition, participants who were interviewed and recorded were required to sign a consent form (translated into Swedish when required) permitting me to use this data. The consent form made clear that any names of participants would be anonymized and that withdrawal of their approval could be granted at any time before April 2016.

6 As the refugees were in a more vulnerable position than the Swedish participants of my study, I did not have the same access to any hidden transcript of the Syrians. However, with villagers openly speaking about the Syrians as undesirable, we see the open articulation of outrage on the part of the Syrians, pointing to the unease that had built up on their part. The last section of chapter 4 – in which one Syrian woman exclaimed that they "are not a human fucking zoo" – discusses the relational element of the processes of distancing between the villagers and Syrians.

7 I use the term "governable subject" throughout the book not as a metaphor but as a theoretical concept based in the work of Nikolas Rose and his reflections on governmentality. This concept stresses that there is no pre-given self prior to subjectification and thus emphasizes the salutary elements of the Swedish national myth of moral superpowerfulness, and its role in shaping subjects who self-identify as tolerant, generous, and standing in solidarity with those who are suffering.

8 I utilize the notions of "good" and "decent" interchangeably throughout when describing citizens to refer to actors operating within the "governmentality of righteousness." I use "citizen" instead of "person" to draw explicit links with the national myth and the way in which this national myth

creates a certain subjectivity and generates certain self-images, particularly one in which it is somewhat bad taste to criticize asylum policy. The good and decent citizen also embodies a relational element – not the idea that a person's behaviour is somehow inherently good or decent in itself but the idea that it is judged good or decent by others, which is important.

9 I borrow the term "worthy" or "deserving" guest from the literature on Maussian hospitality, particularly that of Rozakou (2012). This notion emphasizes the need on the part of the Swedish villagers for reciprocity from the refugees and the hierarchical power relationship between the villagers, who fashion themselves as "hosts" and the refugees who are deemed "guests." The guests are thus obliged to play by all the rules of hospitality as they are temporarily placed in the moral universe of the host. I expand on the empirical manifestations of this phenomenon in chapter 3 and on the theoretical and conceptual implications of this idea of worthy or deserving guest in chapter 5. Similarly, the notion of the "ungrateful" refugee comes directly from my field, voiced numerous times by the volunteers in the Friends of Syria. It is inherently linked to the idea of the refugees as worthy or deserving with the desire for refugees to always show gratitude to their hosts as one of the most important features of the relationship of debt and patronage at play. The most notable example is the story of Ahmed, who attempted to swap a jacket he had been given for another, only to be chastized by one of the volunteers for not appreciating the sacrifices the Swedish people had made to give him a jacket in the first place.

CHAPTER TWO

1 This chapter focuses on comparative statistics from the period leading up to and during my fieldwork: February 2013 to September 2014. These statistics, and Sweden's position on permanent residency for Syrian refugees as well as its approach to refugee resettlement in conjunction with the European Union and the unhcr, has changed since the time of writing. I address these changes, and how they affect the governmentality of righteousness, in the concluding chapter.

2 Sociologically, this transformation of solidarity with regard to asylum policy could also be seen as a reaction by the Social Democrat government to the successful lobbying of the Swedish Trade Union Confederation in 1968, which required all non-Nordic migrants to acquire a work permit and housing before entering the country, with the aim of preventing unemployment among Swedish residents (Pred 2000, 41). However, these stricter rules did not extend to refugees or those Sweden chose to admit for humanitarian

reasons such as "draft dodging." In the early 1970s, therefore, with widespread recession and lowering of growth rates, Olof Palme's government began to increase the number of migrants admitted under these criteria, beginning with large numbers of Chilean intellectuals at risk under Pinochet's regime (Pred 2000, 42–3). This new reconfiguration of the country's immigration scheme, coupled with Palme's active stand against foreign interventions, helped reinforce the notion of solidarity once again, this time linked with a common humanity and egalitarian intent (Pred 2000, 42).

3 Important to point out here is that before 1970, the vast majority of immigration to Sweden was a result of labour migration, whereby Swedish companies actively recruited from neighbouring European countries (Kamali 1997). Immigration controls were introduced in 1967, coinciding somewhat with the oil crisis of 1973, and labour migration practically ceased in the immediate period following these events. Therefore, post-1970, the bulk of Swedish immigration was the result of refugee intake and family reunification (Kamali 1997, 146). However, in the 1970s, the vast majority (80 per cent) of all refugees came from other European nations, primarily Poland, Czechoslovakia, and Hungary. It was from 1980 onward that significant numbers of immigrants arrived from outside of Europe, with about 50 per cent of immigrants coming from non-European nations (Kamali 1997, 145).

4 Chapter 5 looks at the tensions present within the Swedish notion of solidarity as rational egoism and solidarity as a "gift," arguing that it is the messiness and fluidity of the concept within political discourse that renders the concept an empty signifier and enables its appropriation as humanitarianism and generosity, thus requiring some kind of "counter-gift."

5 In practice, however, there are a greater number of exceptions to the requirement than in other member states, including family members of minors, refugees, quota refugees, persons enjoying international protection, and persons who have a residence permit and have spent four years in Sweden with a residence permit, as well as exemptions in cases where there are exceptional grounds (European Migration Network, 2013).

6 It must be noted that the media response from Denmark regarding the Swedish public portrayal of Denmark as racist was equally scathing in painting Sweden as in denial of its immigration problems and as readily curtailing freedom of speech in relation to migration and asylum. In a response to Sundström's book, mentioned above, Danish journalist Mikael Jalving wrote the book *Absolute Sweden: A Journey in a Wealth of Silence*, released in Swedish under the more neutral title *Absolute Sweden: A Country in Change*. It claimed that the suppression of discussion regarding immigration

and asylum, particularly the marginalization from mainstream debate of the Sweden Democrats, the political elite, and media in Sweden, was in fact inadvertently fuelling extremism.

7 Bourdieu's famous denunciation of the use of opinion polls in his article "Public Opinion Does Not Exist" provides an interesting point of departure to critique the political uses and social effects of these comparative polls. For Bourdieu (1993), the three tacit assumptions at the basis of polls are brought into question: the idea that everyone can or does have an opinion; the notion that all opinions are of equal worth; and lastly, and most importantly, that there exists some sort of *prior consensus* about the problem and about what questions are deemed worthy of asking. In this respect, "public opinion" as presented in the form of spot survey statistics in newspapers "is a pure and simple artefact whose function is to dissimulate the fact that the state of the opinion at a given moment is a system of forces, of tensions." He points out how there is practically no "catch-all problem" that is not re-interpreted in function of the "interests and non-interests of the people to whom the question is posed. With particular regard to the Swedish case, Pred (2000, 85) dismisses similar Eurobarometer results as "denial" and "projection." He points to Eurobarometer polls conducted during the 1990s whereby only 2 per cent of Swedes admitted to being "very racist," the lowest figure in the entire European Union. Furthermore, he points out how denial of racism among individuals in Sweden is most widespread among those generations born in the 1950s who were most intensely subjected to the Social Democrat ideology of "solidarity" and "equality." For Pred (2000, 85), denial of racism reverberates with elements of identity that have long rested on a taken-for-granted view that their country is best in the world at social justice. He points out that it is the social taboos within Sweden on admitting to any form of racism that cause Swedes to feel a great deal of unease and personal conflict in admitting any sort of racist attitude and thus to answer negatively in order to reduce cognitive dissonance. He also lists a wide range of Swedish critics of the methodology of the polls, since subjects, as in most polls, are confronted with a very narrow set of predetermined options rather than being permitted to articulate their own position at length.

8 Interestingly, however, when examining *actual* gender pay gaps, Sweden is situated in the centre of the table, with the fourteenth-highest pay gap between male and female earnings, behind states such as Romania and Poland (Eurostat 2011a, Figure 9); in previous reports, it had the twelfth-highest pay gap (Eurostat 2010, 311) and the thirteenth-highest (Eurostat, 2009, 105).

9 In its most recent evaluation of development aid distributed by its DAC, the OECD "commends Sweden for Sweden for budgeting to reach its 1% ODA/GNI target each year since its last peer review in a climate of global financial crisis" (OECD 2013). This makes Sweden one of only five states in the world to meet the UN target of allocating at least 0.7 per cent of GNI to developmental assistance. With 0.99 per cent allocated in 2012, Sweden was second to Luxembourg (OECD 2013).

10 The only political party to raise any objection to this decision was the Sweden Democrats, who held twenty seats in the Riksdag and who argued that the policy was actually "inhumane" as money could be spent more effectively by being directed toward food, medicine, and shelter for Syrian refugees in Syria's neighbouring countries (Ken Ekoroth, spokesperson for the Sweden Democrats).

11 The concluding chapter 6 provides an analysis of the change in the media position in light of the subsequent refugee crisis and the shift that now renders it acceptable for mainstream media to criticize Swedish asylum policy.

12 This obligation refers primarily to article 78(2)(g) of the Treaty on the Functioning of the European Union (TFEA), which requires "measures on partnership and cooperation" with third countries.

13 This notion of intra-EU solidarity relates to article 80 of TFEA, which states that "policies of the Union ... shall be governed by the principles of solidarity and the fair sharing of responsibility, including its financial implications." According to the European Migration Network, intra-EU relocation has, until now, been carried out in the context of the Intra-EU Relocation from Malta Project (EUREMA). Established by the EU, the program co-funded the relocation activities of member states that agreed to receive from Malta recognized beneficiaries of international protection. In 2011, ten Member States received 227 refugees relocated from Malta via EUREMA. In a second phase of the project in 2012, seven member states pledged 86 places. A further eight collectively pledged to receive 233 refugees via bilateral agreements with Malta.

14 Sweden accepted 1,922 new arrivals in 2009 as part of the UNHCR resettlement program, 1,776 in 2010, 1,885 in 2011, 1,827 in 2012, 1,900 in 2013, and 1,950 in 2014. In 2009, most arrivals came from Iran and Iraq; in 2010 from Somalia, Afghanistan, Eritrea, and Iraq, in 2011 from Somalia, Afghanistan, and Eritrea; in 2012 from Afghanistan, Eritrea, Colombia, and Somalia; and in 2013 from Somalia, Afghanistan, and Eritrea (Eurostat 2013). These numbers have been significantly higher than the EU member state receiving the second-highest number of resettlement refugees, namely the UK, which has accepted about 750

arrivals in the past three years. It must be stressed that the UNHCR resettlement program differs from the 5,000 "humanitarian admission" places offered by Germany in 2013. Though these places are also based on protection criteria in conjunction with the UNHCR, they differ from resettlement places in that they offer temporary admission only (two years) and use a simplified selection process.

15 Integration criteria has been adopted by the Czech Republic, Denmark, the Netherlands, Finland, France, Germany, and Slovenia. In Romania, the potential for integration was applied in 2008, but dropped in 2012 in the revised resettlement program after discussions with the UNHCR. Austria has strict integration criteria, mostly requiring that the resettled refugees are Christians. Denmark also has incorporated the integration potential criteria into legislation and added supplementary criteria of influence: language qualifications, education and work experience, social network, age, and motivation (Section 8 (4) of the Aliens Act, Denmark. According to a recent study, the Dutch minister for immigration, Integration, and asylum proposed in 2012 to the UNHCR that they be permitted to resettle "high profile" refugees such as academics and human rights activists (Perrin and McNamara 2013).

16 Chapter 4 discusses how this notion of gender equality became a legitimate terrain through which the decent Swedish citizen could hierarchize the Syrian refugees in the village of Öreby.

CHAPTER THREE

1 The next chapter discusses the implications of the refusal of Migrationsverket to listen to the concerns of the villagers: the sense of powerlessness it engendered among the inhabitants and its role in generating the taboo.

2 I discuss the notion of a solidarity of irony (Chouliaraki 2010, 2013) further in the following chapter when I examine the practices that pushed at the very limits of the governmentality of righteousness.

3 Scott (1990, 47) draws on Pierre Bourdieu to argue that rules of social etiquette are always infused with power and contain political concessions enabling users to interact with others in an appropriate manner. This "grammar of social intercourse" is most notable in the presence of "powerful strangers," whereby failure to observe these rules is most apparent (Scott 1990, 47–8).

4 Allan Pred (2000) has written extensively of the moral panic created by the Swedish press in building up a "hysteria-like climate" and

constructing the residents of Sjobo as a "danger to society" (Pred 2000, 191). He talks of the central place of Sjobo in the popular geographical imagination of the 1990s. Here, Sjoboites are demonized within a reductionist black-and-white picture of racism so that the majority of Swedes could simply write off the particular municipality as an anomaly.

5 The most striking example of citizens actively resisting a governmental agency due to its controversial actions concerns police use of the REVA policy, whereby they stopped and searched suspected undocumented migrants on the metro and demanded to see their identification. Once this came to light, it was condemned by all political parties except the Sweden Democrats. What is interesting is the huge backlash from the public and the attempts to sabotage police action, such as setting up a Facebook page where people could report exactly where the police were operating that day.

6 As with Scott's "powerful stranger" (1990, 47), as discussed above, "guardians of taste and decorum" impose a dominating effect on social relations, ensuring individuals abide by all the rules of etiquette and politeness.

7 The old myths of "Jantelagen" (Jante's Law) and "Lagom" (moderation) were often hinted at in these conversations with foreigners, wherein the Swedish way is described as viewing negatively any showy displays of individual success or excess. This was often the case, even though today, these ideas of Jantelagen and Lagom are viewed by most as tired, irrelevant clichés from an earlier generation.

8 Chapter 5 draws more on this literature (cf. Fassin 2010; Agier 2011; Redfield 2013) and goes into greater depth on the concept of solidarity as humanitarianism and hospitality in relation to the gift, arguing that though Swedish political discourse conceives solidarity in a rational, egoist way, its appropriation is akin to a Maussian "gift economy," complete with obligations of gratitude and changing stakes.

9 The next chapter discusses the idea of compassion fatigue and the role this played in the relationship between the volunteers and the Syrian refugees. The notion of compassion fatigue is completely undertheorized but, in everyday vernacular, refers to the wearing down of sympathy until it turns into indifference or anger toward the victims of adversity. Emphasizing the ironic element of this relationship, i.e., the way in which the waning of sympathy prevents "us" from feeling good and decent, I label the type of compassion fatigue at play among the Friends of Syria an ironic compassion fatigue. This links together the idea of a governmentality of righteousness, one that sees the production of subjects who view themselves as

good and decent, with the increasingly legitimate ability to articulate the refugees as undesirable, undeserving, and dispensable.
10 Important to note is that this mechanism is not a psychological reaction, but a purely sociological phenomenon in which the member of an "outsider" group pursues an individualist strategy to gain access to an "established" group. Elias and Scotson ([1964] 1994) have written about the desire of some members of the disenfranchised to be integrated so that they come to despise the rest of the group in order to distance themselves from the logics of subordination at play.

CHAPTER FOUR

1 A large body of scholarship relating to "feminist Orientalism" (Zonana 1993) explores the way in which assumptions about the East have been used throughout history to further the Western feminist project, most notably Spivak's (1985) critique of Charlotte Bronte's *Jane Eyre* and Bannerji's (1997) reading of Mary Wollstonecraft's *A Vindication of the Rights of Woman* (1792).
2 Elias and Scotson's ([1964] 1994) groundbreaking work *The Established and the Outsiders* sheds light on this "in group/ out group" dynamic, demonstrating that newcomers become marginalized not due to class, income, or origin but due to relationships of mutual dependency that the "established" form through school, work, places of worship, and social spaces. This power structure survives when transferred from generation to generation in what the authors label the "monopolised transfer of specific abilities" (Elias and Scotson ([1964] 1994).
3 Cohen is but one of a number of scholars to examine the social and political impact of rumours. Morin's (1971) *Rumour in Orléans*, a famous study of young women being abducted and sold into slavery by "Jews" was one of the first to systematically study how rumour and legend reflects the uncertainties and phobias of the communities that produce them, arguing that this particular rumour dovetailed with a town in a period of transition, whereby the provincial ideal was slowly dying. Though rumour has been recognized as one of the most important contributing factors to prejudice and violence (Knopf 1975), Fine (2009) notes the relatively little systematic scholarly analysis devoted to the subject, with research spread between the fields of mass media and communication, sociology, psychology, and anthropology.

CHAPTER FIVE

1 In Scott's (1990, 210) original thesis, the timing of this "breaking the silence" can never be predicted and the conditions under which it occurs can vary; however, he does note the existence of circumstances that lower the danger of speaking out to the extent that the previously conforming would now be emboldened, such as the USSR's *glasnost* campaign, whereby a disgruntled party member openly sent a telegram to Gorbachev to complain about policy.
2 Then–prime minister Fredrik Reinfeldt famously called on the Swedish people to "open their hearts to refugees" while campaigning for the re-election of the conservative *Moderaterna* party in August 2014.
3 The challenge presented to Sweden's moral superpower image by Merkel's Germany in the summer of 2015 is reflected upon in chapter 6. We see the way in which Sweden aligned itself with Germany in standing against the hardline practices of other EU member states and was engaged in a type of cat-and-mouse game of adhering to the Schengen agreement and refraining from introducing border controls.
4 In practice, however, due to a backlog in processing applications, refugees were often left in Migrationsverket accommodation long after being granted residence permits.

CHAPTER SIX

1 The consolidated version of the Schengen Border Codes (Regulation (EU) 2016/399) was adopted only in March 2016. The new regulation introduced a number of amendments. Among others, newly introduced in article 29 was a special procedure for the reintroduction of temporary border controls to be decreed by member states "in exceptional circumstances that put at risk the overall functioning of the Schengen system as such." This provision has been invoked by the Council to recommend prolongations to the temporary internal border controls carried out by the member states concerned.
2 In January 2016, for example, the Danish parliament had approved plans to seize the valuable assets of all asylum seekers arriving in the country in order to help pay for maintenance costs (*Independent* 2016).

References

Agamben, Giorgio. 1998. *Homo Sacer: Sovereign Power and Bare Life*. Palo Alto: Stanford University Press.
Agier, Michel. 2002. "Between War and City towards an Urban Anthropology of Refugee Camps." *Ethnography* 3 (3): 317–41.
– 2011. *Managing the Undesirables*. Cambridge: Polity.
Albro, Robert. 2011. *Anthropologists in the Securityscape: Ethics, Practice, and Professional Identity*. Walnut Creek, CA: Left Coast Press.
Al-Jazeera. 2016. "Denmark and Sweden Tighten Border Controls." 4 January. www.aljazeera.com/news/2016/01/denmark-sweden-tighten-border-control-160104140849704.html (accessed 12 April 2016).
Ålund, Alexandra, and Carl-Ulrik Schierup. 1991. *Paradoxes of Multiculturalism: Essays on Swedish Society*. Aldershot: Avebury.
Amnesty International. 2015. "Syria's Refugee Crisis in Numbers." 4 September. www.amnesty.org/en/latest/news/2015/09/syrias-refugee-crisis-in-numbers/ (accessed 12 April 2016).
Amoore, Louise. 2013. *The Politics of Possibility: Risk and Security Beyond Probability*. Durham, NC: Duke University Press.
Amoore, Louise, and Marieke De Goede. 2008. *Risk and the War on Terror*. London: Routledge.
Andersson, Ruben. 2014. *Illegality, Inc.: Clandestine Migration and the Business of Bordering Europe*. Berkeley, CA: University of California Press.
Appadurai, Arjun. 1996. *Modernity at Large: Cultural Dimensions of Globalization*. Vol. 1. Minneapolis: University of Minnesota Press.
Aradau, Claudia. 2004. "The Perverse Politics of Four-Letter Words: Risk and Pity in the Securitisation of Human Trafficking." *Millennium* 33 (2): 251–77.

Aradau, Claudia, and Tobias Blanke. 2017. "Politics of Prediction: Security and the Time/Space of Governmentality in the Age of Big Data." *European Journal of Social Theory* 20 (3): 373–91.

Aradau, Claudia, Luis Lobo-Guerrero, and Rens Van Munster. 2008. "Security, Technologies of Risk, and the Political: Guest Editors' Introduction." Los Angeles, CA: Sage Publications.

Armstrong, John Alexander. 1982. *Nations before Nationalism*. Chapel Hill, NC: University of North Carolina Press.

Austin, Jonathan Luke. Forthcoming. "A Parasitic Critique for IR." *International Political Sociology*.

Balzacq, Thierry. 2016. "Securitization: Understanding the Analytics of Government." In *Theorizing Internal Security Cooperation in the European Union*, edited by Raphael Bossong and Mark Rhinard, 45–63. Oxford: Oxford University Press.

Balzacq, Thierry, Tugba Basaran, Didier Bigo, Emmanuel-Pierre Guittet, and Christian Olsson. 2010. "Security Practices." *International Studies Encyclopedia Online* 18.

Basaran, Tugba. 2008. "Security, Law, Borders: Spaces of Exclusion." *International Political Sociology* 2 (4): 339–54.

– 2015. "The Saved and the Drowned: Governing Indifference in the Name of Security." *Security Dialogue* 46 (3): 205–20.

Basaran, Tugba, Didier Bigo, Emmanuel-Pierre Guittet, and R.B.J. Walker. 2016. "Transversal Lines." *International Political Sociology: Transversal Lines*: 1.

Bauman, Zygmunt. 1998. *Globalization: The Human Consequences*. New York: Columbia University Press.

BBC. 2005. "Denmark's Immigration Issue." 19 February. http://news.bbc.co.uk/1/hi/4276963.stm (accessed 12 December 2017).

– 2013a. "Sweden's Asylum Offer to Syrian Refugees." www.bbc.co.uk/news/world-europe-24635791 (accessed 12 December 2017).

– 2013b. "'Sweden Will Remain Open to Migrants' – Migration Minister Tobias Billstrom." 23 October. www.bbc.co.uk/news/world-europe-24630951 (accessed 12 December 2017).

– 2015. "General Election 2015: Result." 8 May. www.bbc.co.uk/news/election/2015 (accessed 12 December 2017).

– 2016. "Race and Religious Hate Crimes Rose 41% After EU Vote." 13 October. www.bbc.co.uk/news/uk-politics-37640982 (accessed 12 December 2017).

– 2017. "Conservative Manifesto Summary: Key Points At-a-Glance." 18 May. www.bbc.co.uk/news/election-2017-39960311 (accessed 12 December 2017).

Beckman, Ninna Edgardh, Thomas Ekstrand, and Per Pettersson. 2006. "The Church of Sweden as an Agent of Welfare: The Case of Gävle." In *Churches in Europe as Agents of Welfare: Sweden, Norway, and Finland*, edited by Anne Birgitta Yeung with Ninna Edgardh Beckman and Per Pettersson, 20–85. Uppsala: Uppsala Institute for Diaconal and Social Studies.

Beerli, Monique J. 2018. "Saving the Saviors: Security Practices and Professional Struggles in the Humanitarian Space." *International Political Sociology* 12 (1): 70–87.

Behar, Ruth. 2003. "Ethnography and the Book that Was Lost." *Ethnography* 4 (1): 15–39.

Beier, J. Marshall. 2005. *International Relations in Uncommon Places: Indigeneity, Cosmology, and the Limits of International Theory*. New York: Macmillan.

Bergman, Annika. 2007. "Co-Constitution of Domestic and International Welfare Obligations: The Case of Sweden's Social Democratically Inspired Internationalism." *Cooperation and Conflict* 42 (1): 73–99.

Berthélemy, Jean-Claude. 2005. "Bilateral Donors' Interest vs. Recipients' Development Motives in Aid Allocation: Do All Donors Behave the Same?" *Cahiers de la Maison des Sciences Economiques* 1: 179–94.

Bhambra, Gurminder K. 2010. "Historical Sociology, International Relations and Connected Histories." *Cambridge Review of International Affairs* 23 (1): 127–43.

Bigo, Didier. 2002. "Security and Immigration: Toward a Critique of the Governmentality of Unease." *Alternatives* 27 (1_suppl): 63–92.

– 2007. "Detention of Foreigners, States of Exception, and the Social Practices of Control of the Banopticon." *Borderscapes: Hidden Geographies and Politics at Territory's Edge* 29: 3–34.

– 2014a. "Afterword Security: Encounters, Misunderstandings and Possible Collaborations." In *Anthropology of Security: Perspectives from the Frontline of Policing, Counter-Terrorism and Border Control*, edited by M. Maguire, C. Frois, and N. Zurawski, 189–206. London: Pluto Press.

– 2014b. "The (In)Securitization Practices of the Three Universes of EU Border Control: Military/Navy–Border Guards/Police–Database Analysts." *Security Dialogue* 45 (3): 209–25.

Bigo, Didier, and R. B. Walker. 2007. "Political Sociology and the Problem of the International." *Millennium* 35 (3): 725–39.
Bigo, Didier, and Emma Mc Cluskey. 2018. "What Is a Paris Approach to (In)securitization? Political Anthropological Research for International Sociology." In *The Oxford Handbook of International Security*, edited by Alexandra Gheciu and William C. Wohlforth, 116–30. Oxford: Oxford University Press.
Billig, Michael. 1995. *Banal Nationalism*. London: Sage.
Bloomberg. 2006. "'Love Bridge' Fuels Anti-Immigrant Backlash on Swedish Border." 12 November. www.bloomberg.com/apps/news?pid=newsarchive&sid=a4l9dsYOR42g (accessed 12 April 2016).
Boltanski, Luc. 2000. *Distant Suffering: Morality, Media and Politics*. Cambridge: Cambridge University Press.
Booth, Michael. 2014. *The Almost Nearly Perfect People: The Truth about the Nordic Miracle*. London: Random House.
Bourdieu, Pierre. 1993. *Sociology in Question*. Vol. 18. London: Sage.
Brass, Paul R., David Taylor, and Malcolm Yapp. 2000. "Elite Groups, Symbol Manipulation and Ethnic Identity among the Muslims of South Asia." *Nationalism: Critical Concepts in Political Science* 3: 879.
Brauman, Rony. 1994. *Devant Le Mal: Rwanda, Un Génocide En Direct*. Paris: Arléa.
– 2000. *L'action Humanitaire*. Paris: Flammarion.
Brown, Andrew. 2011. *Fishing in Utopia*. London: Granta Books.
Brubaker, Rogers. 1996. *Nationalism Reframed: Nationhood and the National Question in New Europe*. Cambridge: Cambridge University Press.
– 2010. "Charles Tilly as a Theorist of Nationalism." *The American Sociologist* 41 (4): 375–81.
Burchell, Graham. 2011. "Peculiar Interests: Civil Society and Governing 'the System of Natural Liberty.'" In *The Foucault Effect: Studies in Governmentality*, edited by G. Burchell, G. Gordon, and P. Miller, 119–50. Chicago: University of Chicago Press.
Business Insider. 2015. "The Refugee Crisis Is Killing Britain's Chances of Staying within the EU." 19 October. http://uk.businessinsider.com/hsbc-research-refugee-crisis-could-cause-an-eu-referendum-brexit-2015-10 (accessed 12 December 2017).
Buzan, Barry, Ole Wæver, and Jaap De Wilde. 1998. *Security: A New Framework for Analysis*. Boulder, CO: Lynne Rienner Publishers.
Calhoun, Craig. 1994. *Nationalism and Civil Society: Democracy, Diversity and Self-Determination*. Fairfax, VA: George Mason University Press.

– 1997. *Nationalism*. Minneapolis: University of Minnesota Press.
Campbell, David. 1992. *Writing Security: United States Foreign Policy and the Politics of Identity*. Minneapolis: University of Minnesota Press.
Candea, Matei. 2007. "Arbitrary Locations: In Defence of the Bounded Field-Site." *Journal of the Royal Anthropological Institute* 13 (1): 167–84.
Candea, Matei, and Giovanni Da Col. 2012. "The Return to Hospitality." *Journal of the Royal Anthropological Institute* 18 (s1): S1–S19.
Carrera, Sergio, and Elspeth Guild. 2016. *EU-Turkey Plan for Handling Refugees Is Fraught with Legal and Procedural Challenges*. Brussels: Centre for European Policy Studies.
CASE Collective. 2006. "Critical Approaches to Security in Europe: A Networked Manifesto." *Security Dialogue* 37 (4): 443–87.
CBC. 2014. "Bastion of Tolerance Sweden Opens Doors Wide for Syrian Refugees."25 January.www.cbc.ca/news/world/bastion-of-tolerance-sweden-opens-wide-for-syria-s-refugees-1.2508166 (accessed 12 April 2016).
Certeau, Michel de. 1988. *The Practice of Everyday Life*. Translated by Steven Rendall. Berkeley: University of California Press.
– 1990. *Linvention Du Quotidien: Arts De Faire*. Paris: Gallimard.
Charalambous, Constadina. 2009. "Learning the Language of 'the Other': A Linguistic Ethnography of Turkish-Language Classes in a Greek-Cypriot School." London: King's College London (University of London).
Charalambous, Constadina, Panayiota Charalambous, Kamran Khan, and Ben Rampton. 2015. "Sociolinguistics and Security." In *Working Papers in Urban Languages and Literacy*, edited by Ben Rampton, 1–19. London: King's College London.
Childs, Marquis W. 1966. *Sweden: The Middle Way*. New Haven: Yale University Press.
Chouliaraki, Lilie. 2011. "'Improper Distance': Toward a Critical Account of Solidarity as Irony." *International Journal of Cultural Studies* 14 (4): 363–81.
– 2013. *The Ironic Spectator: Solidarity in the Age of Post-Humanitarianism*. Hoboken, NJ: John Wiley & Sons.
Clifford, James. 1983. "On Ethnographic Authority." *Representations* (2): 118–46.
Cohen, Stanley. 1980. *Folk Devils and Moral Panics: The Creation of the Mods and Rockers*. London: Psychology Press.
– 2001. *States of Denial: Knowing about Atrocities and Suffering*. Hoboken, NJ: John Wiley & Sons.

Coleman, Lara Montesinos. 2015. "Ethnography, Commitment, and Critique: Departing from Activist Scholarship." *International Political Sociology* 9 (3): 263–80.

Coleman, Lara Montesinos, and Doerthe Rosenow. 2017. "Beyond Biopolitics: Struggles over Nature." In *Routledge Handbook of Biopolitics*, edited by Sergio Prozorov and Simona Rentea, 260–78. London: Routledge.

Côté-Boucher, Karine, Federica Infantino, and Mark B. Salter. 2014. "Border Security as Practice: An Agenda for Research." *Security Dialogue* 45 (3): 195–208.

Dagen. 2013. "Viktigt Svenskt Beslut Angaende Syrien." 4 September. www.dagen.se/opinion/ledare/i-korthet/viktigt-svenskt-beslut-angaende-syrien/ (accessed 12 April 2016).

Dagens Nyheter. 2010. "Axen Stolt över Sveriges Migrationslagar." 6 August. www.dn.se/nyheter/sverige/axel-stolt-over-migrationslagar/ (accessed 30 May 2011).

– 2012. "Sverige får högst betyg i integrationspolitik" 23 June. www.dn.se/sverige/sverige-far-hogst-betyg-i-integrationspolitik/ (accessed 6 October 2013).

– 2013. "Ledare: Syriska Flyktingar: Rätt Att Öppna Dörren." 4 September. www.dn.se/ledare/signerat/syriska-flyktingar-ratt-att-oppna-dorren/ (accessed 12 April 2016).

– 2014. "Se 2014 Års Valresultat." 12 September. www.dn.se/valet-2014/se-2014-ars-valresultat/ (accessed 12 April 2016).

– 2015a. "Kraftig Förändring – Fler Vill Se Ökat Flyktingmottagande." 27 September. www.dn.se/nyheter/sverige/kraftig-foran-dring-fler-vill-se-okat-flyktingmottagande/ (accessed 12 April 2016).

– 2015b. "Löfven: 'Mitt Europa Bygger Inte Murar.'" 6 September. www.dn.se/sthlm/lofven-mitt-europa-bygger-inte-murar/ (accessed 12 April 2016).

Dahl, Ann-Sophie. 2006. "Sweden: Once a Moral Superpower, Always a Moral Superpower?" *International Journal* 61 (4): 895–908.

Dahlstedt, Magnus. 2005. "*Reserverad Demokrati: Representation I Ett Mångetniskt Sverige.*" Borea: Borea Bokforlag.

– 2008. "The Politics of Activation: Technologies of Mobilizing 'Multiethnic Suburbs' in Sweden." *Alternatives: Global, Local, Political* 33 (4): 481–504.

Dalby, Simon. 2013. "Biopolitics and Climate Security in the Anthropocene." *Geoforum* 49: 184–92.

Dansk Folkeparti. 2010. "Principprogram." www.danskfolkeparti.dk/Principprogram.asp (accessed 12 April 2016).
Daun, Åke. 1996. *Swedish Mentality*. Pennsylvania: Penn State Press.
Davidshofer, Stéphan, Julien Jeandesboz, and Francesco Ragazzi. 2016. "Technology and Security Practices: Situating the Technological Imperative." *International Political Sociology: Transversal Lines* London: Routledge.
Davidson, Arnold I. 2007. "Introduction." In *Michel Foucault: Security, Territory, Population. Lectures at the College de France,* edited by Arnold I. Davidson xix–xxxiv. New York: Macmillan.
– 2011. "In Praise of Counter-Conduct." *History of the Human Sciences* 24 (4): 25–41.
Davis, Kevin E., Benedict Kingsbury, and Sally Engle Merry. 2010."Indicators as a Technology of Global Governance." *NYU Law and Economics Research Paper* (10–13): 10–26.
De Genova, Nicholas. 2002. "Migrant 'Illegality' and Deportability in Everyday Life." *Annual Review of Anthropology*: 419–47.
– 2005. *Working the Boundaries: Race, Space, and "Illegality" in Mexican Chicago*. Durham nc: Duke University Press.
– 2010. "The Deportation Regime: Sovereignty, Space and the Freedom of Movement." In *The Deportation Regime: Sovereignty, Space and the Freedom of Movement*, edited by N. Peutz and N. De Genova, 33–68. Durham, NC: Duke.
Dean, Mitchell. 2002. "Liberal Government and Authoritarianism." *Economy and Society* 31 (1): 37–61.
– 2010. *Governmentality: Power and Rule in Modern Society*. London: Sage.
Detienne, Marcel, and Jean-Pierre Vernant. 1991. *Cunning Intelligence in Greek Culture and Society*. Translated by Janet Lloyd. Chicago: University of Chicago Press.
Dillon, M., and J. Reid. 1999. "Metis and the Problematic of Hyper Security." Paper presented at the ISA meeting, Washington, DC, February.
Dunn Cavelty, Myriam Anna. 2007. *Cyber-Security and Threat Politics: US Efforts to Secure the Information Age*. London: Routledge.
Durkheim, Emile. (1893) 1964. *The Division of Labour in Society*. New York: Free Press.
Eckl, Julian. 2008. "Responsible Scholarship after Leaving the Veranda: Normative Issues Faced by Field Researchers – and Armchair Scientists." *International Political Sociology* 2 (3): 185–203.

Elias, Norbert, and John L. Scotson. (1964) 1994. *The Established and the Outsiders*. Vol. 32. London: Sage.

Enloe, Cynthia. 2000. *Maneuvers: The International Politics of Militarizing Women's Lives*. Berkeley: University of California Press.

– (1990) 2014. *Bananas, Beaches and Bases: Making Feminist Sense of International Politics*. Berkeley: University of California Press.

European Commission. 2006. "Standard Eurobarometer 66/First Results." December. http://ec.europa.eu/public_opinion/archives/eb/eb66/eb66_highlights_en.pdf (accessed 12 April 2016).

– 2010. "Standard Eurobarometer 71/Spring 2009: Future of Europe." January. http://ec.europa.eu/public_opinion/archives/eb/eb71/eb713_future_europe.pdf (accessed 12 April 2016).

– 2011. "Standard Eurobarometer 76/Autumn 2011." December. http://ec.europa.eu/commfrontoffice/publicopinion/archives/eb/eb76/eb76_en.htm (accessed 12 April 2016).

– 2013. "Standard Eurobarometer 79/Spring 2013." July. http://ec.europa.eu/commfrontoffice/publicopinion/archives/eb/eb79/eb79_first_en.pdf (accessed 12 April 2016.

– 2015a. "Commission Proposes Temporary Suspension of Sweden's Obligations under the EU Relocation Mechanism." 15 December. http://europa.eu/rapid/press-release_IP-15-6329_en.htm (accessed 12 April 2016).

– 2015b. "European Commission Statement Following the Temporary Reintroduction of Border Controls by Austria, Particularly at the Hungarian-Austrian Border." 15 September. https://ec.europa.eu/home-affairs/what-is-new/news/news/2015/20150915_1_en (accessed 12 April 2016).

– 2015c. "European Commission Statement Following the Temporary Reintroduction of Border Controls by Germany, Particularly at the German-Austrian Border." 13 September. http://europa.eu/rapid/press-release_STATEMENT-15-5638_en.htm. (accessed 12 April 2016).

– 2015d. "European Commission Statement Following the Temporary Reintroduction of Controls by Slovenia at the Border with Hungary." 17 September. http://europa.eu/rapid/press-release_STATEMENT-15-5667_en.htm (accessed 12 April 2016).

– 2016. "Eurostat 2016: Asylum Quarterly Report." 20 September. http://ec.europa.eu/eurostat/statistics-explained/index.php/Asylum_quarterly_report (accessed 12 April 2016).

European Migration Network. 2013. "Country Report: Sweden." ec.europa.eu/dgs/home-affairs/what-we-do/networks/european_migration_

network/reports/docs/country-factsheets/27.sweden_emn_country_factsheet_2013.pdf (accessed 12 April 2016).
European Resettlement Network. 2013. "Country Profile: Sweden." www.resettlement.eu/country/sweden (accessed 12 April 2016).
European Union Agency for Fundamental Rights (FRA). 2008. "Annual Report 2008." http://fra.europa.eu/fraWebsite/attachments/ar08p2_en.pdf (accessed 12 April 2016).
– 2010. "Annual Report 2010: Conference Edition." http://fra.europa.eu/fraWebsite/attachments/AR_2010-conf-edition_en.pdf (accessed 12 April 2016).
– 2011. "Fundamental Rights of Migrants in an Irregular Situation in the European Union." November. http://fra.europa.eu/fraWebsite/research/publications/publications_per_year/pub-migrants-in-an-irregular-situation_en.htm (accessed 12 April 2016).
Eurostat. 2007. *Europe in Figures: Eurostat Yearbook 2006–2007*. Luxembourg: Office for the Official Publications of the European Communities.
– 2008. *Europe in Figures: Eurostat Yearbook 2008*. Luxembourg: Office for the Official Publications of the European Communities.
– 2009. *Europe in Figures: Eurostat Yearbook 2009*. Luxembourg: Office for the Official Publications of the European Community.
– 2010. *Europe in Figures: Eurostat Yearbook 2010*. Luxembourg: Publications Office for the European Union.
– 2011a. *Europe in Figures: Eurostat Yearbook 2011*. Luxembourg: Publications Office of the European Union.
– 2011b. *Migrants in Europe: A Statistical Portrait of the First and Second Generation*. Luxembourg: Publications Office of the European Union.
– 2012. *Europe in Figures: Eurostat Yearbook 2012*. Luxembourg: Publications Office of the European Union.
– 2013. *Europe in Figures: Eurostat Yearbook 2013*. Luxembourg: Publications Office of the European Union.
– 2016. "News Release 44/2016 - Asylum in the EU Member States. Record Number of over 1.2 Million First-Time Asylum Seekers Registered in 2015." 4 March. https://ec.europa.eu/eurostat/documents/2995521/7203832/3-04032016-AP-EN.pdf/790eba01-381c-4163-bcd2-a54959b99ed6.
Fassin, Didier. 2005. "Compassion and Repression: The Moral Economy of Immigration Policies in France." *Cultural Anthropology* 3 (2): 362–87.
– 2007. "Humanitarianism as a Politics of Life." *Public Culture* 19 (3): 499.

– 2010. "Inequality of Lives: Hierarchies of Humanity: Moral Commitments and Ethical Dilemmas of Humanitarianism." In *In the Name of Humanity: The Government of Threat and Care*, edited by I. Feldman and M. Ticktin, 238–56. Durham, NC: Duke University Press.
– 2012. *Humanitarian Reason: A Moral History of the Present*. Berkeley: University of California Press.
Feldman, Ilana. 2008. *Governing Gaza: Bureaucracy, Authority, and the Work of Rule, 1917–1967*. Durham, NC: Duke University Press.
Financial Times. 2017. "Germany's Election Results in Charts and Maps." 25 September. www.ft.com/content/e7c7d918-a17e-11e7-b797-b61809486fe2 (accessed 12 December 2017).
Foucault, Michel. 1986. "Omnes Et Singulatim: Vers Une Critique De La Raison Politique in Michel Foucault." *Le débat* (41): 5–35.
– 2005. *The Hermeneutics of the Subject: Lectures at the Collège De France 1981–1982*. Vol. 6. New York: Macmillan.
– 2007. *Security, Territory, Population: Lectures at the Collège De France 1977–1978*. Vol. 4. New York: Macmillan.
– 2013. *Lectures on the Will to Know*. New York: Palgrave Macmillan.
Franklin, Marianne I. 2006. *Postcolonial Politics, the Internet and Everyday Life: Pacific Traversals Online*. London: Routledge.
Frowd, Philippe M. 2014. "The Field of Border Control in Mauritania." *Security Dialogue* 45 (3): 226–41.
Frykman, Jonas. 1981. "Pure and Rational. The Hygienic Vision: A Study of Cultural Transformation in the 1930s. The New Man." *Ethnologia Scandinavica Lund*: 36–63.
– 1993. "Becoming the Perfect Swede: Modernity, Body Politics, and National Processes in Twentieth-Century Sweden." *Ethnos* 58 (3–4): 259–74.
Gabrielsen Jumbert, Maria. 2013. "Controlling the Mediterranean Space through Surveillance. The Politics and Discourse of Surveillance as an All-Encompassing Solution to EU Maritime Border Management Issues." *Espace populations sociétés. Space populations societies* (2012/3): 35–48.
Gallup International. 2012. "Global Index of Religiosity and Atheism." www.wingia.com/web/files/news/14/file/14.pdf.
Garelli, Glenda, and Martina Tazzioli. 2017. "The Humanitarian War against Migrant Smugglers at Sea." *Antipode*: 685–703.
Geertz, Clifford. 1973. *The Interpretation of Cultures: Selected Essays*. Vol. 5019. New York: Basic Books.

Germanwatch. 2013. "Global Climate Change Performance Index 2013." https://germanwatch.org/en/download/7158.pdf (accessed 12 April 2016).

Goldstein, Daniel M., Robert Albro, Catherine Besteman, Susan Bibler Coutin, Jennifer Burrell, Diana Fox, John Gledhill, et al. 2010. "Toward a Critical Anthropology of Security." *Current Anthropology* 51 (4): 487–517.

Gouldner, A. 1973. *For Sociology: Renewal and Critique in Sociology Today*. London: Allen Lane.

Green, Nicola, and Nils Zurawski. 2015. "Surveillance and Ethnography: Researching Surveillance as Everyday Life." *Surveillance & Society* 13 (1): 27.

Guardian, The. 2015a. "Sweden Slams Shut Its Open-Door Policy Towards Refugees." 24 November. www.theguardian.com/world/2015/nov/24/sweden-asylum-seekers-refugees-policy-reversal (accessed 12 December 2017).

– 2015b. "Trudeau Welcomes Syrian Refugees but Canada May Not Reach Target." 23 December. www.theguardian.com/world/2015/dec/23/justin-trudeau-welcome-syrian-refugees-christmas-address (accessed 12 December 2017).

– 2016a. "Sweden and Denmark Crack Down on Refugees at Borders." 4 January. www.theguardian.com/world/2016/jan/03/sweden-to-impose-id-checks-on-travellers-from-denmark (accessed 12 December 2017).

– 2016b. "Swedish Police Accused of Covering up Sex Attacks by Refugees at Music Festival." 11 January. www.theguardian.com/world/2016/jan/11/swedish-police-accused-cover-up-sex-attacks-refugees-festival (accessed 12 December 2017).

– 2017a. "'Good' Populism Beat 'Bad' in Dutch Election." 19 March. https://www.theguardian.com/world/2017/mar/19/dutch-election-rutte-wilders-good-populism-bad- (accessed 12 December 2017).

– 2017b. "The Guardian View on the Austrian Elections: An Old Threat in a New Guise." 16 October. https://www.theguardian.com/commentisfree/2017/oct/16/the-guardian-view-on-the-austrian-elections-an-old-threat-in-a-new-guise (accessed 12 December 2017).

Guillaume, Xavier, and Pinar Bilgin. 2016. *Routledge Handbook of International Political Sociology*. Abingdon: Taylor & Francis.

Guillaume, Xavier, and Jef Huysmans. 2013. "Citizenship and Securitizing: Interstitial Politics." In *Citizenship and Security*. 30–46: London: Routledge.

Gullestad, Marianne. 2002. "Invisible Fences: Egalitarianism, Nationalism and Racism." *Journal of the Royal Anthropological Institute* 8, no. 1 (2002): 45–63.

Gustavsson, Jakob. 1998. *The Politics of Foreign Policy Change. Explaining the Swedish Reorientation on EU Membership.* Lund, Sweden: Lund University.

Gusterson, Hugh. 2004. *People of the Bomb: Portraits of America's Nuclear Complex.* Minneapolis: University of Minnesota Press.

Hansen, Peo. 2009. "Post-National Europe – without Cosmopolitan Guarantees." *Race and Class* 50 (4): 20–37.

Hellquist, E. 1922. *Svensk_Etymologisk_Ordbok.* Projekt Runeberg. http://runeberg.org/svetym/0744.html (accessed 16 April 2016).

Hentilä, Seppo. 1978. "The Origins of the Folkhem Ideology in Swedish Social Democracy." *Scandinavian Journal of History* 3 (1–4): 323–45.

Hoeffler, Anke, and Verity Outram. 2011. "Need, Merit, or Self-Interest – What Determines the Allocation of Aid?" *Review of Development Economics* 15 (2): 237–50.

Hook, Steven W. 1995. *National Interest and Foreign Aid.* Boulder, CO: Lynne Rienner Publishers.

Huddleston, J. 2011. "Migrant Integration Policy Index III." Brussels: British Council and Migration Policy Group.

Huysmans, Jef. 2006. *The Politics of Insecurity: Fear, Migration and Asylum in the EU.* London: Routledge.

– 2008. "The Jargon of Exception – on Schmitt, Agamben and the Absence of Political Society." *International Political Sociology* 2 (2): 165–83.

– 2011. "What's in an Act? On Security Speech Acts and Little Security Nothings." *Security Dialogue* 42 (4–5): 371–83.

– 2014. *Security Unbound: Enacting Democratic Limits.* London: Routledge.

– 2016. "Democratic Curiosity in Times of Surveillance." *European Journal of International Security* 1 (1): 73–93.

Huysmans, Jef, and Claudia Aradau. 2013. "Critical Methods in International Relations: The Politics of Techniques, Devices and Acts." *European Journal of International Relations*: 1354066112474479.

Huysmans, Jef, and Joao Pontes Nogueira. 2016. "Ten Years of IPS: Fracturing IR." *International Political Sociology* 10 (4): 299–319.

Inda, Jonathan Xavier. 2008. *Anthropologies of Modernity: Foucault, Governmentality, and Life Politics.* Hoboken, NJ: John Wiley & Sons.

Independent, The. 2015. "Refugee Crisis: Sweden the Only European Country with a Majority Favourable Towards Non-Eu Immigration."

4 September. www.independent.co.uk/news/world/europe/refugee-crisis-sweden-the-only-european-country-with-a-majority-favourable-towards-non-eu-10487466.html (accessed 16 April 2016).
– 2016a. "Cologne Attacks: What Happened after 1,000 Women Were Sexually Assaulted?" 11 February. www.independent.co.uk/news/world/europe/cologne-attacks-what-happened-after-1000-women-were-sexually-assaulted-a6867071.html (accessed 16 April 2016).
– 2016b. "Denmark Approves Controversial Refugee Bill Allowing Police to Seize Asylum Seekers' Cash and Valuables." 26 January. www.independent.co.uk/news/world/europe/denmark-approves-controversial-refugee-bill-allowing-police-to-seize-asylum-seekers-cash-and-a6834581.html (accessed 16 April 2016).
– 2016c. "Refugee Crisis: Sweden Prepares to Expel up to 80,000 Asylum Seekers." 28 January. www.independent.co.uk/news/world/europe/sweden-prepares-to-expel-up-to-80000-asylum-seekers-a6838421.html (accessed 16 April 2016).
– 2016d. "Sweden Has Done So Much for Refugees. Now It's Turned Its Back on Them." 1 January. www.independent.co.uk/news/world/europe/sweden-has-done-so-much-for-refugees-now-its-turned-its-back-on-them-a6792726.html (accessed 16 April 2016).
Ingebritsen, Christine. 2002. "Norm Entrepreneurs Scandinavia's Role in World Politics." *Cooperation and Conflict* 37 (1): 11–23.
Inter-Parliamentary Union (IPU). 2009. "Women in National Parliaments: World Classification 2009." 30 June. www.ipu.org/wmn-e/arc/classif300609.htm (accessed 16 April 2016).
– 2010. "Women in National Parliaments: World Classification 2010." 30 June. www.ipu.org/wmn-e/arc/classif300610.htm (accessed 16 April 2016).
– 2011. "Women in National Parliaments: World Classification 2011." www.ipu.org/wmn-e/classif.htm (accessed 16 April 2016).
– 2012. "Women in National Parliaments: World Classification 2012." www.ipu.org/wmn-e/classif.htm (accessed 16 April 2016).
Jarvis, Lee, and Michael Lister. 2013. "Vernacular Securities and Their Study: A Qualitative Analysis and Research Agenda." *International Relations* 27 (2): 158–79.
Jeandesboz, Julien, and Polly Pallister-Wilkins. 2016. "Crisis, Routine, Consolidation: The Politics of the Mediterranean Migration Crisis." *Mediterranean Politics* 21 (2): 316–20.
Jervis, Robert. 1978. "Cooperation under the Security Dilemma." *World Politics* 30 (2): 167–214.

Jung, Carl Gustav. 2012. *Answer to Job: (from Vol. 11 of the Collected Works of Cg Jung)*. Princeton, NJ: Princeton University Press.

Kamali, Masoud. 1997. *Distorted Integration: Clientization of Immigrants in Sweden*. Uppsala: Centre for Multiethnic Research, Uppsala University.

Kanne, P., and L. Klein Kranenburg. 2015. "'Fort Europa': Hoe Denken Nederlanders over Migratie En Vluchtelingen in Europa En Nederland?" Netherlands: I&O Research.

Kanter, James, and Stephen Castle. 2016. "'Brexit,' Migration, Trade: E.U.'s List of Crises Keeps Growing." *New York Times*. 20 October. www.nytimes.com/2016/10/21/world/europe/brexit-migration-walloons-eus-list-of-crises-keeps-growing.html.

Keohane, Robert O. 1989. "International Relations Theory: Contributions of a Feminist Standpoint." *Millennium* 18 (2): 245–53.

Kohn, Hans. 1961. *The Idea of Nationalism: A Study in Its Origins and Background*. Piscataway, NJ: Transaction Publishers.

Kurier. 2016. "Faymann Ist Erstes Politisches Opfer Der Flüchtlingskrise." 10 May. https://kurier.at/politik/inland/guardian-und-el-pais-faymann-ist-erstes-politisches-opfer-der-fluechtlingskrise/197.940.415 (accessed 16 April 2016).

Lacan, Jacques. (1950) 1992. *The Seminar. Book VII. The Ethics of Psychoanalysis, 1959–1960*. London: Routledge.

Lakoff, Andrew. 2015. "Real-Time Biopolitics: The Actuary and the Sentinel in Global Public Health." *Economy and Society* 44 (1): 40–59.

Lakoff, Andrew, and Stephen J. Collier. 2008. *Biosecurity Interventions: Global Health and Security in Question*. New York: Columbia University Press.

Larner, Wendy, and Richard Le Heron. 2004. "Global Benchmarking: Participating 'at a Distance' in the Globalizing Economy." In *Global Governmentality: Governing International Spaces*, edited by W. Larner and W. Walters, 212–32. London: Routledge.

Lawler, Peter. 1997. "Scandinavian Exceptionalism and European Union." *Journal of Common Market Studies* 35 (4): 565–94.

– 2005. "The Good State: In Praise of 'Classical' Internationalism." *Review of International Studies* 31 (3): 427–49.

– 2007. "Janus-Faced Solidarity Danish Internationalism Reconsidered." *Cooperation and Conflict* 42 (1): 101–26.

Leander, Anna. 2015. "Ethnographic Contributions to Method Development: 'Strong Objectivity' in Security Studies." *International Studies Perspectives*: ekv021.

Levi-Strauss, Claude. 1965. "The Principle of Reciprocity." In *Sociological Theory*, edited by L.A. Coser and B. Rosenberg, 84–94. New York: Macmillan.

Linde-Laursen, Anders. 2007. "Is Something Rotten in the State of Denmark? The Muhammad Cartoons and Danish Political Culture." *Contemporary Islam* 1 (3): 265–74.

Local, The. 2013. "Asylum-Friendly Sweden a Soft-Power Superpower." 21 November. www.thelocal.se/20131121/asylum-friendly-sweden-is-soft-power-super-power (accessed 12 April 2016).

– 2015a. "Support for Nationalists up Despite Refugee Cuts." 17 December. www.thelocal.se/20151217/more-support-for-nationalists-despite-refugee-cuts (accessed 12 April 2016).

– 2015b. "Sweden Could Be Lifted from Eu Refugee Duties." 15 December. www.thelocal.se/20151215/sweden-could-be-excused-from-eu-refugee-duties (accessed 12 April 2016).

Löfgren, Orvar. 1990. "Medierna I Nationsbygget." *Medier och kulturer*: 85–120.

– 1993. "Nationella Arenor." *Försvenskningen av Sverige: Det nationellas förvandlingar*: 22–118.

Lukes, Steven. 2004. *Power: A Radical View*. New York: Palgrave Macmillan.

Lumsdaine, David Halloran. 1993. *Moral Vision in International Politics: The Foreign Aid Regime, 1949–1989*. Princeton: Princeton University Press.

Magalhães, Bruno. 2016. "The Politics of Credibility: Assembling Decisions on Asylum Applications in Brazil." *International Political Sociology* 10 (2): 133–49.

Maguire, Mark, Catarina Frois, and Nils Zurawski. 2014. *Anthropology of Security: Perspectives from the Frontline of Policing, Counter-Terrorism and Border Control*. London: Pluto.

Malinowski, Bronislaw. (1922) 1950. *Argonauts of the Western Pacific*. London: Routledge.

Mauss, Marcel. (1923) 1900. *The Gift: The Form and Reason for Exchange in Archaic Societies*. London: Routledge.

Mearsheimer, John J. 1990. "Back to the Future: Instability in Europe after the Cold War." *International Security* 15 (1): 5–56.

Miller, David. 1995. *On Nationality*. Wotton-Under-Edge: Clarendon Press.

Miller, Peter, and Nikolas Rose. 2008. *Governing the Present: Administering Economic, Social and Personal Life*. Cambridge: Polity.

Moeller, Susan D. 1999. *Compassion Fatigue: How the Media Sell Disease, Famine, War and Death*. London: Psychology Press.

Molina, Irene. 1997. *Stadens Rasifiering: Etnisk Boendesegregation I Folkhemmet*. Uppsala: Geografiska Regionstudier.

Monocle. 2013. "Soft Power Index 2013." 17 November. https://monocle.com/film/affairs/soft-power-survey-2013/ (accessed 12 April 2016).

Moon, Katharine H.S. 1997. *Sex among Allies: Military Prostitution in US-Korea Relations*. New York: Columbia University Press.

Mouritzen, Hans. 1995. "The Nordic Model as a Foreign Policy Instrument: Its Rise and Fall." *Journal of Peace Research* 32 (1): 9–21.

Muftee, Mehek. 2014. "Empowering Refugee Girls: A Study of Cultural Orientation Programs in Kenya and Sudan." *Journal of Multicultural Discourses* 9 (1): 44–60.

Neumann, Iver B. 2012. *At Home with the Diplomats: Inside a European Foreign Ministry*. Ithaca, NY: Cornell University Press.

– 2002. "Returning Practice to the Linguistic Turn: The Case of Diplomacy." *Millennium-Journal of International Studies* 31 (3): 627–51.

New York Times, The. 2015. "The Global Refugee Crisis, Region by Region," 6 September. www.nytimes.com/interactive/2015/06/09/world/migrants-global-refugee-crisis-mediterranean-ukraine-syria-rohingya-malaysia-iraq.html?_r=0 (accessed 12 April 2016).

Noxolo, Patricia, and Jef Huysmans. 2009. *Community, Citizenship, and the "War on Terror": Security and Insecurity*. London: Palgrave Macmillan.

NRC. 2016. "De Draad Kwijt in Het Asieldebat? Dit Zijn De Feiten." 2 February. www.nrc.nl/nieuws/2016/02/02/dit-zijn-de-feiten-over-asielzoekers-in-nederl)6and-a1405200#vraag28 (accessed 12 April 2016).

Nye, Joseph S. 2004. *Soft Power: The Means to Success in World Politics*. New York: PublicAffairs.

Ochs, Juliana. 2011. *Security and Suspicion: An Ethnography of Everyday Life in Israel*. Pennsylvania: University of Pennsylvania Press.

Ojakangas, Mika. 2005. "Impossible Dialogue on Bio-Power: Agamben and Foucault." *Foucault Studies* (2): 5–28.

Organisation for Economic Co-operation and Development (OECD). 2013. "OECD Peer Review 2013." www.oecd.org/dac/peer-reviews/sweden-peer-review-2013.pdf (accessed 12 April 2016).

Ozkirimli, Umut. 2010. *Theories of Nationalism: A Critical Introduction*. London: Palgrave Macmillan.

Pallister-Wilkins, Polly. 2015. "The Humanitarian Politics of European Border Policing: Frontex and Border Police in Evros." *International Political Sociology* 9 (1): 53–69.

Pandolfi, Mariella. 2003. "Contract of Mutual (In)Difference: Governance and the Humanitarian Apparatus in Contemporary Albania and Kosovo." *Indiana Journal of Global Legal Studies* 10 (1): 369–81.

– 2008. "Laboratory of Intervention: The Humanitarian Governance of the Postcommunist Balkan Territories." In *Postcolonial Disorders*, edited by Sandra Teresa Hyde Mary Jo Del Vecchio Good, Sarah Pinto, and Byron Good, 157–88. Berkeley: University of California Press.

PBS. 2016. "Sweden's Welcome to Refugees Disturbed by Violent Backlash." 3 February. www.pbs.org/newshour/bb/swedens-welcome-to-refugees-disturbed-by-violent-backlash/ (accessed 11 May 2017).

Perrin, D., and F. McNamara. 2013. "Refugee Resettlement in the EU: Between Shared Standards and Diversity in Legal and Policy Frames." Florence: European University Institute, Robert Schuman Centre for Advanced Studies.

Pred, Allan. 2000. *Even in Sweden: Racisms, Racialized Spaces, and the Popular Geographical Imagination.* Vol. 8. Berkeley: University of California Press.

Prozorov, Sergei. 2007. "The Unrequited Love of Power: Biopolitical Investment and the Refusal of Care." *Foucault Studies* (4): 53–77.

Pumariega, Andres J., Eugenio Rothe, and JoAnne B. Pumariega. 2005. "Mental Health of Immigrants and Refugees." *Community Mental Health Journal* 41 (5): 581–97.

Ratelle, Jean-François. 2013. "Making Sense of Violence in Civil War: Challenging Academic Narratives through Political Ethnography." *Critical Studies on Security* 1 (2): 159–73.

Redfield, Peter. 2013. *Life in Crisis: The Ethical Journey of Doctors without Borders.* Berkeley: University of California Press.

Regeringen. 2009. "Billstrom Highlights Resettlement Issue." 17 February. www.government.se/sb/d/11810/a/123953 (accessed 12 April 2016).

– 2013. "Billstrom Speaks against Xenophobia." 7 March. www.government.se/sb/d/13759/a/157924 (accessed 12 April 2016).

– 2015a. "The Government's Ten Standpoints to Reform the EU's Refugee Policy." 8 September. www.government.se/articles/2015/09/swedens-ten-standpoints-to-reform-the-eus-refugee-policy/ (accessed 12 April 2016).

– 2015b. "Government Proposes Measures to Create Respite for Swedish Refugee Reception." 24 November. www.government.se/articles/2015/

11/government-proposes-measures-to-create-respite-for-swedish-refugee-reception/ (accessed 12 April 2016).

Reid, Julian. 2005. "The Biopolitics of the War on Terror: A Critique of the 'Return of Imperialism'thesis in International Relations." *Third World Quarterly* 26 (2): 237–52.

Reuters. 2016a. "Germany's Vice Chancellor Says Merkel Underestimated Migrant Challenge." 27 August. www.reuters.com/article/us-europe-migrants-germany-gabriel/germanys-vice-chancellor-says-merkel-under-estimated-migrant-challenge-idUSKCN1120RP (accessed 12 April 2016).

– 2016b. "Trying to Stem Refugee Influx, Sweden Asks: When Is a Child Not a Child?" 3 February. www.reuters.com/article/us-europe-migrants-sweden-idUSKCN0VC1G9 (accessed 12 April 2016).

Rose, Nikolas. 1999. *Governing the Soul: The Shaping of the Private Self*. London: Taylor & Francis/Routledge.

– 2010. *Powers of Freedom: Reframing Political Thought*. Cambridge: Cambridge University Press.

Rosello, Mireille. 2001. *Postcolonial Hospitality: The Immigrant as Guest*. Redwood, CA: Stanford University Press.

Rozakou, Katerina. 2012. "The Biopolitics of Hospitality in Greece: Humanitarianism and the Management of Refugees." *American Ethnologist* 39 (3): 562–77.

Save the Children. 2013. "The Complete Mothers Index 2013." www.savethechildren.org/atf/cf/%7B9def2ebe-10ae-432c-9bd0-df91d2e-ba74a%7D/SOWM-MOTHERS-INDEX-2013.PDF (accessed 12 April 2016).

Schierup, Carl-Ulrik, and Aleksandra Ålund. 2010. *Beyond Liberal Pluralism: Migration and Politics of Exclusion in Europe*. Linköping, Linköping University Electronic Press.

Scott, James C. 1985. *Weapons of the Weak: Everyday Forms of Peasant Resistance*. New Haven: Yale University Press.

– 1990. *Domination and the Arts of Resistance: Hidden Transcripts*. New Haven: Yale University Press.

– 2010. *Seeing Like a State: How Certain Schemes to Improve the Human Condition Have Failed*. New Haven: Yale University Press.

– 2013. *Two Cheers for Anarchism*. Princeton: Princeton University Press.

Scott, James C., Diego Palacios Cerezales, Diogo Duarte, José Manuel Sobral, and José Neves. 2013. "Egalitarianism, the Teachings of Fieldwork and Anarchist Calisthenics." *Análise Social* (207): 447–63.

Smith, Anthony D. 1986. *The Ethnic Origins of Nations*. Hoboken, NJ: Wiley Blackwell.
Spiegel Online. 2016. "Asylpaket Ii: Kabinett Beschließt Verschärfte Flüchtlingsgesetze." 3 February. www.spiegel.de/politik/deutschland/asylpaket-ii-bundesregierung-bringt-verschaerfte-asylgesetze-auf-weg-a-1075424.html (accessed 12 December 2017).
Spivak, Gayatri Chakravorty. 1985. "Three Women's Texts and a Critique of Imperialism." *Critical Inquiry* 12 (1): 243–61.
Summa, Renata. 2016. "Enacting Everyday Boundaries in Post-Dayton Bosnia and Herzegovina: Disconnection, Re-appropriation and Displacement(s)." PhD dissertation, PUC-Rio.
Sundström, Lena. 2006. *Varldens Lyckligaste Folk*. Stockholm: Leopard.
Svenska Dagbladet. 2015. "UNHCR: 'Hjälp Sverige Och Tyskland Med Flyktingar.'" 18 August. www.svd.se/unhcr-hjalp-sverige-och-tyskland-med-flyktingar (accessed 12 April 2016).
– 2016. "Löfven: Sverige Har Inte Skuld Till Dominoeffekt." 21 January. www.svd.se/lofven-fornekar-dominoeffekt/om/flykten-till-europa (accessed 12 April 2016).
Sverige-Radio. 2015. "Löfven and Merkel: Taking in Refugees Is a Question of Values." 8 September. http://sverigesradio.se/sida/artikel.aspx?programid=2054&artikel=6250480 (accessed 12 April 2016).
SVT. 2015. "Regeringen: Ny Lagstiftning För Färre Asylsökande." 24 November. www.svt.se/nyheter/inrikes/regeringen-utokade-id-kontroller-vid-gransen (accessed 12 April 2016).
Sydsvenskan. 2015. "Tält Åt Flyktingar Sätts Upp På Revinge." 15 October. www.sydsvenskan.se/lund/talt-at-flyktingar-satts-upp-pa-revinge/ (accessed 12 April 2016).
Telegraph, The. 2015. "Beware the Rise of Radical Right as Migrants Arrive in Europe, Says German Spy Chief." 27 September. www.telegraph.co.uk/news/worldnews/europe/germany/11895225/Beware-the-rise-of-radical-Right-as-migrants-arrive-in-Europe-says-German-spy-chief.html (accessed 12 December 2017).
– 2016. "The Rise of the Far Right in Europe is not a False Alarm." 19 May. www.telegraph.co.uk/news/2016/05/19/the-rise-of-the-far-right-in-europe-is-not-a-false-alarm/ (accessed 12 December 2017).
– 2017. "Austrian Election Results: Conservative Sebastian Kurz on Course to Become Europe's Youngest Leader." 15 October. www.telegraph.co.uk/news/2017/10/15/austrian-election-conservative-sebastian-kurz-course-become/ (accessed 12 April 2016).

Ticktin, Miriam. 2006. "Where Ethics and Politics Meet." *American Ethnologist* 33 (1): 33–49.
Tilly, Charles. 1994. "A Bridge Halfway: Responding to Brubaker." *Contention: Debates in Society, Culture, and Science* 4 (1): 15–19.
– 1999. *Durable Inequality*. Berkeley: University of California Press.
– 2002. *Stories, Identities, and Political Change*. London: Rowman & Littlefield Publishers.
Tomasson, Richard F. 2002. "How Sweden Became So Secular." *Scandinavian Studies* 74 (1): 61–88.
Tomlinson, John. 2011. "Beyond Connection: Cultural Cosmopolitan and Ubiquitous Media." *International Journal of Cultural Studies* 14 (4): 347–61.
Towns, Ann. 2002. "Paradoxes of (In)Equality: Something Is Rotten in the Gender Equal State of Sweden." *Cooperation and Conflict* 37 (2): 157–79.
Trägårdh, L., and H. Berggren. 2015. Är Svensken Människa?: Gemenskap Och Oberoende I Det Moderna Sverige. Stockholm: Norstedts.
Trägårdh, Lars. 2007. *State and Civil Society in Northern Europe: The Swedish Model Reconsidered*. Vol. 3. New York: Berghahn Books.
Transparency International. 2013. "Global Corruption Perceptions Index 2013." www.transparency.org/cpi2013/results (accessed 12 April 2016).
United Nations Development Programme (UNDP). 2013a. "Development Index2013."http://hdr.undp.org/en/content/content/human-development-report-2013 (accessed 12 April 2016).
– 2013b. "Human Development Reports: Sweden." http://hdr.undp.org/en/countries/profiles/SWE (accessed 12 April 2016).
United Nations High Commissioner for Refugees (UNHCR). 2014. "Syrian Refugees in Europe: What Can Europe Do to Ensure Solidarity?" www.refworld.org/pdfid/53b69f574.pdf (accessed 12 April 2016).
Valverde, Mariana. 1998. *Diseases of the Will: Alcohol and the Dilemmas of Freedom*. Cambridge: Cambridge University Press.
Van Dijk, Teun A. 1998. *Ideology: A Multidisciplinary Approach*. London: Sage.
Vanhuele, Dirk, Joanne van Selm, and Christina Boswell. 2013. "The Implementation of Article 80 TFEU on the Principle of Solidarity and Fair Sharing of Responsibility, Including Its Financial Implications, between the Member States in the Field of Border Checks, Asylum and Immigration." Brussels: European Parliament.

Vaughan-Williams, Nick, and Daniel Stevens. 2016. "Vernacular Theories of Everyday (In)Security: The Disruptive Potential of Non-Elite Knowledge." *Security Dialogue* 47 (1): 40–58.

Veyne, Paul. 1997. "Foucault Revolutionizes History" In *Foucault and His Interlocutors*, edited by Arnold I. Davidson, 146–82. Chicago: University of Chicago Press.

– 2013. *Foucault: His Thought, His Character*. Hoboken, NJ: John Wiley & Sons.

Visit Sweden. 2013. "A Platform for the Swedish Brand." www.visitsweden.com/sweden/brandguide/The-brand/The-Platform/A-platform-for-the-Sweden-brand/ (accessed 12 April 2016).

Vrasti, Wanda. 2008. "The Strange Case of Ethnography and International Relations." *Millennium-Journal of International Studies* 37 (2): 279–301.

– 2013. *Volunteer Tourism in the Global South: Giving Back in Neoliberal Times*. London: Routledge.

Wæver, Ole. 1993. *Securitization and Desecuritization*. Copenhagen: Centre for Peace and Conflict Research Copenhagen.

Waltz, Kenneth Neal. 2001. *Man, the State, and War: A Theoretical Analysis*. New York: Columbia University Press.

Weber, Max. (1922) 1947. *The Theory of Social and Economic Organisation*. Translated by A.M. Henderson and Talcott Parsons. New York: Free Press.

Weldes, Jutta. 1999. *Cultures of Insecurity: States, Communities, and the Production of Danger*. Vol. 14. Minneapolis: University of Minnesota Press.

World Values Survey. 2013. "Findings and Insights: Inglehart-Welzel Cultural Map." www.worldvaluessurvey.org/WVSContents.jsp?CMSID=Findings (accessed 12 April 2016).

Zabusky, Stacia E. 2011. *Launching Europe: An Ethnography of European Cooperation in Space Science*. Princeton: Princeton University Press.

Zeitung, Suddeutsche. 2016. "Fremdenfeindliche Gewalt Bleibt Hoch." 25 September. www.sueddeutsche.de/news/politik/extremismus-fremdenfeindliche-gewalt-bleibt-hoch-dpa.urn-newsml-dpa-com-20090101-160925-99-582806 (accessed 12 April 2016).

Zuckerman, Phil. 2008. *Society without God: What the Least Religious Nations Can Tell Us about Contentment*. New York: New York University Press.

Index

Absolute Sweden: A Journey in a Wealth of Silence, 190n6. See also Jalving, Mikael
Aleppo, 94, 98
Aliens Act (Denmark), 193n15
Alternative for Germany (AfD) (German political party), 7, 178
Amnesty International, 7
anthropology: activist, 14; critical, 13, 142; of hospitality, 75; of humanitarianism, 75, 139, 159, 167, 170; linguistic, 44; political, 44, 148, 153, 170, 185; scholars of, 8; of security, 12, 26, 148, 152–3, 184
anti-immigration: parties, 7, 135, 137–8, 147, 169–70, 178–9; rhetoric, 31, 42, 89, 131, 144, 149
Arbetsförmedlingen, 134, 165
Argonauts of the Western Pacific, 158
Är svensken människa? Gemenskap och oberoende i det moderna Sverige, 50
Austria: refugee intake, 178–9
Austrian People's Party, 179
Berggren, Henrik, 24, 39, 50, 161

Bigo, Didier, 9–14, 23, 68, 139, 153, 184, 187n1
Bildt, Carl, 34, 40–1
Bilgin, Pinar, 8, 9
Billström, Tobias, 59, 62, 63, 64
border controls: temporary introduction, 175, 177
Bourdieu, Pierre, 50, 191n7, 193n3
Bronte, Charlotte, 195n1
Buma, Sybrand, 182

Cameron, David, 180
children, 70–1, 92, 93–4, 96–7, 109, 113–19; ethnic minority, 77–9; removal from parents, 40; rights in Sweden, 66, 117
Christian Democratic Appeal (Dutch political party), 181
Christian Democratic Union (German political party), 178
Christian Social Union (Bavarian political party), 178
Church of Sweden, 51–2, 71
citizenship, 37, 57, 66, 125, 189n8
Cold War, 8, 35, 40
Commission on the Future of Sweden, 51

compassion fatigue, 106, 125–31, 137, 174, 194n9
Conservative Party (UK political party), 180
Copenhagen School, 9, 187n1
crime, 39, 154

Dagen, 60, 61
Dagens Nyheter, 39, 40, 41
Danish People's Party, 46. *See also* Kjaersgaard, Pia
de Certeau, Michel, 16, 76, 112, 151
democracy, 32, 36, 39, 49, 55; social, 29, 34
Denmark, 45–7
Dera'a, 84, 94
Domination and the Arts of Resistance, 124
Douglas, Mary, 155
Durkheim, Emile, 157

Elias, Norbert, 195
Engström, Hillevi, 59
Enzensberger, Hans Magnus, 39
The Established and the Outsiders, 195. *See also* Elias, Norbert and Scotson, John L.
ethnography, 3–6, 14–15, 140, 143, 148, 152
European Commission, 48, 163, 177
European Council on Foreign Relations, 171
European Migration Network, 41, 190n5, 192n13
European Resettlement Network, 65, 66. *See also* refugee resettlement

European Union, 171; Agency for Fundamental Rights, 55, 56, 57; Treaty on the Functioning of, 62
European Urban Knowledge Network, 56
Eurostat, 56, 191n8
everyday, 11–14, 16–18, 148–9, 152–5, 165–7, 184–6

Fälldin, Thorbjörn, 81
far right: definition, 4; political parties, 42
Feminist Initiative (Swedish political party), 135
folkhemmet (the people's home), 34
Försäkringskassan, 134
Foucault, Michel, 16, 18, 42–3, 69, 73–5, 107–8
Freedom Party (Austrian political party), 7, 179
Friends of Syria, 82, 85, 92, 106, 113, 115, 141; breakdown of relations with refugees, 131–4, 136–7, 147, 150, 165; decline of, 21–3, 169; introduction to, 69, 72–3
Front National (French political party), 7

gender: equality, 120; roles, 117–18
Gender Development Index, 55
Gender Empowerment Measure, 55
Germanwatch: Climate Change Performance Index, 54
Germany, 7, 34, 59, 61, 171, 174, 176–8
The Gift (Essai sur le don), 155
Gorbachev, Mikhail, 196n1

governmentality of righteousness, 23–5, 42, 68–70, 73–7, 79, 83–4, 105–38, 156
Green Party, 60
Guillaume, Xavier, 8, 9, 12
Guterres, António, 177

Hama, 84, 94, 133
Hansson, Per Albin, 34
hate crime: Islamophobia, 47; xenophobic, 7, 47, 64, 171, 178
hidden transcripts, 16–18, 109–15, 133–4, 137–8, 139, 143, 145, 156–7, 168, 173, 176, 184–5
Homs, 84, 94
Huysmans, Jef, 5, 8, 9, 10, 11, 12

immigration, 62, 179, 190n6; control of, 5; controversy, 10; countries of, 6; effects on Scandinavian societies, 45–6
insecurity, 11, 13. See also security
international political sociology (IPS), 8–13, 154; definition, 8
Inter-Parliamentary Union, 55
invandrare (immigrant), 36
Iran, 127, 141, 182
Iraq, 126, 127, 128, 135, 182
Iraq War, 63
Islamic State of Iraq and the Levant, 176

Jabhat al-Nusra, 95
Jalving, Mikael, 190n6
Jämtland shooting, 120–2, 124, 147
Jane Eyre, 195. See also Bronte, Charlotte
Jobbik (Hungarian political party), 7
Johansson, Morgan, 176

Kjaersgaard, Pia, 46

Labour (UK political party), 180
language, 39, 41, 44–5, 60, 66, 89, 114–16
Latakia, 94–5
Lega Nord (Italian political party), 7
legislation, 35, 46, 55, 64
Le Pen, Marine, 7
Löfven, Stefan, 176, 177, 183

Mauss, Marcel, 155. See also *The Gift*
Merkel, Angela, 176–7, 178
metis, 24–5, 139–40, 148–56, 161, 169–70, 183–5
Migrant Integration Policy Index, 56, 57
migration, 10
Migrationsverket (Swedish Migration Agency), 63, 65, 80–2, 97, 109–10, 126–7, 193n1, 196n4
moral panic, 105–6, 119–25, 131, 136–8, 146–7, 168–70, 173; mechanism of, 109
multiculturalism, 36

nationalism: Danish, 31, 45; French, 30; Norwegian, 31; in politics, 171; Swedish, 27–8, 29–33; Western, 30
Netherlands: public response to refugee crisis, 180–1
New York Times, 171

opinion polls, 47–54; Eurobarometer, 47–9, 191n7; Gallup, 49; World Values Survey, 49, 50, 161

Öreby, 15, 20–3, 25–6, 67, 69–70; arrival of refugees, 72–3, 75, 77, 117, 125, 144; location, 84; media interest, 131–2, 142; physical description, 70–1; resident concerns, 111–17, 121–2, 126, 136; Residents' Association, 92–2, 126

Palme, Olof, 28, 34, 39, 190n2
Party for Freedom (Dutch political party), 181
People's Party for Freedom and Democracy (Netherlands), 181
Pope Francis, 3
poverty, 55
public transcript, 16–18, 147, 152, 166, 168, 173, 176; definition, 76, 77–83, 104; of solidarity, 106, 110, 114, 116, 150

racism, 41, 64, 70, 80, 107, 116
reflexivity, 26, 140–4, 148, 169
refugee crisis, 23, 145, 172, 174–7, 179–80, 185–6
refugee resettlement, 61, 62–6, 69, 156; local disquiet with, 86–8, 90–1, 97, 125, 173
Rose, Nikolas, 19, 188n7
Rousseau, Jean-Jacques, 51
Rumour in Orléans, 195n3
Rutte, Mark, 181, 182

Save the Children, 54
Schengen Borders Code, 175, 196n1
Scotson, John L., 195n2
Scott, James C., 16–19, 70, 76, 79, 82, 112, 124, 137, 147, 151–2
Second World War, 7, 29, 65, 171

security, 9–10, 11, 13; critical studies of, 14–16, 35. See also International Political Sociology
Security, Territory, Population, 107, 108. See also Foucault, Michel
Seeing Like a State, 102. See also Scott, James C.
sexual offences: crimes, 178, 181; fear of harassment, 113, 116
Sjobo, 80–1, 150
Social Democrats, 34, 36, 40, 46, 52, 60
solidarity, 6, 8, 24–6, 34–5, 37–8, 106–7, 139–40, 155–69, 172–4; as irony, 128–31; discourses of, 153; female, 118; ideal of, 61–2, 64, 77–9, 80, 84–91; national myth, 51, 67, 96, 103; performance of, 113; rationalities of, 182–4; with developing world, 52; with refugees, 63, 72, 73, 83
Sundström, Lena, 47
Sweden: admission to EU, 41; asylum policies, 23–4, 38, 41–2, 56–7, 59–66, 78, 102, 156; change of identity, 39, 42; characteristics of, 29, 48; exceptionalism, 42, 63, 64, 66–7, 96, 151; foreign policy, 40; local elections, 35; parliament, 7, 41; rights to refugees, 7, 164; secularism, 51–3; social conditions, 54; welfare state, 40
Sweden Democrats, 4, 7, 39, 71, 146, 174; 2014 election, 135–6, 147, 192n10, 194n5
Swedish Trade Union Confederation, 189n2
Sydsvenskan, 60, 71
Syrian Civil War, 56, 59, 63, 67, 171; escalation, 7

taboo, 111–12, 113, 118, 136
Trägårdh, Lars, 50, 51, 161
Transparency International: International Corruption Perceptions Index, 54
Treaty on the Functioning of the European Union (TFEU), 62, 192n12
Turkey, 101, 126, 129, 131, 181, 182; measures to ease European refugee crisis, 174

Ullenhag, Erik, 25
United Kingdom: asylum applications, 179; attitudes to immigration, 180; Brexit referendum, 179, 180; Immigration Act 2016, 180
UK Independence Party, 180
United Nations, 48, 56, 192n9; Global AgeWatch Index, 54; High Commission for Refugees, 7, 61, 63, 162–3, 177, 193n14; Human Development Index, 54. *See also* Guterres, António
United States, 6, 44, 53, 145; foreign policy, 35

Världens Lyckligaste Folk, 47. See *also* Sundström, Lena
Vaughan-Williams, Nick, 11, 12, 154
victimhood, 160, 167
Vietnam, 29, 182
A Vindication of the Rights of Women, 195n1. *See also* Wollstonecraft, Mary

War on Terror, 40
Wilders, Geert, 181. *See also* Party for Freedom
Wollstonecraft, Mary, 195n1
World Justice Project, 55